POST-SECULAR
SOCIETY

POST-SECULAR SOCIETY

Peter Nynäs, Mika Lassander, and Terhi Utriainen
editors

Transaction Publishers
New Brunswick (U.S.A.) and London (U.K.)

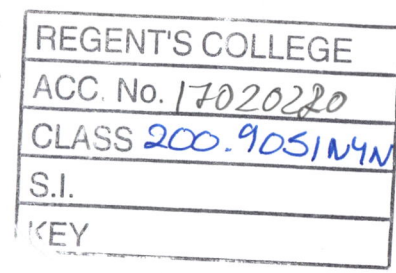
Library of Congress Catalog Number: 2011039931
ISBN: 978-1-4128-4610-3
Printed in the United States of America

Library of Congress Cataloging-in-Publication Data

Post-secular society / Peter Nynäs, Mika Lassander, and Terhi Utriainen, editors.
    p. cm.
  ISBN 978-1-4128-4610-3
  1. Religion and sociology. 2. Postsecularism. I. Nynäs, Peter. II. Lassander, Mika. III. Utriainen, Terhi.
  BL60.P595 2012
  200.9'051—dc23

                         2011039931

Contents

1

Trajectories of Post-Secular Complexity: An Introduction

Marcus Moberg, Kennet Granholm, and Peter Nynäs

[C]ontrary to conventional theories of secularization there is an enduring place for religion within the public spheres of modern democratic polities.[1]

This volume is motivated by the need to explore the post-secular. The erosion of religion—most commonly conceptualized through the notion of secularization—was long held to constitute an inevitable feature of modernity and to be an ultimately unavoidable consequence of modernization. Central to classical notions of secularization was also the presumption of an inherent "incompatibility between some features of 'modernity' and religious belief."[2] The validity of this claim has, however, become increasingly questioned in light of comparative empirical research in recent decades. Indeed, more recent debates on the changing face of religion in late modernity have yielded a more nuanced understanding of secularization as a multidimensional phenomenon that takes different forms depending on the varying trajectories of modernization and social differentiation across different historical, national, social, and cultural contexts. In addition, it has become increasingly clear that secularization needs not only to be understood as a phenomenon that occurs on different—and not necessarily causally related—societal, organizational, and individual levels, but also as a phenomenon that often occurs concurrently with counterdevelopments in postinstitutional forms of religion and spirituality.[3]

More recently, broader debates in the sociological study of religion have become increasingly occupied with the apparent resurgence of religion in the public sphere. Indeed, as José Casanova concluded almost two decades ago, although many modern societies are clearly marked by a general decline in institutional forms of religion, it does not automatically follow from this that religion as such loses influence and relevance either in the political arena, in the culture of a society, or in the everyday lives of individuals.[4] The growth and proliferation of immigrant religions, charismatic movements, new religious movements, and noninstitutional spiritualities further challenges the claims made by earlier monolithic theories of secularization. In the face of apparently contradictory trends of continuing religious decline and enduring religious vitality, scholars have proposed various alternative interpretive frameworks, such as desecularization, resacralization, de-Christianization, and the emergence of a post-secular society.[5]

The chapters in this volume all take as their point of departure scholarly reflections on the post-secular. However, contrary to some voices in the study of religion today, we do not regard the notion of secularization as having entirely lost its explanatory potential. Rather, we would argue that the notion of secularization demands still more reflection, and particularly with regard to the multidimensional and contested relationship between categories such as the "religious" and the "secular"/"secularity." As Michael Warner et al. assert in their discussion of Charles Taylor's *A Secular Age*, "secularity is not just a net reduction in religious belief or practice /.../ but a change in the very conditions of belief."[6] The aim of this volume is thus not to revoke the notion of secularization, but rather to strive to exemplify a more nuanced and multifocal perspective. This aim is exemplified by Casanova in the first chapter of this volume, which addresses the ambiguities that emerge from the idea of the persistence of an ethos of secularity in modern societies.

The contributions to this volume are held together by one overarching question in particular. As the general notion of secularization has proved clearly to be in need of considerable revision, what alternative (although related) ways of conceptualizing the societal and cultural place of religion within contemporary societies might we consider? Faced with this admittedly undecided and controversial question, we find it relevant to approach the issue through striving to integrate more closely multiple perspectives and thematic spheres in religious studies.

We use the concept "trajectories," therefore, to emphasize the need to follow different and novel paths when striving to make sense of the contemporary religious landscape and more closely examine the potential of the concept of the post-secular in this context. We want to emphasize that we do not employ the term "post-secular" in order to propose that we are now living in some kind of totally "new" reality that is somehow decidedly different from a previous "secular" reality or condition. Rather, we are more interested in exploring the potential usefulness of the term when aiming to *conceptualize* the apparent contemporary resurgence of religion in the public sphere as well as in relation to the changing conditions and parameters of religious life for individuals and groups.

It has become clear that the broader scholarship on contemporary religious life needs to remain attentive to a range of complex and often interrelated macro-level changes occurring in contemporary Western societies. As being central among these, we would regard, firstly, more recent overarching transformations of the global political economy following accelerating globalization over the past few decades and the resulting increased interconnectedness of societies with regard to the economy, politics, culture, media, and populations. Secondly, we also find it important to pay close attention to changing structures of power and authority between religious communities and other societal institutions and the implications of such developments for collective and individual religious agency, religious identity formation, and community and network construction. Thirdly, the increasing rethinking of secularist principles of governance and the general erosion of the hegemony of secularist discourse across a range of social and cultural fields also needs to be examined in detail. Such work may well require that we as scholars are willing to openly question and, when necessary, transform our underlying philosophies and received epistemological paradigms.[7] Indeed, as a result of this, the very category of religion may have to be further problematized, reworked, and rethought.

The Concept of the Post-Secular

Thus far, the wider debates on the concept of the post-secular have primarily been social–philosophical and social–theoretical in character and have mainly been concerned with ideologically challenging received understandings of "the secular" and secularist principles of governance. Following Michele Dillon, these debates could therefore be described as mainly having been concerned with philosophically addressing "the dilemmas posed by religious otherness."[8] As such, they have been particularly focused on re-framing "the ongoing tensions between religious cultures and civic political life."[9] All of these above elements constitute part and parcel of the concept of post-secularity as developed in the more recent social–philosophical writing of Jürgen Habermas—without a doubt the single-most influential and widely debated version of the concept to have been developed so far.[10]

In Habermas' writing, the term "post-secular" primarily describes a general shift involving a more recent and widespread rise in "public consciousness" regarding religion and religion-related issues throughout "the affluent societies of Europe or countries such as Canada, Australia and New Zealand, where people's religious ties have steadily or rather quite dramatically lapsed in the post-World War II period."[11] This emphasis on a rise in public "consciousness" must be regarded an important one, especially when considering that Habermas rather paradoxically goes on to stress that "in terms of *sociological indicators* /. . ./ the religious behaviour and convictions" of populations in these regions "have by no means changed to such an extent as to justify labelling these societies 'post-secular.'"[12] It is also worth noting that Habermas does not regard the concept to be applicable to the United States where religion in general (and Christianity in particular) appears largely to have retained considerable social and cultural significance. This growing public consciousness, argues Habermas, has been brought about by the following three "stimuli" in particular: (1) the increasing coupling of religion with global conflicts, which "undermines the secularistic belief in the *foreseeable disappearance* of religion and robs the secular understanding of the world of any triumphal zest"; (2) the more recent proliferation of religious voices and discourses on different national levels in connection with value-laden civil and political issues and controversies; and (3) following increasing immigration, particularly by people "from countries with traditional cultural backgrounds" (which appears to imply Muslim immigration in particular).[13] In order to adequately grasp and conceptualize this new situation, argues Habermas, both traditional secularist ideologies and monolithic theories of secularization prophesizing the gradual, but ultimately inevitable submission of religion to secular ideologies and values will have to be thoroughly reevaluated and revised.[14]

The concept of post-secularity as developed by Habermas thus retains quite close connections to broader contemporary sociological theorizing on the current and future societal position of religion, and the "de-privatization" of religion in particular.[15] Similar to such perspectives, Habermas' notion of post-secularity is primarily based on the premise that the above-mentioned Western societies have experienced some kind of more profound historical shift involving an increasing blurring of previously more clearly marked and differentiated "secular" and "religious" spheres.

These ideas undoubtedly also signal a highly notable shift in Habermas' thinking with regard to the possibility of religious voices and ideologies contributing to rational civil public debate in modern liberal constitutional democracies. However, they also necessarily need to be understood in close relation to his broader social–philosophical thinking, both earlier and more recent (including its purely normative aspects). The focus here has primarily been on social justice and the importance of the "public sphere" when considering the preconditions for a viable rational, inclusive, and participatory democracy.[16]

Indeed, in a very compressed form, Habermas' main argument is that in order for a rational and inclusive democracy to be achieved in societies which are deemed post-secular (i.e., societies that are marked by a general rise in public consciousness regarding religion and religion-related issues), both secular and religious individuals and groups need fully to recognize the right of each other to participate in and contribute to the wider civic and political life. In order to be able to do so adequately, Habermas contends, both need to engage in a mutual "complementary learning process," each reflexively striving to understand, respect, and accommodate the positions and arguments of the other. Ultimately, however, Habermas can nevertheless be said to cling on to a secularist position when he adds that "in a constitutional state, all norms that can be legally implemented must be formulated and *publicly justified* in a language that all the citizens understand."[17] When engaging in public civic and political debate, as Michele Dillon expresses it, religious individuals and groups therefore need to be able to translate "their religious norms into a secular idiom."[18]

Although these ideas are primarily social–philosophical (and normative) in character, their "more inclusive view of religion as an emancipatory political and cultural resource," as Dillon notes, has made them the subject of much debate among sociologists of religion as well.[19] However, from a sociology of religion perspective, Habermas' notion of post-secularity undoubtedly also contains a range of problematic aspects, most of which follow from his overly intellectualized and rationalized view of religion. For example, when examining the wider public debate surrounding some contested issue in some particular social context that involves both "religious" and "secular" parties, it is not always clear what constitutes a "religious" idea or argument as opposed to a "secular" one.[20] Following Dillon, we can therefore also certainly question how reasonable it is to assume that religious individuals in modern Western liberal democracies necessarily conceive of themselves as either religious *or* secular citizens, especially when considering that many religious institutions and communities have a long-standing tradition of participation in civil and political life.[21]

Indeed, these critical remarks also largely apply to many of the philosophically oriented debates on post-secularity more generally. As Bryan S. Turner argues, "philosophers tend /.../ to concentrate on religious beliefs rather than on practice and they almost never look at religious objects."[22] Consequently, within wider debates on post-secularity, "there is a marked tendency to look at formal theologies, official statements of belief and formal institutions."[23] Moreover, as commentators within these debates "rarely refer to any actual findings of social science," they also typically tend to neglect "major developments in modern religiosity" such as the "growth of 'post-institutional spirituality' and the development of all forms of popular religion."[24] As noted above, problematic aspects of this kind are, at least partly, although arguably far from satisfactorily, recognized in Habermas' own version of the concept. Even so, from a sociological point of view, Turner is quite right in stating that arguments about the post-secular character of contemporary Western societies, as well as other closely associated broader arguments such as those having been presented by influential commentators such as Charles Taylor,[25] have rarely moved beyond the terrain of "abstract speculations."[26]

It is clear that the concept of post-secularity is still in need of much further clarification and refinement if it is to serve as a framework through which to conceptualize the continued social significance and growing public visibility of religion throughout much of the Western world. As Justin Beaumont argues, as a starting point we might begin by taking the concept as generally referring "to the limits of the secularization thesis /.../ and the ever growing realization of radically plural societies in terms of religion, faith and belief within and between diverse urban societies."[27] More specifically, however, argues Beaumont, we could "consider postsecular as the indication of diverse religious, humanist and secular positionalities" and principally focus on examining the "interrelations between these dimensions."[28]

In addition to the above, we would also need to consider more closely what we mean by "secularization" in this context. For example, it may well prove useful to distinguish between what Turner calls "political" and "social" secularization. While the former would primarily refer to issues regarding religious institutions and political arrangements, the latter would instead primarily refer "to issues about social values, practices and customs, namely to everyday life or what we might call the social sphere" or the arena "that is the ensemble of rituals, practices and sites where religion is practised."[29] At the same time, however, we also need to acknowledge the difficulty in upholding easy distinctions between different social "spheres" (e.g., "public," "private," and "domestic") when it comes to religion and religious life and practice.

An important matter for further consideration, therefore, is the issue of exactly *where* signs, elements, or aspects deemed characteristic of post-secularity can best be located and identified, and subsequently *empirically* observed and investigated. As already noted, it is evident that, in order for the concept of post-secularity to have any greater explanatory value, it necessarily needs to be refined in a way that allows for both firm contextualization and empirical grounding.[30] One obvious arena of such contextualized empirical investigation would be the public debate revolving around some particular contested issue in some particular society. As Kim Knott observes, such an investigation could, for instance, focus on the "language of opposition" which often marks public debates involving religious and secular voices.[31] Beaumont also points to the importance of contextualization and empirical grounding when he writes that "it is in the *urban* that the shift from secular to postsecular in terms of public space, building use, governance and civil society is most intensely observed and experienced."[32]

However, if we want to develop a more contextualized and firmly empirically grounded understanding of post-secularity that is attentive both to the changing locations and changing general character of contemporary religious life and practice, we need to cast our net wider still. As argued by Dillon, "if the term post-secular is theoretically robust /. . ./ it should be able to help us understand the more general relevance of religion as *a public cultural resource*" as well as something that necessarily needs to be understood in relation to people's actual lived experiences and practices.[33] Turner also expresses some similar ideas when he, as briefly discussed above, criticizes the broader debates on post-secularity for having been too narrowly focused on religion as a matter of "belief to the exclusion of religious practice."[34]

Some clarification in regard to the concept of the post-secular has been provided in recent publications that have explored it in relation to more specific topics and issues such as politics, the urban, philosophy, and theology.[35] Having said that, there are also cases where the term "post-secular" has been employed merely as a catchword,[36] or has been used in a directly descriptive sense as referring to an actual condition or state of affairs.[37] As already noted, considering the complexities involved, it is our view that the concept of the post-secular and its explanatory and analytical potentials and limitations needs to be explored along multiple trajectories, focusing on a broad range of social and cultural phenomena. Crucially, however, when examining the post-secular it is of outmost importance not to confuse concept with reality. The question of whether or not the concept could or should be taken to refer to an actual "condition," "reality," or "state of affairs" is largely an empirical question that, for the time being at least, remains largely unsubstantiated and thus unresolved. The prefix "post" in our use of the term therefore primarily refers to a *scholarly position* that is determined by a reflective and critical distance to generalized and simplistic applications of various secularization theses in combination with renewed empirical research efforts concentrating on decisive changes at societal, cultural, and individual levels.

In line with this general agenda, the chapters in this volume examine the application of the concept of the post-secular in relation to ongoing transformations in the very category of "religion"; the growing public visibility of religion, religious actors, and discourses, the impact of the present-day media environment on contemporary religious life and practice, the changing power relations between religious and other societal institutions, and the changing environments and parameters of collective and individual religious agency.

Religion, the Secular and Liquidity

Having set out the general agenda for this volume, we will now shed light on some of the main trajectories explored in its individual chapters. Our discussion will also touch upon some additional, potentially relevant themes which will largely be left for future research to address.

In the introductory part of this chapter we claimed that there is a need to explore alternative ways of conceptualizing the place of religion within contemporary societies. One important aspect of this concerns what can be defined as the need for a critical position in relation to epistemological paradigms.[38] For example, problematizing received understandings of the very category of "religion" has become a topical question in research on religion. For instance, with reference to Bauman's concept of "liquid modernity", Teemu Taira and Turner propose that the term "liquid religion" could prove fruitful when exploring developments in postinstitutional religiosity, and the increasing blurring of the boundaries between the religious and the secular, the public and the private.[39]

For example, focusing in particular on the case of Wicca in Finland, Taira has explored religion as a discursive technique and classificatory tool in relation to the channeling of social and practical interest. As he writes:

> Although Wicca does not go completely against the grain of modernity by keeping private religion and public issues relatively separate, it brings unpleasant ambivalence to our understanding of the nature of religion and its location in society. It shakes up the comfortable everyday life where everything should be in its proper place. In this sense, Wicca is a prime example of ambivalence and fluidity characterising liquid modern life.[40]

The fluidity and liquidity that both Taira and Turner depict as being characteristic of sections of the contemporary religious landscape also surface in the contributions to this volume, as does the related ambivalence and tensions inherent in received categories such as "religion" and "the secular," the "public," and the "private." However, this fluidity should not necessarily be regarded a feature of non- or postinstitutional religiosity only. On the contrary, it might certainly be of value to explore such developments and consider new conceptual tools in religious studies in general. For example, in the final chapter of this volume, Mika Lassander highlights the need to constantly reflect on possible reconfigurations of the category of religion and to abandon outdated categories and explanatory models when necessary. Rather than defining religion as an independently real object with certain specific generic properties, Lassander approaches religion as a quasi-object that is neither entirely socially constructed nor an objective fixed structure, neither inherently social nor inherently psychological. Instead, religion is approached as a hybrid that cannot be divided or reduced into social or psychological components without each acknowledging the other.

Lassander emphasizes the model of vernacular religion, which makes explicit the view that an individual's religion is a process dependent on what that individual does with the religion, how s/he talks about it, what actors—human and nonhuman—are involved, how they are engaged, and how they translate information. In addition, Lassander also proposes that actor-network theory would help us to better understand the bidirectional influences that determine these processes, as well as how they need not necessarily be tied to things that are usually presumed to be religious. This kind of mapping of networks and processes might surely prove productive when striving to understand people's beliefs and worldviews in social and cultural environments which are marked by increasing complexity and rapid change. One of the potential values of this perspective is the possibility that it might take us some steps further in ongoing discussions concerning the category of religion and the concepts of the religious and the secular.

In our above discussion about the concept of post-secularity, an important but problematic aspect was identified with regard to Habermas' thoughts on the subject. On the one hand, in a post-secular society as envisaged by Habermas, religious and secular individuals and groups face the challenge of recognizing each other's (and thereby indirectly their own) right to contribute to wider civil and political debate through striving to engage in a mutual learning process so as to be able to accommodate and better understand the positions of the other. On the other hand, the very same pluralist society in which this is meant to happen is itself dependent on the maintenance of a publicly justified language which is shared by all citizens. This involves an ongoing tension in terms of discursive conflicts that have contributed to the eruption of the religious in the public sphere.

Steven D. Smith discusses this in depth in his book *The Disenchantment of Secular Discourse*. In the final chapter he poses a quite common and general question when he writes that "outside the sphere of secular public discourse /. . ./ there are circles of discourse that are metaphysically and theologically much thicker /. . ./. So the challenge, it seems, is /. . ./ to figure out whether and how and on what terms to admit such thicker belief into public discourse."[41] Smith's question is topical in many Western cultural and societal contexts since it addresses problematic issues such as plurality versus shared norms and the preconditions for the organization of a publicly justified civil language.

The philosophical and political discussion about plurality and the quest for a publicly justified language is, from another perspective, closely related to the long-standing discussion about sovereignty and understandings of sovereignty in terms of vertical vs. horizontal (e.g., popular) sovereignty.[42] In his chapter in this volume, Casanova discusses how European societies are becoming increasingly religiously pluralistic, how the model of the homogeneous nation-state is being called into question. Historically, however, "The Westphalian principle—*cuius regio eius religio*—was not significantly altered either by the critical transition from royal to national or popular sovereignty after the French Revolution, or by the expansion and consolidation of democracy in Western European societies after World War II."

William E. Connolly has also addressed contemporary claims about the paradox of sovereignty becoming stark in late modernity. He argues that the question of sovereignty has grown both more acute and more elusive in contemporary societies because of extra and intra state processes, generated by transnational corporations, supranational regulatory instances, and global media networks, and refers to sovereignty "as composed of a plurality of forces circulating through and under the positional sovereignty of the official arbitrating body."[43] In other words, the contemporary condition as depicted here from a perspective of sovereignty also implies that we are required to account for a society that is characterized by a cluster of discursive public processes rooted not only in more or less established institutions, but also in highly significant broader social movements and cultural trends that strive to transform their particular positions into legitimate societal values and practices.

Tuomas Martikainen's chapter provides a relevant contribution to this discussion and sets out an additional important trajectory. From a perspective of power and rule in late modern societies, Martikainen argues that we are witnessing significant changes in the social location of religion and that we are entering a new phase of state–religion relations, affected by, in particular, neoliberalization and globalization. Turner, among others, has made a similar observation and highlighted how modern nation-states have become increasingly forced to organize and regulate religion through a diversity of policies. He refers to this as the "management of religions."[44] However, in order to gain an adequate understanding of the development of such management strategies, the various effects of the implementation of neoliberalist policies need to be taken into account. This means directing attention to the ways in which the development of such strategies unfold in particular social and cultural environments that have become increasingly characterized by a move away from institutionalized practices toward an ethos of entrepreneurial freedom.[45] We will return to the relevance of exploring neoliberal politics and culture later in this introductory chapter. At this point we would like to further underline another theme. As Martikainen states in his chapter:

> [a] self-reflexive stance on currently fashionable academic vocabulary (as also used in this text) is necessary, as concepts such as "social capital," "governance," and "transnationalism," are themselves significantly products of this very same change in the global power regime, in the same way as the terms "society," "nation-state," and "religion" have their roots in modernity.

As highlighted here, the scholarly perspectives and concepts we apply are bound to and embedded in particular times and locations. From the above it is evident that in a post-secular society, encounters between voices affiliated with religious or nonreligious orientations become a much more complex issue than merely one concerning the bridging of differences with regard to formal theologies or worldviews. Hence, to continue regarding different religions simply as rational belief systems with incompatible truth claims implies a simplification and problematic distortion of what is undoubtedly a multifaceted phenomenon.[46] A reevaluation of the traditional understanding of religious pluralism is also clearly called for as the relativism of the late modern or postmodern age gives way to a stronger sense of religious integrity among several minority groups in society.[47] Neither Habermas nor Connolly provides a clear route out of the discursive conflicts that inevitably seem to erupt in those pluralist societies which are deemed to be post-secular. However, according to Connolly, pluralist societies require a "deep pluralism": "[t]o renegotiate the ethos of sovereignty in the contemporary context requires an audacious pluralization of the sacred and a corollary relaxation of what it takes to defile the sense of the sacred embraced by you, me, or others."[48] His emphasis on the role of the sacred is somewhat similar to Turner's,[49] although Turner might be said to draw the conclusion of what Connolly calls the pluralization and relaxation of the sacred when writing that the world of the sacred appears to be shrinking and the separation of the sacred and profane evaporating in contemporary societies.

However, we might need to be a bit cautious when considering this argument. Ruth Illman and Laura Wickström's chapter provides thought-provoking insights into this complexity by highlighting contemporary religious environmentalism and examining the blurring of the boundaries between the secular and the religious when observed in the context of people's quests for holistic unity between spiritual and worldly dimensions of reality. The authors demonstrate how contemporary religious/spiritual environmentalism seems to strongly advocate a rediscovering of the sacredness of the environment and a reenchantment of nature that often entails a reconfiguration of elements of secular and religious values. People are increasingly prone to blur the boundaries between different sectors of knowledge and in juxtaposing scientific, religious, esoteric, and therapeutic discourses and practices.[50]

In her chapter, Katja Valaskivi also addresses a similar liquidity or reconfiguration of the secular and the religious. She explores global innovationism—a secular subsystem of the economy, politics, and science—in terms of a secular belief or rationalized symbolic universe with religious connotations. Based on her empirical analysis she points to how innovationism involves the organization and maintenance of core values and how it is connected to the social imaginary and the management of hope and threat in societies in which religion has become a matter of individual choice. Although Valaskivi's contribution concentrates on a field that is usually perceived to be somewhat remote from the "religious" sphere in terms of organization and practice, her case nevertheless clearly provides an important insight into contemporary social changes and reconfigurations that need to be taken into account when exploring the notion of the post-secular.

It is worth emphasizing once again that the contemporary religious landscape is inherently complex and provides researchers with not only a theoretical challenge but also a methodological one. For instance, as a result of the profound changes now occurring it becomes difficult to focus only on religious groups, organizations, or movements; many current developments with obvious implications for any consideration of the post-secular are to be found in the field of noninstitutional forms of religion and alternative/holistic spiritualities.[51] Further, if we follow the trajectories explored by Illman and Wickström and Valaskivi, we need to acknowledge how both spiritual practices and spiritualized secular positions (of both a collective and individual nature) connect to broader ideological, political, and cultural trends in society. That is to say that we should not automatically assume the existence of a religious "sphere" that is distinct or separate from broader social, cultural, political, and economic "spheres." This becomes evident when philosophical normative perspectives are abandoned in favor of perspectives that focus more directly on discursive processes that cut through post-secular culture and society.

Indeed, observations such as these are heavily dependent on empirical research that would aim to bring us closer to the subjects, politics, and movements involved in (or which become affected by) the reconfiguring of the religious and the secular. Taking such directions in research seems to become more and more important in light of the increasingly pressing need to reevaluate and reformulate received and taken-for-granted theories and concepts. For example, in researching beliefs and practices in contemporary society in the United Kingdom, Abby Day deliberately avoided asking direct questions about, for example, belief in God, or about religious practices such as prayer or worship. Instead, she promoted open discussion about broader beliefs and practices and found that even apparently nonreligious people still found religion to be an important marker of personal and social identity. What some might dismiss as "nominal" or "marginal" religion is, she argued, far from blurry, empty or insignificant, but rich in cultural and relational meaning and "arguably the largest form and fastest-growing style of Christian belief and belonging in the world."[52]

In particular, two of the chapters in this volume contribute to these discussions in a decisive way. Terhi Utriainen, Måns Broo, and Tuija Hovi's chapter on contemporary well-being practices sheds light on a relevant tension within the post-secular. They suggest that, in addition to the notion of individual freedom, a sense or construction of "destiny" can be identified as an important aim in modern life and many contemporary well-being practices. Anne Birgitta Pessi and Nadia Jeldtoft also highlight the multifaceted nature of individual experiences in their chapter when arguing that authenticity and a sense of belonging to a moral community continues to matter for individuals at the level of lived religion.

These are important contributions which both address a central issue also put forward by Utriainen, Broo, and Hovi: "[t]oday, both identity and agency are often seen in terms of choices to be made, but there are important conditions as well as contours around individual choice-making." This observation indirectly calls for future research to reinvestigate the interplay between the religious and the secular on the one hand, and that between gender, ethnicity, social class, sexuality, ability, and age on the other.[53] We need to examine the notion of the

14

post-secular in a way that does not blind us to the interconnectedness of the individual, the subject, and the social. Connolly has addressed similar issues in terms of the politics of becoming, referring to how "new cultural identities are formed out of unexpected injuries, energies and institutionally congealed injuries."[54]

The above complexities surely need to be addressed from several vantage points and positions. For instance, Rosi Braidotti argues for the necessity of a position that "does not condition the emergence of the subject on negation but on creative affirmation" and on "vital generative forces."[55] However, this does not imply that we should ignore the structuring and conditioning forces and power-relations within both religious and secular institutions and in their interplay. It might be assumed that a post-secular condition (presuming the actuality of such a condition for the sake of argument) raises many challenges for late modern subjects. The labor market is becoming more insecure and transitive, social life is becoming ever more fragmented and intimate relationships increasingly fragile (while still remaining important), and identities are not given once and for all but need to be endlessly (re)constructed and reinforced. Some analyses of post-secular urban culture have depicted it in critical terms as being disorienting or generating increasing disconnectedness, as being marked by a lack of subjectivity or authenticity, a glorification of the superficial, the fragmentary, diffuse, and disassociated.[56] In some cases critical interpretations have been related to commercialization and consumer culture.[57] From this perspective, post-secular urban culture is regarded as an ultimate manifestation of the spirit of late modern capitalism, historically rooted in this-worldly asceticism, as outlined by Max Weber. Linda Woodhead and Ole Riis also discuss late modern society in terms of tensions and contradictions on the part of subjects. They argue that "different domains of a polycentric society pursue their values self-referentially" and that "[m]any individuals find their lives dispersed between competing symbolic and social systems, while seeking a unified and consistent biography," which causes a paradox of demands for freedom and autonomy in combination with calls for commitment and surrender.[58] They claim, however, that this condition also leads to increased reflexivity.

At this point we can take a step back and reflect more in depth on Smith's[59] earlier question from another position. On the basis of the above discussion, it can be claimed that the question about whether or how it would be feasible to suggest carving out space for alternative discourses to enter public secular discourse is somewhat misleading or even based on a set of erroneous assumptions. Is this really an alternative at hand? Who would be able to make such a choice? Even though the question ever more often tends to surface in a growing variety of contexts, we need to keep in mind that this question remains embedded in a largely normative philosophical context characterized by a higher level of abstraction. It is also primarily connected to Smith's main concern, i.e., matters related to the academic field of law.

This becomes obvious when we follow another important trajectory and thoroughly investigate the relevance of media for contemporary society and culture, and in particular for religion in relation to public discourse. Smith also makes a similar observation about how media allows for religious discourses to take a strong role in the public sphere, but he does not develop this idea further and addresses it more or less as a matter of quality and from a normative position. Smith's way of addressing the relevance of media is limited to the notion of "richness" and "depth." On the one hand, he finds the growing public debate relevant but, on the other hand, he discusses it in terms of a "current degradation" and "symptoms" even though he also states "they might well be viewed (and often have been viewed) as potential contributors to a richer and deeper public discourse."[60]

As has been indicated several times above, we do not find this to be a satisfying enough position for our purposes of investigating different trajectories of the post-secular. The problem is that while both Smith and Connolly point out important directions and address the complexity of the contemporary condition, they do not explore these directions in any detail. In contrast, we find it important to take a position closer to the one articulated by Lynch et al., who write that "[c]ontemporary media and culture encourage the 'deregulation' of religious ideas and symbols, allowing them to circulate through society in ways that are increasingly beyond the control of religious institutions"—and, we would add, beyond the control of many or most societal, political, and cultural institutions.[61] One implication of this might be that Smith's assumption that we have the opportunity to make a choice, i.e., to limit or open the secular public discourse for this or that, is problematic. This is particularly so when we look at the issue from a social–scientific and not primarily philosophical perspective.

A common feature of the religious landscape that is addressed in the chapter by Liselotte Frisk and Peter Nynäs is the invitation to work with oneself, more specifically with one's mind, body, and spirit, as well as with one's emotions, goals, values, and relations. This has been referred to as "the subjective or expressive turn of culture,"[62] the "de-differentiation of the person"[63] or "self-realization."[64] Recognizing that religious agency and identity construction are not reconfigured and formed in a vacuum, it has become important to integrate studies of popular culture and consumer culture in the study of religion. As argued by several scholars,[65] popular culture has come to play an ever more important role in the dissemination of a wide range of religious and spiritual beliefs, ideas, practices, and identities. These developments also highlight the need to focus more firmly on the ways in which people's actual religious and spiritual beliefs are reflected in the various forms of media and popular culture that they use and consume. Moreover, this also involves exploring the different ways and degrees to which media and popular culture may become formative and determinative of the religious life and practice of different individuals and groups.[66]

Against this background, the chapter by Marcus Moberg and Kennet Granholm provides a further contribution to broader discussions about the concept of the post-secular, its potentials, and limitations. Moberg and Granholm explore how attention to the contemporary nexus of religion, media, popular culture, and consumer culture could contribute to a more empirically and context-oriented understanding of the post-secular and afford it more substance in relation to other related current theoretical concepts within the wider sociological study of religion. They suggest that if current debates on post-secularity were to be coupled with a more sustained focus on the impact of media, popular culture, and consumer culture on contemporary religious life and practice, then we might well arrive at new interpretations of the actual composition and general character of the contemporary Western religious landscape. Concerning the notion of deregulation and circulation raised above with reference to Lynch et al., this perspective does not rule out a focus on power relations.[67] On the contrary, it is clearly pointed out by Moberg and Granholm that a changing media landscape has affected power relations between religious groups and other institutions, thereby having made possible new and innovative forms of both collective and individual religious agency.

In addition to the need for exploring the effects of media and understanding changing power relations, it is important to examine further the relevance of neoliberal politics and culture. This was already highlighted with regard to Martikainen's chapter and it also forms a prominent background theme in Valaskivi's analysis of the global secular subsystem of innovationism. Gauthier et al. provide an interesting and brief overview of how the relationship between religion and economics (consumer culture) has been articulated, describing several positions, such as research focusing on the negative effects of consumer culture on religion, research that examines the ways in which consumer culture has stimulated change in religious institutions, as well as an emerging body of work on religion, neoliberalism, and changing welfare provision.[68] All these positions provide further potentially fruitful ways of exploring trajectories of the post-secular, not least since the ideologies and practices of neoliberalism to an ever larger extent affect more and more aspects of our lives. In order to be able to further explore this field in a systematic manner, it might be worthwhile in the future to investigate different ways of accommodating neoliberalism. Carrette and King, for example, provide an agenda for such an endeavor.[69]

However, from a critical point of view, this trajectory would also need to be integrated at the level of epistemology and methodology. Carrette and King claim that "[r]eligion is re-branded in order to support the ideology of capitalism."[70] While remaining cautious of the pitfalls of overly deterministic arguments, this idea should be taken seriously also when reflecting on our own engagement with our own field of study. If neoliberalism has become a dominant ideology strongly rooted in Western cultures and societies, we need to pose the question as to what extent it also affects our own ways of investigating, interpreting, and describing contemporary religious landscapes? This issue is raised in Frisk and Nynäs' contribution, which sheds light on commonly held scholarly views of contemporary religious trends on the one hand, and the need to critically consider the ideological connotations and views of humankind and society that are embedded in these on the other. They claim that this requires a nuanced conceptual reflection and also ethical considerations.

In conclusion, current scholarly discussions about religion in the public sphere and in particular the notion of the post-secular form the background of this book. The chapters are held together by one topical question in particular. As the general notion of secularization clearly has proved to be in need of rethinking and revision, what new pathways of understanding the societal and cultural place of religion within contemporary societies might we consider? In line with this question, the chapters in this volume examine the application of the concept of the post-secular in relation to ongoing transformations in the very category of "religion," the growing public visibility of religion, religious actors and discourses, the impact of the present-day media environment on contemporary religious life and practice, the changing power relations between religion and other societal institutions, and the changing environments and parameters of collective and individual religious agency.

The wider reflections on the concept of the post-secular have primarily been social–philosophical and social–theoretical in character. Therefore, we have underlined above that, in order for the concept of post-secularity to gain any greater explanatory and analytical value, it necessarily needs to be further developed in ways that allows for both firm contextualization and empirical grounding. An important issue that is explored in this volume, therefore, is the issue of where signs, elements, or aspects deemed characteristic of post-secularity can best be located and identified, and subsequently empirically observed and investigated.

It has become clear that the broader scholarship on contemporary religious life needs to remain attentive to a range of complex and often interrelated macro-level changes occurring in contemporary Western societies. Through the discussion and examples in this introductory chapter we have shed light on at least some of the elements of this complexity. Faced with the challenges outlined and briefly discussed in this introductory chapter, we find it relevant to approach the issue through striving to follow different trajectories, to more closely integrate multiple perspectives and thematic spheres in religious studies, and to openly question and transform our underlying philosophies and received epistemological paradigms when necessary.

Notes

1. Matthias Koenig and Paul F. A. de Guchteneire, eds., *Democracy and Human Rights in Multicultural Societies* (Aldershot: Ashgate, 2007), 12.
2. Charles Taylor, *A Secular Age* (Cambridge, MA: The Belknap Press of Harvard UP, 2007), 543.
3. E.g., Grace Davie, *The Sociology of Religion* (London: Sage, 2007); Bryan S. Turner, *Religion and Modern Society: Citizenship, Secularisation and the State* (Cambridge: Cambridge University Press, 2011).
4. José Casanova, *Public Religions in the Modern World* (London: The University of Chicago Press, 1994).
5. E.g., Peter L. Berger, ed., *The Desecularization of the World: Resurgent Religion and World Politics* (Washington, DC: The Ethics and Public Policy Center, 1999); Davie, *Sociology of Religion*; Turner, *Religion and*

Modern Society; Jürgen Habermas, "Notes on Post-Secular Society," *New Perspectives Quarterly* 25 (Fall 2008).

6. Michael Warner and others, "Editors' Introduction," in *Varieties of Secularism in a Secular Age*, ed. Michael Warner, Jonathan Vanantwerpen, and Craig Calhoun (Cambridge, MA and London: Harvard University Press, 2010), 9.

7. Turner, *Religion and Modern Society*.

8. Michele Dillon, "Can Post-Secular Society Tolerate Religious Differences?" *Sociology of Religion* 71 (2010): 141.

9. Ibid., 142.

10. Jürgen Habermas, "Religion in the Public Sphere," *European Journal of Philosophy* 14 (2006): 1–25; "Notes on Post-Secular Society," 17–29.

11. Habermas, "Notes on Post-Secular Society," 17.

12. Ibid.

13. Ibid., 20.

14. For a more detailed discussion of Habermas' account of the concept of post-secularity, see, for example, Austin Harrington, "Habermas and the 'Post-Secular' Society," *European Journal of Social Theory* 10 (2007): 543–60; Gregor McLennan, "Spaces of Postsecularism," in *Exploring the Postsecular: The Religious, the Political and the Urban*, ed. Arie L. Molendijk, Justin Beaumont, and Christopher Jedan (Leiden: Brill, 2010), 41–62; Dillon, "Can Post-Secular Society Tolerate Religious Differences?" 139–56.

15. E.g., José Casanova, "Religion, European Secular Identities, and European Integration," in *Religion in an Expanding Europe*, ed. Timothy A. Byrnes and Peter J. Katzenstein (Cambridge: Cambridge University Press, 2006), 65–92.

16. Jürgen Habermas, *The Structural Transformation of the Public Sphere* (1964; repr., Cambridge: Polity Press, 1992); cf. Harrington, "Habermas and the 'Post-Secular' Society," 547–48; Bernice Martin, "Contrasting Modernities: 'Postsecular Europe and Enspirited Latin America,'" in *Exploring the Postsecular*, 67; Dillon, "Can Post-Secular Society Tolerate Religious Differences?", 144.

17. Habermas, "Notes on Post-Secular Society," 28.

18. Dillon, "Can Post-Secular Society Tolerate Religious Differences?," 146.

19. E.g., Ibid., 145.

20. Ibid.; cf. James W. Boettcher and Jonathan Harmon, "Introduction: Religion and the Public Sphere," *Philosophy & Social Criticism* 35 (2009): 12.

21. E.g., Justin Beaumont, "Transcending the Particular in Postsecular Cities," in *Exploring the Postsecular*, 4.

22. Bryan S. Turner, "Religion in a Post-secular Society," in *The New Blackwell Companion to the Sociology of Religion*, ed. Bryan S. Turner (Chichester: Blackwell, 2010), 650.

23. Ibid.

24. Ibid.

25. Taylor, *Secular Age*.

26. Turner, "Religion in a Post-secular Society," 650.

27. Beaumont, "Transcending the Particular in Postsecular Cities," 6; cf. Hent de Vries, "Introduction: Before, Around, and Beyond the Theologico-Political," in *Political Theologies: Public Religions in a Post-Secular World*, ed. Hent

de Vries and Lawrence E. Sullivan (New York: Fordham University Press, 2006), 7.

28. Beaumont, "Transcending the Particular in Postsecular Cities," 6.

29. Turner, "Religion in a Post-secular Society," 652–53.

30. E.g., Ibid., 649–67; Dillon, "Can Post-Secular Society Tolerate Religious Differences?"; cf. de Vries, "Introduction Before, Around, and Beyond the Theologico-Political," 3.

31. Kim Knott, "Cutting Through the Postsecular City: A Spatial Interrogation," in *Exploring the Postsecular*, 34.

32. Beaumont, "Transcending the Particular in Postsecular Cities," 3, our emphasis; See also Knott, "Cutting Through the Postsecular City."

33. Dillon, "Can Post-Secular Society Tolerate Religious Differences?" 142, our emphasis; cf. Beaumont, "Transcending the Particular in Postsecular Cities," 7.

34. Turner, "Religion in a Post-secular Society," 658.

35. Arie L. Molendijk and others, eds., *Exploring the Postsecular: The Religious, the Political and the Urban* (Leiden: Brill, 2010); Hent de Vries and Lawrence E. Sullivan, eds., *Political Theologies: Public Religions in a Post-secular World* (New York: Fordham University Press, 2006).

36. E.g., Stefanie Knauss and Alexander D. Ornella, eds., *Reconfigurations: Interdisciplinary Perspectives on Religion in a Post-Secular Society* (Münster: Lit Verlag, 2007).

37. Hans-Georg Ziebertz and Ulrich Riegel, "Post-Secular Europe – a Concept Questioned," in *Europe: Secular or Post-Secular?* ed. Hans-Georg Ziebertz and Ulrich Riegel (Berlin: Lit Verlag, 2008), 27.

38. E.g., Davie, *Sociology of Religion*, 9–10.

39. Zygmunt Bauman, *Liquid Modernity* (Cambridge: Polity Press, 2000); Teemu Taira, "Religion as a Discursive Technique: The Politics of Classifying Wicca," *Journal of Contemporary Religion* 25, no. 3 (October 2010); Turner, *Religion and Modern Society*, ix.

40. Taira, "Religion as a Discursive Technique," 387–88.

41. Steven D. Smith, *The Disenchantment of Secular Discourse* (Cambridge, MA: Harvard University Press, 2010), 215.

42. See, e.g., Taylor, *A Secular Age*; Wendy Brown, "Sovereignty and the Return of the Repressed," in *The New Pluralism: William Connolly and the Contemporary Global Condition*, ed. David Campbell and Morton Schoolman (Durham, NC: Duke University Press, 2008).

43. William Connolly, *Pluralism* (Durham, NC: Duke University Press, 2005), 145.

44. Turner, *Religion and Modern Society*, 175–84.

45. David Harvey, *A Brief History of Neoliberalism* (Oxford: Oxford University Press, 2005), 7.

46. Willy Pfändtner, *Understanding Religious Diversity. A Contribution to Interreligious Dialogue from the Viewpoint of Existential Philosophy* (Uppsala: Uppsala University, 2005).

47. Aimee Upjohn Light, "Post-Pluralism through the Lens of Post-Modernity," *Journal of Inter-Religious Dialogue* 1 (2009): 67–71, http://irdialogue.org/journal; Davie, *Sociology of Religion*, 159–60.

48. Connolly, *Pluralism*, 147.

49. Turner, *Religion and Modern Society*, xii–xiii, 278–79.
50. Inger Furseth, *From Quest for Truth to Being Oneself. Religious Change in Life Stories* (Frankfurt am Main: Peter Lang, 2006).
51. Cf. Steven Sutcliffe, *Children of the New Age. A History of Spiritual Practices* (London: Routledge, 2003).
52. Abby Day, *Believing in Belonging: Belief and Social Identity in the Modern World* (Oxford: Oxford University Press, 2011), 9.
53. Giselle Vincett and others, "Women, Religion and Secularization: One Size Does Not Fit All," in *Women and Religion in the West. Challenging Secularization*, ed. Kristin Aune, Sonya Sharma, and Giselle Vincett (Aldershot: Ashgate, 2008), 1–19.
54. William E. Connolly, "Suffering, Justice, and the Politics of Becoming," *Culture, Medicine and Psychiatry* 20 (1996): 261.
55. Rosi Braidotti, "In Spite of the Times: The Postsecular Turn in Feminism," *Theory Culture & Society* 25 (2008): 19.
56. E.g., Pasi Mäenpää, *Narkissos kaupungissa: tutkimus kuluttajakaupunkila isesta ja julkisesta tilasta* [Narcissus in the City: A Study of the Consumer Citizen and the Public Sphere] (Helsinki: Tammi, 2005); Graham Ward, *Cities of God* (London: Routledge, 2000); J. Pahl, *The Desire to Acquire: Or, Why Shopping Malls are Sites of Religious Violence* (2007), http://divinity. uchicago.edu/martycenter/publications/webforum/052007/desire_to_ acquire.pdf (accessed December 18, 2011); Danièle Hervieu-Legér, *Religion as a Chain of Memory* (Cambridge: Polity Press, 2000).
57. David R. Loy, "The Religion of the Market," *Journal of the American Academy of Religion* 65, no. 2 (1997): 275–90.
58. Ole Riis and Linda Woodhead, *A Sociology of Religious Emotion* (Oxford: Oxford University Press, 2010), 204.
59. Smith, *Disenchantment of Secular Discourse*, 215.
60. Ibid., 6.
61. Gordon Lynch and others, "Introduction," in *Religion, Media and Culture: A Reader*, eds. Gordon Lynch, Mitchell Jolyon, and Anna Strhan (London and New York: Routledge, 2012), 1.
62. Paul Heelas and Linda Woodhead, *The Spiritual Revolution. Why Religion is Giving Way to Spirituality* (Oxford: Blackwell Publishing, 2005), 2–5.
63. Davie, *Sociology of Religion*, 231.
64. Hervieu-Legér, *Religion as a Chain of Memory*, 36.
65. E.g., Christopher Partridge, *The Re-enchantment of the West (vol. 1): Alternative Spiritualities, Sacralization, Popular Culture and Occulture* (London: Continuum, 2004); Christopher Partridge, *The Re-enchantment of the West (vol. 2): Alternative Spiritualities, Sacralization, Popular Culture and Occulture* (London: Continuum, 2005); Stewart M. Hoover, *Religion in the Media Age* (New York: Routledge, 2006); Gordon Lynch, *The New Spirituality. An Introduction to Progressive Belief in the Twenty-first Century* (New York: I.B. Tauris, 2007).
66. E.g., Hoover, *Religion in the Media Age*, 290.
67. Lynch and others, "Introduction," 1–6.
68. François Gauthier et al., "Introduction: Religion et société de consummation/ Religion in Consumer Society," *Social Compass* 28 (2011): 291–301.

69. Jeremy Carrette and Richard King, "Spirituality and the Re-branding of Religion," in *Religion, Media and Culture*, 60–69.
70. Ibid.

Bibliography

Barker, Victoria. "After the Death of God: Postsecularity?" *Journal of Religious History* 1 (2009): 82–95.

Bauman, Zygmunt. *Liquid Modernity*. Cambridge: Polity Press, 2000.

Beaumont, Justin. "Transcending the Particular in Postsecular Cities." In *Exploring the Postsecular: The Religious, the Political and the Urban*, edited by Arie L. Molendijk, Justin Beaumont, and Christopher Jedan, 3–17. Leiden: Brill, 2010.

Berger, Peter L., ed. *The Desecularization of the World: Resurgent Religion and World Politics*. Washington, DC: The Ethics and Public Policy Center, 1999.

Boettcher, James W., and Jonathan Harmon. "Introduction: Religion and the Public Sphere." *Philosophy & Social Criticism* 35 (2009): 5–22.

Braidotti, Rosi. "In Spite of the Times: The Postsecular Turn in Feminism." *Theory, Culture & Society* 25 (2008): 1–24.

Brown, Wendy. "Sovereignty and the Return of the Repressed." In *The New Pluralism: William Connolly and the Contemporary Global Condition*, edited by David Campbell and Morton Schoolman, 250–73. Durham, NC: Duke University Press, 2008.

Carrette, Jeremy, and Richard King. "Spirituality and the Re-branding of Religion." In *Religion, Media and Culture: A Reader*, edited by Gordon Lynch, Mitchell Jolyon, and Anna Strhan, 60–69. London and New York: Routledge, 2012.

Casanova, José. *Public Religions in the Modern World*. London: The University of Chicago Press, 1994.

———. "Religion, European Secular Identities, and European Integration." In *Religion in an Expanding Europe*, edited by Timothy A. Byrnes and Peter J. Katzenstein, 65–92. Cambridge: Cambridge University Press, 2006.

Connolly, William E. *Pluralism*. Durham, NC: Duke University Press, 2005.

———. "Suffering, Justice, and the Politics of Becoming." *Culture, Medicine and Psychiatry* 20 (1996): 251–77.

Davie, Grace. *The Sociology of Religion*. London: Sage, 2007.

Day, Abby. *Believing in Belonging: Belief and Social Identity in the Modern World*. Oxford: Oxford University Press, 2011.

Dillon, Michele. "Can Post-Secular Society Tolerate Religious Differences?" *Sociology of Religion* 71 (2010): 139–56.

Furseth, Inger. *From Quest for Truth to Being Oneself. Religious Change in Life Stories*. Frankfurt am Main: Peter Lang, 2006.

Gauthier, François, Tuomas Martikainen, and Linda Woodhead. "Introduction: Religion et société de consummation/Religion in Consumer Society." *Social Compass* 28 (2011): 291–301.

Habermas, Jürgen. "Notes on Post-Secular Society." *New Perspectives Quarterly* 25 (Fall 2008): 17–29.

———. "Religion in the Public Sphere." *European Journal of Philosophy* 14 (2006): 1–25.

———. *The Structural Transformation of the Public Sphere*. 1964. Reprint, Cambridge: Polity Press, 1992.

Harrington, Austin. "Habermas and the 'Post-Secular' Society." *European Journal of Social Theory* 10 (2007): 543–60.

Heelas, Paul, and Linda Woodhead. *The Spiritual Revolution. Why Religion is Giving Way to Spirituality.* Oxford: Blackwell Publishing, 2005.

Hervieu-Legér, Danièle. *Religion as a Chain of Memory.* Cambridge: Polity Press, 2000.

Hoover, Stewart M. *Religion in the Media Age.* New York: Routledge, 2006.

Knauss, Stefanie, and Alexander D. Ornella, eds. *Reconfigurations: Interdisciplinary Perspectives on Religion in a Post-Secular Society.* Münster: Lit Verlag, 2007.

Knott, Kim. "Cutting Through the Postsecular City: A Spatial Interrogation." In *Exploring the Postsecular: The Religious, the Political and the Urban,* edited by Arie L. Molendijk, Justin Beaumont, and Christopher Jedan, 19–38. Leiden: Brill, 2010.

Koenig, Matthias, and Paul F. A. de Guchteneire, eds. *Democracy and Human Rights in Multicultural Societies.* Aldershot: Ashgate, 2007.

Loy, David R. "The Religion of the Market." *Journal of the American Academy of Religion,* 65, no. 2 (1997): 275–90.

Lynch, Gordon. *The New Spirituality. An Introduction to Progressive Belief in the Twenty-first Century.* New York: I.B. Tauris, 2007.

Lynch, Gordon, Mitchell Jolyon, and Anna Strhan. "Introduction." In *Religion, Media and Culture: A Reader,* edited by Gordon Lynch, Mitchell Jolyon, and Anna Strhan, 1–6. London and New York: Routledge, 2012.

Mäenpää, Pasi. *Narkissos kaupungissa: tutkimus kuluttajakaupunkilaisesta ja julkisestaTilasta* [Narcissus in the City: A Study of the Consumer Citizen and the Public Sphere]. Helsinki: Tammi, 2005.

Martin, Bernice. "Contrasting Modernities: 'Postsecular' Europe and Enspirited Latin America." In *Exploring the Postsecular: The Religious, the Political and the Urban,* edited by Arie L. Molendijk, Justin Beaumont, and Christopher Jedan, 63–89. Leiden: Brill, 2010.

McLennan, Gregor. "Spaces of Postsecularism." In *Exploring the Postsecular: The Religious, the Political and the Urban,* edited by Arie L. Molendijk, Justin Beaumont, and Christopher Jedan, 41–62. Leiden: Brill, 2010.

Molendijk, Arie L., Justin Beaumont, and Christopher Jedan, eds. *Exploring the Postsecular: The Religious, the Political and the Urban.* Leiden: Brill, 2010.

Pahl, Jon. *The Desire to Acquire: Or, Why Shopping Malls are Sites of Religious Violence.* 2007. http://divinity.uchicago.edu/martycenter/publications/webforum/052007/desire_to_acquire.pdf (accessed December 18, 2011).

Partridge, Christopher. *The Re-enchantment of the West (vol. 1): Alternative Spiritualities, Sacralization, Popular Culture and Occulture.* London: Continuum, 2004.

———. *The Re-enchantment of the West (vol. 2): Alternative Spiritualities, Sacralization, Popular Culture and Occulture.* London: Continuum, 2005.

Pfändtner, Willy. *Understanding Religious Diversity. A Contribution to Interreligious Dialogue from the Viewpoint of Existential Philosophy.* Uppsala: Uppsala University, 2005.

Riis, Ole, and Linda Woodhead. *A Sociology of Religious Emotion.* Oxford: Oxford University Press, 2010.

Smith, Steven D. *The Disenchantment of Secular Discourse*. Cambridge, MA: Harvard University Press, 2010.

Sutcliffe, Steven. *Children of the New Age. A History of Spiritual Practices*. London: Routledge, 2003.

Taira, Teemu. "Religion as a Discursive Technique: The Politics of Classifying Wicca." *Journal of Contemporary Religion* 25, no. 3 (October 2010): 379–94.

Taylor, Charles. *A Secular Age*. Cambridge, MA: Harvard University Press, 2007.

Turner, Bryan S. *Religion and Modern Society: Citizenship, Secularisation and the State*. Cambridge: Cambridge University Press, 2011.

———. "Religion in a Post-secular Society." In *The New Blackwell Companion to the Sociology of Religion*, edited by Bryan S. Turner, 649–67. Chichester: Blackwell, 2010.

Upjohn Light, Aimee. "Post-Pluralism through the Lens of Post-Modernity." *Journal of Inter-Religious Dialogue* 1 (2009): *http://irdialogue.org/journal (accessed* December 18, 2011).

Vincett, Giselle, Sonya Sharma, and Kristin Aune. "Women, Religion and Secularization: One Size Does not Fit All." *In Women and Religion in the West. Challenging Secularization*, edited by Kristin Aune, Sonya Sharma, and Giselle Vincett, 1–23. Aldershot: Ashgate, 2008.

de Vries, Hent. "Introduction: Before, Around, and Beyond the Theologico-Political." In *Political Theologies: Public Religions in a Post-Secular World*, edited by Hent de Vries and Lawrence E. Sullivan, 1–88. New York: Fordham University Press, 2006.

de Vries, Hent, and Lawrence E. Sullivan, eds. Political Theologies: Public Religions in a Post-secular World. New York: Fordham University Press, 2006.

Ward, Graham. *Cities of God*. London: Routledge, 2000.

Warner, Michael, Jonathan Vanantwerpen, and Craig Calhoun. "Editors' Introduction." In *Varieties of Secularism in a Secular Age*, edited by Michael Warner, Jonathan Vanantwerpen, and Craig Calhoun, 1–31. Cambridge, MA and London: Harvard University Press, 2010.

Ziebertz, Hans-Georg, and Ulrich Riegel. "Post-Secular Europe – a Concept Questioned." In *Europe: Secular of Post-Secular?* edited by Hans-Georg Ziebertz and Ulrich Riegel, 9–41. Berlin: Lit Verlag, 2008.

2

Are We Still Secular? Explorations on the Secular and the Post-Secular*

José Casanova

The term "post-secular" like every other term composed of the prefix "post" is full of ambiguities. The prefix "post" may indicate simply a subsequent phase within the same phenomenon, such as the postmodern phase of modernity or the postindustrial phase of advanced capitalist societies. Alternatively, it may point to something radically different, to a new epoch that transcends, goes beyond, and leaves behind a phenomenon without having yet a label to characterize the new. But the ambiguity in the term "post-secular" derives not only from the unclear meaning of the prefix, but much more from the ambiguities and outright contradictions in the multiple meanings of the term "secular."

When we ask ourselves whether we are still secular, the meaningful answer can only be "it depends." It depends whether we are no longer secular, perhaps because we are religious again, in which case the prefix "post" would also be problematic. Or perhaps we are still secular, but in a new reflexive way that justifies the use of the prefix. In any case it should be obvious that the meaning of "post-secular" will depend from the meaning of the term "secular." Moreover, it will also depend on the connotation of "we," namely, who and which societies and institutions are included in this reflexive interrogation? Finally, it will also depend whether the focus of our investigation is directed at the qualifier "still," that is, if the central question is whether we are in the midst of an epochal change in the secular Zeitgeist.

In the following presentation, I would like to proceed by addressing each of these three types of questions: (1) In which different ways one may be said to be "secular,"? (2) Who is included in the secular "we,"? and (3) Are we "still" secular or can one perceive a shift towards some "post-secular" condition?

Three Meanings of Secular

I would like to introduce an analytical distinction between three different meanings of the word "secular," or three different ways in which one may be said to be secular, to which would correspond three different understandings of the process of secularization.

1. Living in the secular world and in secular time

This is the broadest possible sense of the term "secular," which is derived from the medieval Christian theological transformation of the Latin term "saeculum." Originally, the Latin world saeculum, as in *per saecula saeculorum* only meant an indefinite period of time, but eventually it became one of the terms of a dyad, religious/secular, which served to structure the entire spatial and temporal reality of Medieval Christendom into a binary system of classification separating two worlds, the religious–spiritual–sacred world of salvation and the secular–temporal–profane world. Thus, the distinction between the "religious" or regular clergy, who withdrew from the world into the monasteries to lead a life of Christian perfection, and the "secular" clergy who lived in the world along with the laity.

In this respect, to secularize means to "make worldly," to convert religious persons or things into secular ones, as when a religious person abandons the monastic rule to live in the world, or when monastic property is secularized. This is the original Christian theological meaning of the term "secularization" that may serve, however, as the basic metaphor of the historical process of Western secularization. This historical process needs to be understood as a particular reaction to the structuring dualism of Medieval Christendom, as an attempt to bridge, eliminate, or transcend the dualism between the religious and the secular world. Even in the West, however, this process of secularization follows two different dynamics.

One is the dynamic of internal Christian secularization which aims to spiritualize the temporal and to bring the religious life of perfection out of the monasteries into the secular world. It tends to transcend the dualism by blurring the boundaries between the religious and the secular, by making the religious secular and the secular religious through mutual reciprocal infusion. This path was initiated by the various medieval movements of Christian reform of the saeculum, was radicalized by the Protestant Reformation and has attained its paradigmatic expression in the Anglo-Saxon Calvinist cultural area, particularly in the United States.

The other, different, indeed almost opposite, dynamic of secularization takes the form of laicization. It aims to emancipate all secular spheres from clerical–ecclesiastical control and in this respect it is marked by a laic–clerical antagonism. Unlike in the Protestant path, however, here the boundaries between the religious and the secular are rigidly maintained, but those boundaries are pushed into the margins, aiming to contain, privatize, and marginalize everything religious, while excluding it from any visible presence in the secular public sphere, now defined as the realm of *laïcité*, freed from religion. This is the paradigmatic French–Latin–Catholic path of secularization, but it will find diverse manifestations throughout continental Europe.

With many variations, these are the two main dynamics of secularization, which culminate in our secular age. In different ways both paths lead to an overcoming of the medieval Christian dualism through a positive affirmation and revaluation of the saeculum, that is, of the secular age and the secular world, imbuing the immanent secular world with a quasi-transcendent meaning as the place for human flourishing. In this broad sense of the term "secular," we are all secular and all modern societies are secular and are likely to remain so for the foreseeable future, one could almost say *per saecula saeculorum*.

2. Within the immanent frame of the secular age: To be or not to be religious, that is the question!

There is a second narrower meaning of the term "secular," that of self-sufficient and exclusive secularity, when people are simply "irreligious," that is, devoid of religion and closed to any form of transcendence beyond the purely secular immanent frame. Here, secular is not anymore one of the units of a dyadic pair, but is constituted as a self-enclosed reality. To a certain extent, this constitutes one possible end-result of the process of secularization, of the attempt to overcome the dualism between religious and secular, by freeing oneself of the religious component.

In his recent work, *A Secular Age*, Charles Taylor has reconstructed the process through which the phenomenological experience of what he calls "the immanent frame," becomes constituted as an interlocking constellation of the modern differentiated cosmic, social, and moral orders.[1] All three orders, the cosmic, the social, and the moral, are understood as purely immanent secular orders, devoid of transcendence, and thus functioning *etsi Deus non daretur*, "as if God would not exist." It is this phenomenological experience that, according to Taylor, constitutes our age paradigmatically as a secular one, irrespective of the extent to which people living in this age may still hold religious or theistic beliefs.

The question is whether the phenomenological experience of living within such an immanent frame is such that people within it will also tend to function *etsi Deus non daretur.* Taylor's phenomenological account of the secular "conditions" of belief is meant to explain the change from a Christian society around 1500 CE in which belief in God was unchallenged and unproblematic, indeed "naïve" and taken for granted, to a post-Christian society today in which belief in God not only is no longer axiomatic but becomes increasingly problematic, so that even those who adopt an "engaged" standpoint as believers tend to experience reflexively their own belief as an option among many others, one moreover requiring a explicit justification. Secularity, being without religion, by contrast tends to become increasingly the default option, which can be naively experienced as natural and, thus, no longer in need of justification.

This naturalization of "unbelief" or "nonreligion" as the normal human condition in modern societies corresponds to the assumptions of the dominant theories of secularization, which have postulated a progressive decline of religious beliefs and practices with increasing modernization, so that the more modern a society the more secular, i.e., the less "religious," it is supposed to become. That the decline of religious beliefs and practices is a relatively recent meaning of the term "secularization" is indicated by the fact that it does not yet appear in the dictionary of most modern European languages.

The fact that there are some modern non-European societies, such as the United States or South Korea, that are fully secular in the sense that they function within the same immanent frame and yet their populations are also at the same time conspicuously religious, or the fact that the modernization of so many non-Western societies is accompanied by processes of religious revival, should put into question the premise that the decline of religious beliefs and practices is a quasi-natural consequence of processes of modernization. If modernization per se does not produce necessarily the progressive decline of religious beliefs and practices, then we need a better explanation for the radical and widespread secularity one finds among the population of Western European societies.[2]

Secularization, in this second meaning of the term "secular," being "devoid of religion," does not happen automatically as a result of processes of modernization, but needs to be mediated phenomenologically by some other particular historical experience. The meaning of "post-secular" in this context, however, would be that of individuals as well as societies becoming religious again, undergoing processes of religious revival, which would reverse previous secular trends. Peter Berger has used the expression "de-secularization of the world," while David Martin asks whether "secularization has gone into reverse."[3] There is little evidence, however, that individuals or societies in the heartland of secularization, Western Europe, are becoming post-secular in the sense of becoming religious again. As Martin has pointed out, not even in the most secular of societies, East Germany, can one find any evidence of any religious revival.[4]

3. Secularism as stadial consciousness

Self-sufficient secularity, that is, the absence of religion, has a better chance of becoming the normal taken-for-granted position if it is experienced not as an unreflexively naïve condition, as just a fact, but actually as the meaningful result of a quasi-natural process of development. As Taylor has pointed out, modern unbelief is not simply a condition of absence of belief, nor merely indifference. It is a historical condition that requires the perfect tense, "a condition of 'having overcome' the irrationality of belief."[5] Intrinsic to this phenomenological experience is a modern "stadial consciousness," inherited from the Enlightenment, which understands this anthropocentric change in the conditions of belief as a process of maturation and growth, as a "coming of age" and as progressive emancipation. For Taylor, this stadial phenomenological experience serves in turn to ground the phenomenological experience of exclusive humanism as the positive self-sufficient and self-limiting affirmation of human flourishing and as the critical rejection of transcendence beyond human flourishing as self-denial and self-defeating.

In this respect, the historical self-understanding of secularism has the function of confirming the superiority of our present modern secular outlook over other supposedly earlier and, therefore, more primitive religious forms of understanding. To be secular means to be modern, and, therefore, by implication to be religious means to be somehow not yet fully modern. This is the ratchet effect of a modern historical stadial consciousness, which turns the very idea of going back to a surpassed condition into an unthinkable intellectual regression.

The function of secularism as a philosophy of history, and thus as ideology, is to turn the particular Western Christian historical process of secularization into a universal teleological process of human development from belief to unbelief, from primitive irrational or metaphysical religion to modern rational postmetaphysical secular consciousness. Even when the particular role of internal Christian developments in the general process of secularization is acknowledged, it is in order to stress the universal significance of the uniqueness of Christianity as, in Marcel Gauchet's expressive formulation, the religion that produces "the exit from religion."[6]

I would like to propose that this secularist stadial consciousness is a crucial factor in the widespread secularization that has accompanied the modernization of Western European societies. Europeans tend to experience their own secularization, that is, the widespread decline of religious beliefs and practices among their midst as a natural consequence of their modernization. To be secular is not experienced as an existential choice which modern individuals or modern societies make, but rather as a natural outcome of becoming modern. In this respect, the theory of secularization mediated through this historical stadial consciousness tends to function as a self-fulfilling prophecy. It is, in my view, the presence or absence of this secularist historical stadial consciousness that explains when and where processes of modernization are accompanied by radical secularization. In places where such secularist historical stadial consciousness is absent or less dominant, as in the United States or in most non-Western postcolonial societies, processes of modernization are unlikely to be accompanied by processes of religious decline. On the contrary, they may be accompanied by processes of religious revival.

Within the context of the third meaning of the term "secular," that of secularist secularity, post-secular would imply reflexively abandoning or at least questioning the modern secularist stadial consciousness which relegates "religion" to a more primitive, more traditional, now surpassed stage of human and societal development. This appears to be the sense in which Habermas uses the term "post-secular," not as a change in society itself, as a reversal of secular trends, but as a change in consciousness, as "an altered self-understanding of the largely secularized societies of Western Europe, Canada, or Australia."[7]

Post-secular here would mean, first of all, becoming reflexively aware of what Habermas calls a "secularistic self-misunderstanding."

Now that we have introduced a distinction between those three different meanings of being secular: (a) that of *mere secularity*, that is, the phenomenological experience of living in a secular world and in a secular age, where being religious may be a normal viable option; (b) that of *self-sufficient and exclusive secularity*, that is, the phenomenological experience of living without religion as a normal, quasi-natural, taken for granted condition; and (c) that of *secularist secularity*, that is, the phenomenological experience not only of being passively free, but actually of having been liberated from "religion" as a condition for human flourishing, we may be in a better position to answer satisfactorily the question, "how secular are we?"

How Secular Are "We"?

As a matter of fact, in every society at any time some people are likely to be more "religious" than others. This may be a constant, even after taking account of changes in the meaning and nature of religiosity across time and space. In this respect, individuals in any society may be more or less religiously inclined, or in the expressive formulation of Max Weber, more or less "religiously musical or unmusical."

Arguably, Italy, where 31 percent of its population affirms to have had a deep religious experience or the experience of religious transcendence, is the country with the most religiously musical population of all Europe.[8] Only in five other European countries does the proportion of those who claim a similar religious experience surpass 20 percent, that is, one-fifth of the population. Surprisingly, in this small group of countries with the highest level of experiential individual religiosity, one finds France with 24 percent and the Netherlands with 22 percent, two countries that in every other respect are supposedly among the most secularized of Europe. In any case, both percentages are still higher than the number of professed atheists in both countries, which are, respectively, 19 percent and 17 percent of the French and Dutch populations. West Germany and Britain occupy the European middle ground, 16 percent of their population claim to have had a religious experience, while the proportion of those who declare themselves atheists are, respectively, 11 percent and 10 percent. The population of former East Germany occupies the very bottom in the scale of religiosity or the very top in the scale of European secularity. Only 10 percent of East Germans claim to have had some deep personal religious experience. By contrast, a majority, 51 percent, confesses to be atheist.

In fact, a majority, that is, over 50 percent of the population in every European country, with the exception of East Germany and the Czech Republic, still declares "belief in God." But the range of belief and unbelief in Europe is significantly wide. At the high end, over 90 percent of the population in Poland, Ireland, and Portugal declare themselves believers. In the Scandinavian countries, France, the Netherlands, and Russia, the number of believers goes down to the fifties. Britain and West Germany, with 69 percent and 65 percent, respectively, occupy the European middle ground.

In summary, one may say that although a majority of the population in most European countries still maintains some kind of general belief in God, the depth and extent of individual religiosity in Europe is rather low in so far as those who profess belief in a personal God, those who pray with some regularity, and those who claim to have had some personal religious experience are a small minority in most European countries. In this respect, unlike in the United States where one finds high levels of individual religiosity even among the unchurched, a majority of the population in most European countries can be characterized as simply secular and nonreligious.

The drastic decline in church attendance across Europe since the 1950s constitutes the strongest evidence for the defenders of the traditional theory of secularization. Less than 20 percent of the population in the majority of European countries attends church regularly, while in East Germany, Russia, and in the Scandinavian countries the proportion of regular churchgoers decreases to the single digits. When compared with the very different evidence of continuing vitality in congregational, associational religion in the United States across all denominations—Protestant and Catholic, Jewish and Muslim, and now Hindu and Buddhist, it is obvious that this is the fundamental difference between American and European religiosity. Secularization in Europe takes primarily the form of "unchurching" (*Entkirchlichung*), which should be understood as a form of liberation from the type of territorialized confessional religiosity which was the legacy of the Westphalian system. European Christianity, for all kinds of reasons, never made the full historical transition from territorial national churches based on the territorial parish or Pfarrgemeinde, to competing denominations of civil society based on voluntary religious associations, a modern form of religious community.

The analytical distinction between "church" and "denomination" is the key to any comparative analysis of religious developments and patterns of secularization in Europe and the United States. Following Max Weber's definition, sociologically, a "church" is an ecclesiastical institution which claims the monopoly of the means of salvation over a territory. The territorialization of religion and the corresponding confessionalization of state, nation, and peoples are the fundamental facts and formative principles of the Westphalian system of sovereign territorial states which emerged in early modern Europe out of the so-called Wars of Religion. The principle *cuius regio eius religio* is the general formative principle of such system, a principle moreover which was already well established before the wars of religion and even before the Protestant Reformation, as shown by the expulsion of Jews and Muslims from Spain by the Catholic monarchs in order to establish a territorial Catholic state ruling over a homogeneously religious Catholic society. What the Peace of Westphalia represented was the generalization of this dual model of confessionalization of states, nations, and peoples and territorialization of ecclesiastical religion among the emerging European territorial states. Every early modern European state (with the exception of the Polish–Lithuanian Commonwealth) was defined confessionally as Catholic, Anglican, Lutheran, Calvinist, or Orthodox. In this respect, religious homogenization and, in many instances, ethno-religious cleansing stand at the very origin of the modern European state.

This is the fundamental factor of early modern European history which will determine the various patterns of European secularization. Comparatively speaking, European secularization can be best understood as a process of successive deconfessionalizations of state, nation, and peoples, which was phenomenologically experienced as a process of liberation from confessional identities. This is what determines the historically unique character of European secularization, which is now increasingly being recognized as a form of "European exceptionalism" rather than as a general model of modernization that is likely to be replicated elsewhere. In fact, the European pattern of secularization can hardly be replicated in other contexts in which there was no previous historical pattern of confessionalization of states, nations, and peoples requiring their secularization, that is, their deconfessionalization.

If my assumption is correct, it would imply that the various different patterns of European secularization and the various patterns of civil society formation across Europe are very much related to the various patterns of deconfessionalization of state, nation, and peoples. Those patterns are historically complex and although generally path dependent, they also traverse recognizable breakthroughs at historical turning points which offer structural opportunities to change course or revise the particular path of secularization. It is this common phenomenological experience of having passed through stages of deconfessionalization which permeates the typically European stadial consciousness which understands the process of secularization as a process of progressive emancipation from religion.

In fact, without taking into account the long-term European pattern of confessionalization of states, peoples, and territories, it is not possible to understand the difficulties which every continental European state has, irrespective of the fact whether they have maintained formal establishment or are constitutionally secular, and the difficulties which every European society has, the most secular as well as the most religious ones, in accommodating religious diversity, and particularly in incorporating immigrant religions.[9] This is one of the fundamental differences between Europe and the United States, which never underwent a process of confessionalization and developed a radically different model of religious denominationalism.

Paraphrasing Karl Marx in "On the Jewish Question," one could say that if America can be characterized simultaneously as the model of "perfect disestablishment" and the "land of religiosity par excellence," European societies offer by contrast the inverse combination of different forms of "imperfect disestablishment" and "lands of secularity par excellence."[10] The United States never had to undergo a formal process of separation of church and state, since it never had either a confessional state or an established state church, from which the state had to separate itself. Unlike most Europeans, Americans also did not need to undergo a process of deconfessionalization from any national ecclesiastical institution, since even the established colonial churches, Congregational, Presbyterian, and Anglican, remained minoritarian institutions and the majority of the population remained unchurched. The American state was born as a modern secular state, without having to undergo any process of deconfessionalization and the dual constitutional formula of no establishment of religion at the state level and free exercise of religion in society guaranteed the development of denominationalism as a system of free and open religious pluralism in society.

American denominationalism is a system of mutual recognition of deterritorialized voluntary religious institutions and associations within civil society without any state regulation or interference other than through the courts when there are legal conflicts within or among religious organizations. The American state not only has no office of regulation or registration of religious associations, but does not even have the right to register or survey the religious denomination of its individual citizens.

Tocqueville's remains the classic and still unsurpassed analytical sociological account we have of the modern system of American religious pluralism and its affinities with the model of a pluralist and democratic civil society. Like so many other European visitors, Tocqueville was immediately struck by the vitality of religion in America and by the "innumerable multitude of sects" he found there. But unlike so many later European visitors and professional observers who tended to minimize or explain away the relevance of this phenomenon by referring to "American exceptionalism," as if the vitality of religion in America was simply the exception that confirmed the general rule of European secularization, Tocqueville saw it clearly as a "novel" situation, that is, as the product of modern developments and not simply as a traditional residue that was eventually bound to disappear with progressive modernization, and, therefore, as a challenge to the premise of European secularization.

Indeed, by tying his explanation of the striking pluralism and vitality of religion in America to a historical theory of modern individualism, to a historical theory of modern civil society, and to a historical theory of modern civil religion, Tocqueville offers a more persuasive institutional theory of the unique vitality of the very particular American system of religious denominationalism, than contemporary supply-side theories of the American religious markets which are based (a) on dubious anthropological presuppositions of a single and universal type of rational human action based on the utilitarian calculation of costs and benefits; (b) on an ahistorical theory of religious markets according to which the demand for religious commodities is universally constant, what changes is the supply along with changes in the level of regulation and free competition in the religious market; and (c) on an ahistorical theory of a self-differentiated and self-regulated religious market that appears disembedded from the American state, from the legal–constitutional system, from the American nation, and from American culture, and is, therefore, a model which presumably can be exported to any society in the world or can naturally flourish once state regulation of religious markets disappears.

It should be obvious that the different models of religious denominationalism within a pluralistic civil society and confessional national churches with limited pluralism have important consequences for the constitution of civil society on both sides of the Atlantic but also for the development of inclusionary, more egalitarian, and solidaristic welfare states in Europe and the weak development of a welfare state in the United States. As the polemical debates around the attempts of the Obama administration to reform the American health system clearly indicate, the very discursive legitimation of what is a taken-for-granted principle in most European nation-states, namely, the principle of a public national health system which guarantees a minimum egalitarian access of health care for all its citizens, is immediately suspect as an etatist, socialist un-American project, and susceptible to the most irrational debates. What is surprising is not that conservative Republicans may oppose the Democratic project of reforming the national health system, but that their arguments still find such a resonance within American public opinion.

One can certainly find close elective affinities between the antietatist model of state–civil society relations and the model of free exercise of religion protected from any kind of state regulation or control. But secularist interpretations of the relation between the absence of a welfare state in America and the persistence of religion invert, in my view, the nature of the relationship. It is not, as Norris and Inglehart tend to argue, that Americans are still so religious because of their existential insecurity due to the absence of a welfare state, but rather that Americans have defeated so far every attempt to institutionalize the welfare state because of the model of a self-organized and privately regulated civil society which is so intrinsically related with their model of religious denominationalism.[11]

Empirically, all the evidence for the positive correlation between modernization and secularization comes from Western Christian (i.e., post-Christian) societies, primarily Western European countries with the addition of Canada, Australia, and New Zealand (that is, European settler colonial societies). Japan is the only non-Western society that would seem to corroborate Inglehart's thesis. But in the case of Japan, as in the case of China, one could offer a more convincing socio-cultural explanation for what appears to be already inordinate evidence of secularity well before the precipitation of processes of modernization.

Indeed, China and the United States are the two great outliers in opposite directions in Inglehart's figures, which put into question the entire theory. Given the basic assumption that "people who experience ego-tropic risks during their formative years (posing direct threats to themselves and their families) or socio-tropic risks (threatening their community) tend to be far more religious than those who grow up under safer, comfortable, and more predictable conditions,"[12] and given the catastrophic experience of material existential insecurity suffered by broad sectors of the Chinese population throughout the twentieth century, one should expect high levels of religiosity among the Chinese population, particularly among older generations. Yet, the evidence tends to point in the opposite direction. China, along with Japan, perhaps for similar reasons, appears to be one of the most secular societies on earth, at least as measured by the Western Christian categories of religiosity used by the World Values Survey.[13]

Both, the evidence of a society like China that may have been both "secular" and economically undeveloped, and the evidence of a society like the United States which seems to have become progressively more rather than less religious as it became more economically developed, seem to put into question the intrinsic correlation between modernization and secularization. American religion is not a survival from a premodern traditional society, but is a product of American modernity. Thus, the expectation that religiosity will also eventually decline as the material conditions of the American population become more secure, is highly problematic. None of the three explanations of American exceptionalism offered by Norris and Inglehart seem very convincing.

The economic insecurity connected with high levels of economic inequality does not sound convincing, when all sectors of the American population, from the most privileged to the most disprivileged, evince inordinate high levels of religiosity, at least in comparison with most Western European societies. As I have already indicated, the argument that Americans are still so religious because they do not have yet a welfare state, inverts in my view the more plausible direction of the correlation between the system of American denominationalism and the weakness of the welfare state in America.

As to the argument that Americans may be inordinately religious due to the constant flow of poor immigrants from undeveloped countries, it is empirically equally problematic for several reasons. There is no evidence of any decline of American religiosity from the late 1920s to 1965, when the gates of immigration to America for all practical purposes were closed, a period which also coincides with a limited institutionalization of the welfare state. There is no evidence of an increase in American religiosity after 1965, when the gates of immigration became wide open again. The assumption that immigrants may be more religious because they come from undeveloped countries is also problematic, since half of all post-1965 new immigrants tend to have higher levels of education and income than the average American. Moreover, there is compelling historical evidence that immigrants to America in all waves of successive immigration, throughout the nineteenth century as well as in the late twentieth century, become increasingly more religious, not less, as they settle in the new country. In fact most immigrant groups, Protestants and Catholics, Jews and Muslims, Hindus and Buddhists, today as in the past, claim to be more consciously and reflexively religious in the United States than they were in their old countries before immigration.

Moreover, while Norris and Inglehart offer irrefutable evidence of a very strong statistical correlation between levels of socio-economic development and general levels of secularization among Western European societies, the theory cannot explain satisfactorily the still significant variations in levels of secularization among otherwise similarly developed European societies. Neither levels of modernization nor levels of existential security can explain convincingly why East Germany and West Germany, or the Czech Republic and Poland (two similarly developed Catholic post-Soviet Slavic societies), or France and Italy (two similarly developed Latin Catholic societies), or the Netherlands and Switzerland (two similarly developed biconfessional Calvinist–Catholic societies) evince such radically different levels of secularization. It seems that patterns of historical relations between church, state, and nation can offer more convincing explanations of the variations.

Are We "Still" Secular or Are We Entering a "Post-Secular" Global Age?

Insofar as answering this question requires projecting one's gaze and one's interpretation of what appear to be contemporary trends into the future, one can offer at best some cautiously speculative answers, well aware that the social sciences have a dismal record of historical forecasting, that history remains contingent and, therefore, unpredictable and that the future remains, therefore, fundamentally open.

Concerning the first meaning of the word "secular," that of living phenomenologically within the immanent frame of a secular world, not only are we in the West still secular and are likely to remain so for the foreseeable future, but even most non-Western societies are also becoming increasingly secular, in the sense that the cosmic order is increasingly defined by modern science and technology; the social order is increasingly defined by the interlocking of citizenship "democratic" states, market economies, and mediatic public spheres; and the moral order is increasingly defined by the calculations of rights-bearing individual agents, claiming human dignity, liberty, equality, and the pursuit of happiness. Indeed, globally one must admit that the whole world is becoming simultaneously both more "religious" and more "secular" as the Western Christian binary system of classification of religious–secular reality became globalized. Indeed, the categories of "religious" and "secular" have became recently globalized for the first time in all non-Western cultures.

Concerning the second meaning of "secular," there is little evidence of any significant religious revival among the population of Western European societies, except among immigrant groups. At best one could say that the rate of religious decline has slowed down or has been halted. Actually, the rate of secularization in many European societies may have reached a point of no return. Religion as "a chain of memory," using the formulation of the French sociologist Daniele Hervieu-Leger, appears broken almost without repair and large generations of young Europeans are growing up without any personal relationship with or even knowledge of the Christian religious tradition. Not only the Christian churches, but most importantly families have lost their role in the process of religious socialization. Barring any unforeseeable religious revival, it is unlikely that the process of European secularization, that is, the unchurching of the European population may be reversed. In this respect, it is premature to speak of European societies as post-secular.

And yet, something fundamental is happening to the European secular Zeitgeist. Neither the naïve, unreflexive secularity which accepted being without religion as the quasi-natural, modern condition, nor the secularist self-understanding which turned the particular process of European Christian secularization into a universal normative development for all of humanity are simply tenable, that is, can be simply taken for granted without questioning or reflexive elaboration anymore.

We are not "religious" again, yet. But we have certainly become obsessed with religion as a question, particularly as a public issue. The fact that we are asking the question, "Are we still secular or are we post-secular?" is in itself evidence that a change has taken place in the secular Zeitgeist, that we have crossed a threshold and that we cannot be simply unreflexive secularists anymore. We can of course reassert our secularism again, even aggressively and militantly, as the new atheists are doing.[14] But this in itself is a response to what is viewed as an unwelcome and dangerous return of the repressed, of something we thought we had overcome and left behind.

There are many reasons for this new reflexive and inquisitive attitude. I will only mention three.

a. Globalization

The first and most obvious one can be subsumed under the code word "globalization." In our global age it has become increasingly evident that European secular developments are not a universal norm for the rest of the world, that as the rest of the world modernizes, people are not becoming more secular like us, but are becoming more religious, or actually they are becoming simultaneously both more secular and more religious, which of course only muddles and confuses our binary categories.

It is not anymore the United States only which appears to be an exception to the European rule of secularization, but the rest of the world appears to be equally exceptional to the point in which we are now talking of European exceptionalism. But we should be cautious with the new discourse of European exceptionalism. When it comes to "religion" and its antonym "the secular," there is no global rule. We must humbly recognize that many of our received categories, derived from our Christian-secular European developments, fail us when we try to understand developments in the rest of the world, in that rather than facilitating understanding actually lead to fundamental misunderstanding. Neither the category of religious fundamentalism, nor the term proposed by Peter Berger "the de-secularization of the world" as if secularization had gone into reverse, nor even the expression "return of religion" or "religious revival" as we were simply witnessing the return of the old traditional religions, none of these categories are very helpful in trying to understand contemporary religious developments around the world. We need first a "de-secularization" of our consciousness and of our secularist and modernist categories before we can develop better concepts to understand the novelty and the modernity of these developments.

Moreover, the discourse of European exceptionalism is also problematic because even internally within Europe there is no single European rule of secularization.

It is the secularist self-understanding of European modernization, which has constructed such a rule of European secularization. The historical reality is that of multiple and complex patterns of secularization and religious revivals across Europe, many of them also intrinsically implicated with global colonial developments beyond Europe. This brings us to the second main reason for our renewed reflexive and polemical interest in religion.

b. European integration

The process of European integration, the expansion to the East, and the possible entry of Turkey have made evident that there is no European rule. None of the national models, the French or the German, the Dutch or the Italian, the Danish or the British, can serve as a general European model. The acrimonious debates around the preamble to the European constitution makes obvious the confusion about the so-called fundamental European values, the problematic notion that one much choose between Christian and secular values, or between Christianity and the Enlightenment as the source of the supposedly universal European values.

One must add the puzzling prospect of Turkey joining the European Union, of a Muslim democratic Turkey which may well meet all the formal criteria and tests to join the European club and yet cannot be fully European because it is neither Christian nor secular.

c. Immigration and increasing religious pluralism

Finally, there is the novel reality that European societies due to interrelated processes of religious individuation and more importantly increasing immigration are becoming either for the first time or again after many centuries religiously pluralistic. The model of the homogeneous nation-state inherited from the Westphalian system is being put into question. The Westphalian principle *cuius regio eius religio* was not significantly altered either by the critical transition from royal to national or popular sovereignty after the French Revolution, or by the expansion and consolidation of democracy in Western European societies after World War II.

The manifest difficulty which all European societies show in the integration of Muslim immigrants can be viewed as an indication of the problems which the model of the European nation-state has, whether it is formally secular or not, in regulating deep religious pluralism. One must question the problematic notion that the European secular state is de facto a religiously neutral state and, therefore, already contains within itself the proper solution to the management of religious pluralism in society.

We need to be more reflexively aware of the complex historical process of Western Christian secularization and its relation to allegedly general processes of modernization. We must avoid the false dichotomies built into our binary categories, either religious or secular, either traditional or modern. Above all, we must be more critically reflexive of the stadial consciousness built into our "secular self-interpretation of modernity." Becoming post-secular does not mean necessarily becoming religious again, but questioning our stadial consciousness, destabilizing if not our secular immanent frame, at least the possibilities of transcendence within the immanent frame, and being open, receptive, at least curious to all the manifold forms of being religiously human.

Notes

*   A more elaborate version of this paper is being published as "Exploring the Post-Secular: Three Meanings of 'the Secular' and Their Possible Transcendence," in *Habermas and Religion*, ed. Craig Calhoun, Eduardo Mendieta, and Jonathan Van Antwerpen (Cambridge, UK: Polity Press, 2012).

1.   Charles Taylor, *A Secular Age* (Cambridge, MA: Harvard University Press, 2008). My analysis in the following section draws upon my review of Taylor's work, José Casanova, "A Secular Age: Dawn or Twilight," in *Varieties of Secularism in a Secular Age*, ed. Michael Warner, Jonathan Van Antwerpen, and Craig Calhoun (Cambridge, MA: Harvard University Press, 2010), 265–81.

2.   Peter Berger, Grace Davie, and Effie Fokas, *Religious America, Secular Europe? A Theme and Variations* (Burlington, VT: Ashgate, 2008).

3.   Peter Berger, ed., *The Desecularization of the World* (Washington, DC: Ethics and Public Policy Center, 1999); David Martin, "Has Secularization Gone into Reverse?" in *The Future of Christianity. Reflections on Violence and Democracy, Religion and Secularization* (Farnham: Ashgate, 2011), 85–104.

4. David Martin, "East Germany: The World's Most Secular Society," in *The Future of Christianity*, 149–64.
5. Taylor, *A Secular Age*, 269.
6. Marcel Gauchet, *The Disenchantment of the World: A Political History of Religion* (Princeton, NJ: Princeton University Press, 1997).
7. "A Postsecular World Society? On the Philosophical Significance of Post-secular Consciousness and the Multicultural World Society," An Interview with Juergen Habermas. By Eduardo Mendieta. *SSRC the Immanent Frame*, 4.
8. I am using the figures provided in Andrew Greeley, *Religion in Europe at the End of the Second Millennium* (New Brunswick, NJ: Transaction Publishers, 2003), 3. Greeley uses a composite of the results from the 1981 and 1990 European Values Study (EVS) and the 1991 and 1998 International Social Survey Programme (ISSP). Those are at best approximate indicators of trends. For a more detailed analysis, see José Casanova, "The Religious Situation in Europe," in *Secularization and the World Religions*, ed. Hans Joas and Klaus Wiegandt (Liverpool: Liverpool University Press, 2009), 206–28.
9. José Casanova, "Immigration and the New Religious Pluralism: A EU/US Comparison," in *The New Religious Pluralism and Democracy*, ed. Thomas Banchoff (New York: Oxford University Press, 2007), 59–83.
10. Berger, Davie, and Fokas, *Religious America, Secular Europe*.
11. Pippa Norris and Ronald Inglehart, *Sacred and Secular. Religion and Politics Worldwide* (New York: Cambridge University Press, 2004).
12. Ibid., 4.
13. There is, moreover, significant evidence of various kinds of religious revivals within contemporary China (*quigong* movements as well as evangelical Christianity, Taoism as well as folk religion, Confucianism as well as Buddhism) as it experiences dramatic rates of economic growth and increasing levels of socio-economic development across large sectors of the Chinese population, which are similar to developments associated with South Korean and, to a lesser extent, Japanese modernization. Cf. Vincent Goossaert and David A. Palmer, *The Religious Question in Modern China* (Chicago, IL: The University of Chicago Press, 2011); Fenggang Yang, *Religion in China: Survival and Revival Under Communist Rule* (New York: Oxford University Press, 2011); Mayfair Mei-Hui Yang, ed., *Chinese Religiosities* (Berkeley, CA: University of California Press, 2008).
14. Cf. Richard Dawkins, *The God Delusion* (New York: Houghton Mifflin, 2008); Christopher Hitchens, *God Is Not Great* (New York: Hachette Book Group, 2009).

Bibliography

Berger, Peter, ed. *The Desecularization of the World*. Washington, DC: Ethics and Public Policy Center, 1999.

Berger, Peter, Grace Davie, and Effie Fokas. *Religious America, Secular Europe? A Theme and Variations*. Burlington, VT: Ashgate, 2008.

Casanova, José. "Immigration and the New Religious Pluralism: A EU/US Comparison." In *The New Religious Pluralism and Democracy*, edited by Thomas Banchoff, 59–83. New York: Oxford University Press, 2007.

———. "The Religious Situation in Europe." In *Secularization and the World Religions*, edited by Hans Joas and Klaus Wiegandt, 206–28. Liverpool: Liverpool University Press, 2009.

———. "A Secular Age: Dawn or Twilight?" In *Varieties of Secularism in a Secular Age*, edited by Michael Warner, Jonathan Van Antwerpen, and Craig Calhoun, 265–81. Cambridge, MA: Harvard University Press, 2010.

Dawkins, Richard. *The God Delusion*. New York: Houghton Mifflin, 2008.

Gauchet, Marcel. *The Disenchantment of the World*. Princeton, NJ: Princeton University Press, 1997.

Goossaert, Vincent, and David Palmer. *The Religious Question in Modern China*. Chicago, IL: University of Chicago Press, 2011.

Greeley, Andrew. *Religion in Europe at the End of the Second Millennium*. New Brunswick, NJ: Transaction Publishers, 2003.

Habermas, J, and E Mendieta. "A Postsecular World Society? On the Philosophical Significance of Postsecular Consciousness and the Multicultural World Society." In *The Immanent Frame*. Interview by Mendieta Eduardo, (2010): http://blogs.ssrc.org/tif/wp-content/uploads/2010/02/A-Postsecular-World-Society-TIF.pdf (accessed February 27, 2012).

Hitchens, Christopher. *God Is Not Great*. New York: Hachette Book Group, 2009.

Martin, David. *The Future of Christianity. Reflections on Violence and Democracy, Religion and Secularization*. Farnham: Ashgate, 2011.

Norris, Pippa, and Ronald Inglehart. *Sacred and Secular: Religion and Politics Worldwide*. New York: Cambridge University Press, 2004.

Taylor, Charles. *A Secular Age*. Cambridge, MA: Harvard University Press, 2007.

Yang, Fenggang. *Religion in China: Survival and Revival under Communist Rule*. New York: Oxford University Press, 2011.

Yang, Mayfair Mei-Hui, ed. *Chinese Religiosities*. Berkeley, CA: University of California Press, 2008.

3

Characteristics of Contemporary Religious Change: Globalization, Neoliberalism, and Interpretative Tendencies

Liselotte Frisk and Peter Nynäs

Introduction

In this chapter we focus on changes in contemporary religion and in particular in relation to the globalization process. Globally, one aspect of recent religious change is that fundamentalist religious movements are thriving, aiming at reviving tradition, and making religion influential again in contemporary society. While these movements can be conceived of as responses to globalization in the particularistic mode, in this chapter we will explore the more vague religious expressions of Western culture, related to New Age and the spirituality discourse, as responses to globalization in the universalistic mode. In addition to this, we will also discuss the concepts of New Age and spirituality, and argue that essentializing a New Age category no longer makes sense in a globalized society. Instead, we attempt a focus on the dichotomy of institutionalized religion on one hand, and uninstitutionalized, or popular religion, on the other hand.

Finally, we will raise some critical questions. In the final part of the chapter we will point to some significant similarities between, on the one hand, the characteristics of contemporary religious change and, on the other, neoliberal politics and culture. We claim that this does not merely indicate vital similarities between the two, as well as ways in which neoliberal politics and culture have affected religious change. Rather, we emphasize the need to critically reflect on the interpretative role of the scholar and the demands for reflexivity and the ethical considerations that follow. Our interpretations involve implicit or explicit conceptions of man and society. These are embedded in the discourses we rely on, in this case a neoliberal framework. This does not deny the directions of contemporary religious change that have been put forward by many scholars, but requires a continuous, nuanced, and critical conceptual awareness.

The New Age Concept and the Discourse of Spirituality: Different Voices

The New Age subculture has been called "a major phenomenon in popular religion, with a considerable cultural and religious significance."[1] However, in spite of much research and discussion, its nature and contents have remained vague. New Age has been categorized as "religion", "a religion", "a movement", or several movements.[2] Some scholars have likened New Age to a "smorgasbord" where everyone is free to compose his or her own plate.[3] But what is presented on the "smorgasbord" in the first place—what is New Age and what is not—has remained problematic. Several authors claim, however, that there is a certain coherence of beliefs and structure, which legitimate the use of an essentializing label for these currents.[4] Others focus on one essential trait: e.g., healing, self-spirituality, or the literal significance of the concept of New Age,[5] that a new age is on the way.[6] Still others question if New Age is at all a real and identifiable phenomenon, or merely an artificial construction created by scholars or the media.[7]

One of the most radical critics of the concept of the New Age, who also discusses concepts as "popular religion," "spirituality," and "alternative spirituality," is Steven Sutcliffe, who in his 2003 book claims that the formulation of a New Age movement simply essentializes a set of mixed and divergent social processes, and that New Age as a movement is a constructed, etic category. Sutcliffe suggests the removal of New Age from the field of "movement studies" and a reevaluation of it as a harbinger of a shift in contemporary religious practice to small groups and a discourse of spirituality.[8] Sutcliffe sees New Age as a codeword for the heterogeneity of alternative[9] spirituality, best classified as a subtype of popular religion. Some typical concerns of religion in a popular mode are, according to Sutcliffe, grass roots activism, strategies for everyday living, ideals of spiritual autonomy and egalitarianism, and an ideology of direct, unmediated access to experiences.[10] Sutcliffe argues that a popular, functional everyday spirituality increasingly displaces New Ageism, and is a product of its genealogy. "Spirituality" has, according to Sutcliffe, emerged as a hybrid discourse, constructed from alternative and popular sources, and is associated with lived experience and inner discourse, in contrast to a religion which is associated with systems and dogma. Sutcliffe speaks of the emergent spiritual discourse as being *dissident*, striving at finding something other, more and better than institutionalized religion; being *lay*, having a domestic setting which undermines traditional boundaries between public and private space; being *populist*, recognizing the supremacy of the will of the people; and being *functional*, emphasizing short-term achievements of goals and the active creation of meaning in everyday life.[11]

The recent discourse of spirituality has also been discussed by several other interpreters of contemporary popular religion. Paul Heelas, for example, claims that a spiritual revolution is gradually taking place, as religion gives way to spirituality.[12] By "religion," Heelas means "obedience to a transcendent God and a tradition that mediates his authority," while he defines "spirituality" as the "experience of the divine as immanent in life." While the former is under threat, the latter is, according to Heelas, thriving, and is doing well both among those who are not involved with institutionalized religion, and within the field of traditional religion itself.[13] Heelas views New Ageism as symptomatic of a wider, spiritual revolution, widespread in mainstream culture. The New Age is, according to Heelas, just the most visible tip of a much larger iceberg.[14]

Linda Woodhead argues along much the same lines, claiming that a "turn to life" is one of the most significant trends in religion and spirituality, as well as in the wider culture, in the West since World War II. Woodhead characterizes the "turn to life" as having two poles: one personal, living out one's own life in all its fullness, "selfing," to do things "in my own way"—and one cosmic pole, turning to the life force, of which the small self is ultimately only an aspect. The turn to life also places more emphasis on nature and/or on human relationships. It is this-worldly and "holistic," and there is also an emphasis on a radical egalitarianism, a radical empowerment of each individual.[15] Woodhead emphasizes, as does Paul Heelas, that this "turn to life" is effective not only in alternative, post-Christian, and countercultural movements, but it is also becoming widely influential in postwar Christianity in the West, especially in its more liberal wing, and in feminist theology as well. Punishment, hell, damnation, and demonology have almost dropped out of the picture, as has a strong emphasis on asceticism and self-mortification. Experience, egalitarianism, and this-worldly development continue to eclipse earlier emphases on sacrifice and denial in this life in preparation for a more real life to come.[16]

Woodhead discusses the "turn to life" in terms of "the flight from deference," meaning a flight from submission to a higher authority, as well as a flight from the deferral of personal gratification. The flight from deference is, according to Woodhead, not confined to the religious sphere: The World Values Survey of 1990 indicates a decline in deference to many institutions which would formerly have commanded respect. A loss of confidence in governmental,[17] party-political, and religious institutions is evident.[18]

In their book, Heelas and Woodhead are taking this theory one step further, discussing an ongoing, major cultural shift, meaning a turn away from "life lived in terms of external or 'objective' roles, duties and obligations, and a turn towards life lived with reference to one's own subjective experiences."[19] They find some support for this thesis, at least as tendencies.[20] Several other authors also discuss the discourse of spirituality along much the same lines as Heelas and Woodhead. "Spirituality" is presented as being a more personal and individual concept than "religion", more anthropological than theological, syncretistic and pluralistic, antihierarchical, and innerworldly.[21]

Globalization and Contemporary Religious Change

Although there are reasons to be critical of some of the above representations[22]—"a major cultural shift" may, for example, be far too strong an expression—there are nevertheless several indications that there are tendencies toward a change of focus in aspects of contemporary religion. In the words of Eileen Barker: "something important is going on, which students of religion ought to recognise."[23]

As to the changes, each author describes them a little differently, but there are a few characteristics that several of them bring up. In this paper, we will focus on six of these characteristics: *Eclecticism* and syncretism, emphasis on *personal experience* at the expense of ideology or dogma, noninstitutionalism or religiosity in the *private* mode, radical *egalitarianism* or recognizing each person as his/her own spiritual authority, *self-spirituality* or a shift from God to human being, and emphasis on *this-worldliness* rather than emphasizing life after death. Below we will, based on field observations and the above discussed authors, discuss these characteristics as six interlinked processes of change in the light of globalization theories, as we believe this is one of the most important explanations for these changes. Globalization is of course only one of the processes triggering this shift, but we think that as a major cause it has been quite neglected in the discussion so far.

Together with some of the above discussed authors, we reject the concept of New Age as an essentialized category, and focus instead on the whole field of unofficial or popular religiosity[24] in contrast to the institutionalized[25] religions. The different elements of popular religion are today, as a consequence of globalization, increasingly interrelated and mixed. It is questionable if it makes sense any more to distinguish or essentialize special categories such as New Age. There certainly are some characteristics which historically belonged to the cultic milieu of New Age, but these characteristics are today so well spread and mixed with other elements in popular religion, that we would argue that, while it might have made sense in the 1970s and even in the 1990s to speak about "new religiosity" or even "New Age," it does not make sense today. Communication in the globalized world is increasingly dense, and because of the syncretism and ecumenism in uninstitutionalized popular religiosity in the post-Christian western culture, today all these elements are mixed to a degree that it makes no sense to speak about "new religiosity"[26] as a separate category. At the most, one could speak of different tendencies in popular, uninstitutionalized religiosity.

Moreover, this syncretistic tendency is also slowly making it more and more unsatisfactory to speak of different religions as essentialized categories, even if this process is much slower. The religious change discussed above relates to both institutionalized and uninstitutionalized religion, but more to the latter category, as there is an inherent resistance to change in institutionalized religion.

Six Interlinked Processes of Religious Change
Related to Globalization

From Particular to Eclectic

Several authors, for example, Olav Hammer and Ursula King, note the eclecticism of the contemporary spirituality discourse/New

Age. Many different religions are used eclectically as *resources* rather than identified exclusively with one religious tradition being the only *source*.[27] Irving Hexham, professor of religious studies, and Karla Poewe, professor of anthropology, who discuss New Age in a global-ized context, write that one of the main characteristics of New Age is that it consists of fragments of different cultures. New Age selectively combines aspects of many traditions to create a new culture, a process which is only possible under strongly globalized conditions.[28]

Today, communication is worldwide and increasingly dense. People, cultures, societies, and civilizations that were previously more or less isolated from one another are now in regular contact.[29] Structurally, the contemporary, strongly globalized conditions explain the existence of elements of several cultures in one place. But to explain why this leads to eclecticism, we have to look at a special process of globaliza-tion as described by the sociologists of religion Roland Robertson and Peter Beyer and called *relativization*. Through the process of globalization, particular societies are set in a wider system of societies, resulting in the relativization of both societies and individuals.[30] All particular cultures are relativized, including the religions.[31] Individuals form their religious identity in the knowledge that their religion is only one among several possibilities.[32] This process, together with the radical empowerment of the individual discussed below, gives rise to the wild eclecticism we see today in popular culture. As elements of one religious culture are as good as other elements of another reli-gious culture, the individual can pick according to individual choice. However, this choosing is of course not completely at random: some religious cultures—like, for example, Western esotericism, Indian religion, Chinese religion, and Native American religion—are more represented in popular Western religious culture than, for example, African or Arabic religions. Global currents are more inclined to flow in certain directions, depending on, for example, aspects of power, and on aspects of prevalent discourses, such as the discourse of Orientalism.[33] This eclecticism also gives rise to an extreme toler-ance: if all religions are relative, they are all equally true. Further, this characteristic undermines religions such as Christianity, which claim to have a *particular* truth.

This eclecticism also in some sense makes the boundaries between different religions more vague. The difference between religions has, for the individual, become increasingly unimportant. In some contexts, elements from different religions are mixed, without awareness even that there is a mixture. This is so far evident especially with religions like Hinduism and Buddhism, which have some similarities and about which there is limited knowledge in the West.[34]

From Dogma to Experience

It is characteristic in a globalized world that many different belief systems and ideologies coexist side by side. Many of them oppose each other, and it must be clear to the individual that not all of them could be true. For example, if you go to heaven after death, you cannot at the same time reincarnate. As a consequence, for the individual, the plausibility of *all* belief systems is undermined. The solution, for the individual, is to change focus away from dogmas and belief systems and toward other aspects of religion. The ideological dimension loses importance, and, together with the radical empowerment of the individual, discussed below, the dimension of subjective experience stands out as the most important aspect of contemporary religion.

Another argument for the decline in importance of the belief dimension in contemporary religion is that several recent and large-scale quantitative studies of religious beliefs show that there is a good deal of uncertainty in religious belief and this is spreading in Western society. The "don't know" answers, as well as "believe a little," and "maybe" answers are well represented.[35] This might also be an expression of a change of emphasis from dogma to experience.

From Collective to Personal

In popular spirituality, there is also a new emphasis on the personal individual, as opposed to collective institutions. Religious establishments have, for the postwar generation, broken down or at least substantially weakened in influence.[36] As Linda Woodhead notes, the results of the World Values Survey indicate a decline in deference to many institutions—governmental, party-political, and religious. Woodhead argues that the social, political, and economic transformation from at least the 1970s onward all serve to empower more and more individuals to make decisions for themselves. Much of religion has thus moved from the public to the private sphere.

Peter Beyer argues that globalization structurally favors the privatization of religion (although it also could provide fertile ground for the renewed public influence of religion). For religion to be publicly influential, it is required that religious leaders have control over a service that is indispensable in today's world, in the same way that health professionals, political leaders, scientific or business experts do. The structures of modern/global society greatly weaken most of the ways that religious leaders have accomplished this before. The central structural feature of modern and global society is, according to Beyer, differentiation on the basis of function. There is a difference between how a subsystem relates to the society as a whole—which Beyer calls "function"—and how it relates to other subsystems—"performance." In the context of the religious subsystem, "function" refers to "pure" religious communication, whereas "performance" occurs when religion is applied to problems generated in other systems (e.g., the economy and politics). Beyer means that "performance" is a problem for religion today, because of its special nature of encompassing holism, which runs counter to the specialized and instrumental pattern of other dominant functional systems. The major applications dominated by religious experts in the past—for example, higher education or healing—have been taken over by experts of other functional domains.[37] Therefore, Beyer argues that religion has a comparatively difficult time in gaining public influence, and is more visible in the private, personal sphere.[38]

From Hierarchical to Egalitarian

Steven Sutcliffe is one of the scholars who emphasizes that contemporary spirituality is populist, meaning that it recognizes the supremacy of the will of the people, and that the authority to interpret is reclaimed by lay doers and thinkers.

This egalitarianism may also be connected to the prevalent globalization. Peter Beyer argues that a global society has no outsiders who can serve as the social representatives of evil, danger, or chaos. The person who used to be the outsider is now a neighbor. According to Beyer, under globalized conditions there are two main responses for religion: the conservative option, which reasserts the reality of the devil (and persons/cultures who are seen as outsiders or evil) and the liberal option, which dissolves the devil. Liberal religion seeks to address the problems engendered by the global system, but on the basis of the prevailing global values and not in opposition to them. Liberal religion thus correlates with the structural tendencies of a global society, and according to Beyer the liberal option might be seen as the trend of the future. Liberal religion is ecumenical and tolerant, and more or less agrees that there are comparable possibilities for enlightenment and salvation in different religions. The possibility of salvation, enlightenment, or wisdom is for all; everyone is included. Liberal religion works for the fuller inclusion of all people in the benefits of the global community.[39]

Tolerance and inclusivity go together well with egalitarianism and democratic values. Everyone's voice commands the same respect today. Therefore, the reasons for heeding authorities diminish, or even disappear. The individual is radically empowered, and knows as much as the priest about spiritual matters—not through studies or revelation, but through inner experience.

From Theological to Anthropological

In popular religiosity there is a radical emphasis on the human being. According to Ursula King, spirituality has moved away from the theological to the anthropological dimension. Salvation in popular religion is conceived of as more of an inner realization than as related to an outer divinity.[40] The individual has become radically empowered, a process connected to and interlinked with the processes of privatization and egalitarianism. Characteristic of this is that the spiritual potential of every human being is affirmed, and that spiritual growth is conceived of as closely related to the individual's psychological development and maturation. Some scholars, like Paul Heelas, even mean that "self-sacralization" or "selfing" is the very basic characteristic of contemporary popular spirituality today.

The new emphasis on the human being also means that religion has become more secular, interlinked with the sixth and final process discussed below. Contemporary religion is manifesting itself in far more secular ways than before, of which the emphasis on the human being, at the expense of supernatural beings, is but one aspect.

From after Death to This-worldliness

According to Linda Woodhead, the "turn to life" is one of the most significant trends in religion and spirituality in the West since World War II. Today the emphasis in religion is on this world, not on the world to come. In popular spirituality, the divine is conceived of as immanent in both the individual and in this world. Aspects of this world, such as nature or intimate relationships, are seen as sacred.[41] Together with the flight from the deferral of personal gratification and the emphasis of the divine immanent in this world, Woodhead points out that also subjects like punishment, hell, damnation, and demonology have almost completely dropped out of the picture, in popular spirituality as well as in institutionalized religion. According to Peter Beyer, the globalization of society does not lead mainly to the death of God, but to the death of the devil, because of the liberal tendency to be all-inclusive. Without forces of evil, the forces of order and good also become more difficult to identify, undermining, or relativizing, for instance, moral codes.[42]

Alver et al. point out that popular spirituality today expresses itself not only in contexts we are used to calling religious, but also everywhere in secular culture. There are no longer any sharp borders between the religious and the secular, between holy and profane. The profane is sacralized, and the sacred is rendered profane. The sacred is no longer confined to church, or to life after this life, but is conceived of as immanent in the human individual, in nature, and in intimate relationships.[43]

Globalization—An Outline to a Further Understanding

Globalization is a complex process, generating vastly variable impacts across cultures. This chapter has not considered the processes that Peter Beyer calls the particularistic religious responses to globalization, for example, the Hindu nationalists, the Muslim fundamentalists, or the Christian Right in the United States. To problematize Beyer's classification, however, the particularistic responses to globalization also in different ways absorb globally transmitted cultural values—most of them, for example, use media technology characteristic of globalization.[44]

There are also cultural responses which are core elements of the global economy and society, but at the same time are affirming cultural identities. Elaborating on this theme is Manuel Castells, who uses the idea of the *information society* as a key notion for the contemporary global world. The information society is, according to Castells, based on knowledge generation and information processing, and is organized in networks. Castells writes that the global trend for the informational economy is to connect to its network those who are valuable to it, but disconnect those who are valueless. This results in increasing social injustice in the form of income inequality, polarization, and poverty. Global networks of information and wealth often do not respect the values of historically rooted identities, and has generated a situation in which dominant values threaten other cultural identities. This creates instability and potentially fundamentalist reactions, questions the legitimacy of the development, and creates what Castells calls *resistance identities*.[45]

The core of the theory of the network society is thus the tension between the rise of the network society and cultural identity. The global informational economy threatens cultural identities. Thus, nationalism and religious fundamentalism are basically increasing with the rise of the network society. Castells, however, questions whether the information society always needs to be in conflict with different cultural identities.[46] Further, Castells writes in another book that resistance identities resist—they do not communicate. They are built around sharply distinct principles, defining an "in" and an "out."[47] The social construction of identity always takes place in a context marked by power relationships, and resistance identity is generated by those actors who are in positions/conditions which are devalued and/or stigmatized by the logic of domination, thus building resistance and survival on the basis of principles different from or opposed to, those permeating the institutions of society.[48] For those social actors excluded from or resisting the individualization of identity attached to life in the global networks of power and wealth, cultural communes of religious, national, or territorial foundation seem to provide the main alternative for the construction of meaning. These cultural communes are characterized by three features: they appear as reactions to prevailing social trends, which are resisted on behalf of autonomous sources of meaning; they are defensive identities that function as refuge and solidarity, to create a defense against a hostile, outside world; and, they are culturally constituted, that is, organized around a specific set of values whose meaning and sharing are marked by specific codes of self-identification—the community of believers, the icons of nationalism, and the geography of locality. The constitution of these cultural communes works on raw materials from history, geography, language, and the environment. They are constructed around historically and geographically determined reactions and projects.[49]

According to Castells, religious fundamentalism and cultural nationalism are defensive reactions: reactions against three fundamental threats—globalization, which dissolves the autonomy of the institutions, organization, and communication systems where people live; against networking and flexibility, which blur the boundaries of membership and involvement; and against the crisis of the patriarchal family. When the world becomes too large to be controlled, social actors aim to shrink it back to their size and reach. When networks dissolve time and space, people anchor themselves in places, and recall their historic legacy. When the patriarchal sustenance of personality breaks down, people affirm the transcendent value of family and community, as God's will. These defensive reactions become sources of meaning and identity by constructing new cultural codes out of historical materials.[50]

Castells also describes a third kind of identity besides resistance identity and legitimizing identity, this third kind being introduced by the dominant institutions of society to extend and rationalize their domination—which he calls project identity. A project identity is when social actors build a new identity that redefines their position in society and, by so doing, seek the transformation of the overall social structure. Identities that start as resistance may induce projects, and may also become dominant, thus becoming legitimizing identities.[51]

Ronald Inglehart also writes about the knowledge society in contrast to the industrialized society. Industrialization, says Inglehart, brings rationalization, secularization, and bureaucratization, but the rise of the knowledge society brings another set of changes that move in a new direction, placing an increasing emphasis on individual autonomy, self-expression, and free choice, and giving rise to a new type of society that is increasingly people-centered. Inglehart demonstrates by means of survey data from eighty-one societies containing 85 percent of the world's population, collected from 1981 to 2001 (The World Value Survey), that the basic values and beliefs of the publics of advanced societies differ dramatically from those found in less developed societies—and that these values are changing in a predictable direction as socioeconomic development takes place. Changing values, in turn, have important consequences for the way societies are governed, promoting gender equality, democratic freedom, and a good governance. In the postindustrial phase, there is a shift from survival values to self-expression values (or individualism), which brings increasing emancipation from authority.[52]

To summarize, several components may underlie the specific developments of globalization regarding the religious change described in this article. What direction globalization takes seems to be related to economic and historical developments, and also to power relations. In this case, the parts of the world most affected by globalization in the way described above, have as a base a rapid and stable socioeconomic development, which according to Inglehart leads to individualistic values and effective democracy. It also concerns parts of the world with no recent history of suppression or minority complexes, and a part of the world with more power (economically and otherwise) than other parts, and with a minimal glorious past. Parts of the world with the opposite characteristics—weak socioeconomic development, no power, a glorious history—may be more open (as may parts of cultures with these characteristics) to particularistic responses to globalization.

A Neoliberal Framework?

In the following we will briefly shed light on the basic features of neoliberalism based on how it is presented by David Harvey[53] and Raymond Plant.[54] The aim of this brief presentation is first and foremost to underline some of the shared features between neoliberal thought and culture on the one hand and, on the other, the received understanding of central parts of the contemporary religious landscape. From this background we will finally point to some potentially critical issues concerning our position as scholars of religious studies. As we stated earlier in this chapter, there are reasons to be critical of some of the above representations. Despite tendencies toward a shared understanding of changes in contemporary religion, both difficulties and differences concerning how to express and articulate these are obvious from our discussion. Further, representations of contemporary religion might also suffer from value judgments. Finally, from the discussion about the relevance of globalization we could claim that important societal issues are involved.

Our brief description of neoliberalism should not, however, overrule the fact that within neoliberal thinking we on the one hand have a set of quite divergent theoretical or philosophical positions[55] and, on the other, that the practices and implementations of neoliberal politics varies globally to a large extent.[56] Finally, neoliberal ideologies are inherently connected to the European tradition of political thought, but whether or not characteristic aspects of Western European history are compatible with neoliberal practices is a complex issue.[57]

Neoliberalism is in the first instance a theory of political economic practices. According to Harvey this theory proposes that "human well-being can be best advanced by liberating individual entrepreneurial freedoms and skills within an institutional framework characterised by strong private property rights, free markets, and free trade. The role of the state is to create and preserve an institutional framework appropriate to such practices."[58] Plant's definition does not differ much from Harvey's but he emphasizes that within neoliberal systems political institutions are expected to provide a "framework of general rules which facilitate the pursuit of private ends, however divergent such ends may be."[59] Neoliberalism involves a strong emphasis on the rule of law.

In neoliberalism the notion of a common good is set aside in the preference of an emphasis of individual freedom. There is no idea of a common good in terms of some essential and collectively endorsed moral goal or purpose in society. This often entails an opposition to social justice as an organizing principle in societies and the assertion of social justice is by some proponents seen as a kind of old-fashioned nostalgia rooted in a time and place that allowed for societies to direct individuals and groups to contribute to and facilitate the achievement of a common good.[60] Hence, neoliberalism is not about the "what" of politics, such as specific goals to be collectively attained. It is rather about the "how" of politics, i.e., defining the practices in relation to general terms and conditions for the implementation of a neoliberal politics, together with the rights and duties which will enable individuals to pursue their diverse goals according to these.[61] As Plant writes: "[t]his theory sees freedom as part and parcel of human agency—the ability to construct and carry forward what Hayek calls a 'coherent plan of his own.'"[62] Hence, individuals have a moral right to freedom of action and this right places constraints on the actions of others and on the individual concerned. Exercising this freedom should not infringe the similar rights of all others.[63] This view includes the idea that the individual also has some assured private sphere, that private property is given high priority and an emphasis on the market is the main mechanism by which these conditions are achieved.

Concerning conceptions of human nature it should be clearly stressed that most neoliberal thinkers avoid normativity and understandings of human nature that go beyond focusing on the person as a center of subjective choice.[64] This "realist" stance is also present in other ways. Some neoliberal thinkers lean toward evolutionary perspectives through which neoliberal practices are rendered more or less natural. Hayek, for example, presents the view that we are now living in a condition that can be characterized as a "Great Society." The former tribal-like society was, according to this, based on shared values, informal relations, and solidarity while the new modern condition is based on diversity and anonymity and generates abstract and complex relationships and the need for new forms of interaction.[65]

However, references to a natural development, or a realist, non-normative stance embedded in neoliberal thinking should not allow us to neglect other aspects. The neoliberal global trend is not just a matter of economic practices. It is just as much a matter of a cultural trend, or "an ethic in itself, capable of acting as a guide to all human action, and substituting for all formerly held ethical beliefs."[66] Further, neoliberal economic practices cannot be facilitated and implemented in a vacuum. For a set of ideas and practices to become dominant as common sense, i.e., to be taken for granted and not open to question, it also has to appeal to our intuitions, instincts, values and, desires, as well as to the possibilities inherent in the social world we inhabit. Or to put it in the words of Margaret Thatcher "economics are the method, but the object is to change the soul."[67]

When we look at neoliberalism in terms of culture we can also more easily recognize some overlapping areas between, on the one hand, the received understanding of contemporary religious change presented above and neoliberalism. The main component in this overlapping area is, of course, a strong emphasis on individualism and freedom, a feature of neoliberalism that holds a very prominent place in neoliberal thinking. Plant writes: "[i]ndividualism and liberty are not just subjectively endorsed 'bright ideas,' nor are they metaphysically grounded. Rather, they are complex ideas with equally complex historical roots and very different forms of expression: religious, philosophical, ethical, political, and aesthetic."[68] From the neoliberal perspective, as well as in many cases of contemporary religiosity, it is considered a basic value that individuals themselves can choose the ends, goals, and the goods of their own lives.

The neoliberal emphasis of individualism is the focal point through which other dimensions emerge that connect to significant characteristics of contemporary religious change. Briefly, we can claim that this is evident in particular for the following features: from a neoliberal perspective the possibility of developing a normative "science" is denied and if all ends are determined by individual subjective choice there cannot be such normativity.[69] It is claimed that a person cannot be mistaken about these choices since they are noncognitive. The emphasis on experience is also a feature of neoliberal thinking, derived from the focus on individualism, since individual choices are based on desires, passions, and emotions and not discovered by the exercise of reason.[70] This emphasis of the subjective position involves, of course, an antiauthoritarian position and a recognition of a society strongly marked by complexity and diversity.

Hence, within the neoliberal position we find striking similarities with characteristics of contemporary religious change. Except for individualism and the radical emphasis on the human being, together with the resulting move away from collectivism, we also find forms of egalitarianism and eclecticism. The shift toward subjective experience further involves a specific distanced position in relation to rationalization. The idea of the rule of law takes the form of a moral ideal that is closely related to ideas about the spontaneous order and a fragmented and dispersed nature of knowledge.[71]

The similarities between characteristics of contemporary religious change on the one hand and neoliberal culture and politics on the other are based on general received understandings and explored very briefly in this chapter. Still, we find that they are striking and give reason to raise some general issues. In this chapter we will not, however, pose any questions concerning these similarities as such or, for instance, how neoliberal culture has affected contemporary religious development. Rather, we would like to raise a question about the role of scholarly interpretations.

Even though the scholarly work about contemporary religious change presented and summarized in this chapter is based on thorough reflection and often also on empirical analyses, it still always involves an element of interpretation. Hence, the similarities also need to be understood in terms of the expressive and articulating act of language and discourses.[72] Further, all forms of engagement with politics, or more general conceptions or representations of man and society are associated with and require imagination, no matter how natural or realistic they claim to be. This involves the pursuit of both fantasies and illusions.[73]

This notion involves by necessity the idea that scholars do not only represent more or less well-grounded descriptions of contemporary religious landscapes, but that they also take part in forming and shaping these landscapes for both people involved in religion and scholars of religion. However, this does not to imply that the idea about contemporary change is misguided, or strongly distorted, or that the main direction of contemporary religious change depicted above is wrong. Neither is it a claim that scholars are "doing politics." Rather it is an observation that the kinds of similarities outlined here indicate how scholars are dependent on dominant societal and cultural discourses in their effort to interpret and communicate their findings. This implies that there is a continuous need for an explicit critical distance in combination with a high level of conceptual reflexivity. Conceptions of man are vital elements in research on religion and bear significant underlying attitudinal dimensions.[74] Hence, there are strong ethical implications embedded in how we as scholars make sense of contemporary religious change. These need to be made explicit and evaluated, in particular, as the conception of man and society in neoliberal thought is controversial in several ways.[75] The fact that neoliberal thought dismisses the issue of social justice is of course an additional reason for aiming at a high level of conceptual reflexivity. The neoliberal discourse on interpretations of contemporary religious change might have a negative effect on the scholarly work that is done and make us blind to certain aspects of contemporary development.

Conclusion

Several observations indicate that there are silent changes happening in contemporary religiosity that need more attention from scholars of religious studies. The thesis discussed in this chapter is that globalization is a key factor in this religious change. Essentially the contributions of globalization are connected to the inclusion of all and everything in a globalized world, and the consequential process of relativization. Reasons for such responses to globalization in Western cultures may connect to issues of socioeconomic developments, power, and future-oriented identities, as responses to globalization may also manifest in radically other ways.

Essentialized categories of "religion" and different kinds of religion, whether New Age or Christian, make less and less sense in the global world. All borders blur and elements migrate freely with individual choice as the only limit. Elements of the historical field of alternative religion mix more and more with other elements of religion in the popular mode, and have become part of the current mainstream. As indicated in the introductory chapter, it has become relevant to reflect on religion in terms of liquidity. Hence, with Linda Woodhead, we want to emphasize that the changes discussed in this paper involve a change *in* religion, not *from* religion. Thus, this paper is also a contribution to the secularization debate. As one of the key processes involved in the contemporary religious change is a sacralization of the profane, there is, however, a new difficulty for scholars of religious studies: that of recognizing and sorting out which expressions are religious and which are not. This is also discussed in the introductory chapter of this volume.

Finally, difficulties and differences concerning how to express and articulate contemporary changes in religion makes research vulnerable to dominant cultural and societal discourses and with them limited conceptions of man and society. In what has been discussed here, we might observe some vital similarities between representations of contemporary religion and neoliberal discourse. This is not necessarily only a matter of empirical observation, but also of tendencies in scholarly interpretations. This problematic scholarly condition requires a high level of conceptual reflexivity and ethical sensitivity, especially because of the close connection between contemporary religious development and globalization.

Acknowledgments

Extensive parts of this chapter have been published in the article by Liselotte Frisk (2009): Liselotte Frisk, "Globalization: A Key Factor in Contemporary Religious Change," *JASANAS: Journal of Alternative Spiritualities and New Age Studies* 5 (2009): http://www.asanas.org.uk/files/005Frisk.pdf (accessed December 17, 2011).

Notes

1. Wouter Hanegraaff, *New Age Religion and Western Culture: Esotericism in the Mirror of Secular Thought* (Leiden, New York, and Köln: Brill, 1996), 1.
2. Wouter Hanegraaff, "Spectral Evidence of New Age Religion: On the Substance of Ghosts and the Use of Concepts," *JASANAS: Journal of Alternative Spiritualities and New Age Studies* 1 (2005), 42; Olav Hammer, *På spaning efter helheten. New Age – en ny folktro?* [In Search of the Whole. New Age – A New Folklore?] (Stockholm: Wahlström & Widstrand, 1997), 16–18; Paul Heelas, *The New Age Movement: The Celebration of the Self and the Sacralization of Modernity* (Oxford: Blackwell Publishers, 1996); Michael York, "Wanting to Have Your New Age Cake and Eat It Too," *JASANAS: Journal of Alternative Spiritualities and New Age Studies* 1 (February 2005): http://www.asanas.org.uk/files/001York.pdf (accessed December 17, 2011).
3. Liselotte Frisk, "Vad är New Age? Centrala begrepp och historiska rötter," *Svensk religionshistorisk årsskrift* (1997), 87.
4. Hammer, *På spaning efter helheten. New Age – en ny folktro?*, 18–21; Hanegraaff, *New Age Religion and Western Culture*, 514.
5. Frisk, "Vad är New Age? Centrala begrepp och historiska rötter," 95; York, "Wanting to Have Your New Age Cake and Eat It Too," 29; Heelas, *New Age Movement.*
6. Gordon J. Melton, "A History of the New Age Movement," in *Not Necessarily the New Age. Critical Essays*, ed. Robert Basil Buffalo (New York: Prometheus Books, 1988), 35–36.

7. York, "Wanting to Have Your New Age Cake and Eat It Too," 17.
8. Steven J. Sutcliffe, *Children of the New Age: A History of Spiritual Practices* (London and New York: Routledge, 2003), 5–6.
9. There has also been a scholarly discussion as to whether New Age should be considered "alternative" and "countercultural," or if it should be viewed as "mainstream." For example, James R. Lewis and J. Gordon Melton call New Age "an integral part of a new, truly pluralistic 'mainstream'" (Lewis and Melton 1992, ix), while Hanegraaff means that all New Age trends are intended as alternatives to currently dominant religious and cultural trends, and that there is a persistent pattern of New Age culture criticism, directed against what are perceived as the dominant values of Western culture in general, and of modern Western society in particular (Hanegraaff 1996, 515–16). Sutcliffe argues that the term "alternative" is problematic when used in connection with New Age, as some of its spiritual styles have fully entered popular culture and are circulating in advertising, television, the World Wide Web, paperbacks, and magazines. Sutcliffe suggests the use of "alternative spirituality" for the extensive historical field from which New Age emerged, thereby suggesting that what was alternative yesterday is mainstream today (Sutcliffe 2003, 5). A similar view is taken by Hanegraaff in a later paper, where he says that New Age has developed from a distinct counterculture to a dimension of mainstream culture (2005, 48).
10. Sutcliffe, *Children of the New Age*, 9.
11. Ibid., 214–23.
12. Paul Heelas, "The Spiritual Revolution: From 'Religion' to 'Spirituality,'" in *Religions in the Modern World: Traditions and Transformations*, ed. Linda Woodhead et al. (London and New York: Routledge, 2002), 365.
13. Ibid., 358.
14. Ibid., 361.
15. Linda Woodhead, "The Turn to Life in Contemporary Religion and Spirituality," in *Spirituality and Society in the New Millennium*, ed. Ursula King and Tina Beattie (Brighton/Portland: Sussex Academic Press, 2001), 111–13.
16. Ibid., 113–17.
17. Woodhead traces these changes back to a combination of significant social, political, and economic transformations from the 1970s, or even earlier, which typify "late industrial" society: unprecedented levels of affluence and postsecondary education, the growth of the service sector of the economy, and the information revolution. All these changes serve, according to Woodhead, to empower more and more individuals to make decisions for themselves, to shape their lives as they wish, and to extend the power of choice and consumption into more and more spheres of life (2001, 117–21). In this paper, we focus on globalization as one of the key factors of the contemporary religious change. Globalization is, however, only one factor triggering this change and other aspects of modernization must of course also be taken into account.
18. Woodhead, "The Turn to Life in Contemporary Religion and Spirituality," 117–21.
19. Paul Heelas and Linda Woodhead, *The Spiritual Revolution: Why Religion is Giving Way to Spirituality* (Oxford: Blackwell Publishing, 2005), 2.

20. Ibid.

21. Ursula King, ed., *Spirituality and Society in the New Millennium* (Brighton/ Portland: Sussex Academic Press, 2001), 5–9; Wade Roof Clark and others, *The Post-War Generation and Establishment Religion: Cross-Cultural Perspectives* (Boulder, San Francisco, Oxford: Westview Press, 1995), 247–52; Eileen Barker, "The Church Without and the God Within: Religiosity and/or Spirituality?" in *Religion and Patterns of Social Transformation*, ed. Dinka Marinovi Jerolimov, Siniaa Zrinaak, and Irena Borowik (Zagreb: IDIZ, Institute for Social Research in Zagreb, 2004), 23–47; Hanegraaff, "Spectral Evidence of New Age Religion."

22. We do not find the subjectivization thesis of Heelas and Woodhead convincing, especially as their representation is loaded with subjective judgments: for example, the mode of life as it is represented as "conformity to external authority" (2005, 4) or "neglect of the cultivation of their unique subjective-lives" (7), while the mode of subjective-life is presented as an "authentic connection with the inner depths of one's unique life-in-relation" (4) or to "live in accordance with the deepest, sacred dimension of their own unique lives" (7).

23. Barker, "The Church Without and the God Within," 23.

24. The sociologist of religion Meredith McGuire defines "non-official religion" as a set of religious and quasi-religious beliefs and practices that is not accepted, recognized, or controlled by official religious groups. Whereas official religion is relatively organized and coherent, nonofficial religion is unorganized, inconsistent, heterogeneous, and changeable. Unofficial religion is sometimes called "folk," "common," or "popular," because it is the religion of ordinary people rather than the product of religious specialists in a separate organizational framework. McGuire writes that popular religion is no single entity, and that its elements are diverse (McGuire 1992, 104–5). In this article, we will use the concepts popular, unofficial, and uninstitutionalized religion as interchangeable concepts, not going into, for the moment, the different meanings different labels might have.

25. There are, of course, different degrees of organization and institutionalization, which forms a spectrum from institutionalized to uninstitutionalized, rather than two separate categories. Although popular religion to a great extent is expressed in the private mode, there are also institutional forms and social expressions. Every healer or channeler has her/his embryonic organization, and there is social transmission and interaction in sessions, courses, and lectures. Other social arenas for popular religion are media, books, and the Internet.

26. The label "new religious movements" could of course also be discussed, but we would argue that, in spite of many difficulties, it at least makes more sense to speak about new religious movements as a separate category, as "newness" in connection with religious organizations often relates to some special characteristics, such as a living charismatic leader, a deviating belief system, an authoritarian structure, a dichotomous worldview and tension in relation to society (Barker 2004b).

27. King, *Spirituality and Society in the New Millennium*, 5–9.

28. Irving Hexham and Karla Poewe, *New Religions as Global Cultures: Making the Human Sacred* (Oxford: Westview Press, 1997), 41–43.

29. Peter Beyer, *Religion and Globalization* (London: Sage, 1994), 2.
30. Ibid., 26–27.
31. Ibid., 9.
32. Ibid., 30.
33. Liselotte Frisk, "Globalization or Westernization? New Age as a Contemporary Transnational Culture," in *New Age Religion and Globalization*, ed. Mikael Rothstein (Aarhus: Aarhus University Press, 2001), 38–40.
34. Liselotte Frisk, "The Satsang Network: A Growing Post-Osho Phenomenon," *Nova Religio* 6, no. 1 (October 2002), 78–79.
35. Göran Gustafsson, *Tro, samfund och samhälle: Sociologiska perspektiv* [Faith, Community and Society: Sociological Perspectives] (Örebro: Libris, 1997), 35.
36. Roof and others, *Post-War Generation and Establishment Religion*, 244.
37. Beyer, *Religion and Globalization*, 79–81.
38. Ibid., 71–72.
39. Ibid., 87–104.
40. Liselotte Frisk, "Religion och medicin inom nyreligiositeten: Deepak Chopra och Stephen Levine som två företrädare," *Chakra* 2 (2004), 41.
41. This tendency is interrelated also with other changes in our society, above all the material surplus, triggering a need for religious legitimation.
42. Beyer, *Religion and Globalization*, 72.
43. Bente Gullveig Alver and others, *Myte, magi og mirakel: I møte med det moderne* [Myth, Magic and Miracle: Encounter with Modernity] (Oslo: Pax Forlag, 1999), 7–13.
44. Arvind Rajagopal, *Politics after Television: Hindu Nationalism and the Reshaping of the Public in India* (Cambridge: Cambridge University Press, 2001), 30; Christian Smith, *Christian America? What Evangelicals Really Want* (Berkeley, Los Angeles, and London: University of California Press, 2000).
45. Manuel Castells and Pekka Himanen, *The Information Society and the Welfare State: The Finnish Model* (Oxford: Oxford University Press, 2004), 1–10.
46. Ibid., 127–28.
47. Manuel Castells, *The Power of Identity*, 2nd ed. (Oxford: Blackwell Publishing, 2004), 421.
48. Ibid., 7–8.
49. Ibid., 68–69.
50. Ibid., 69.
51. Ibid., 7–8.
52. Ronald Inglehart and Christian, Welzel, *Modernization, Cultural Change, and Democracy: The Human Development Sequence* (Cambridge: Cambridge University Press, 2005), 1–5.
53. David Harvey, *A Brief History of Neoliberalism* (Oxford: Oxford University Press, 2005).
54. Raymond Plant, *The Neo-liberal State* (Oxford: Oxford University Press, 2010).
55. Ibid.
56. Harvey, *Brief History of Neoliberalism*.
57. Plant, *Neo-liberal State*, 13–16.

58. Harvey, *Brief History of Neoliberalism*, 2.
59. Ibid., 6.
60. Ibid., 94.
61. Ibid., 6–7.
62. Ibid., 71.
63. Ibid., 51.
64. Ibid., 253.
65. Ibid., 31–36.
66. Harvey, *Brief History of Neoliberalism*, 3.
67. Ibid., 23.
68. Plant, *Neo-liberal State*, 12.
69. Ibid., 58.
70. Ibid., 53, 60.
71. Ibid., 25.
72. Charles Taylor, *Human Agency and Language: Philosophical Papers I* (Cambridge: Cambridge University Press, 1985), 131, 263, 290f.
73. Raymond Geuss, *Politics and the Imagination* (Princeton and Oxford: Princeton University Press, 2010).
74. Peter Nynäs, "Människosynen och det kognitiva studiet av religion – en fråga med moraliska implikationer," *Svensk Teologisk Kvartalskrift* (2006).
75. Plant, *Neo-liberal State*.

Bibliography

Alver, Bente Gullveig, Ingvild Saelid Gilhus, Lisbeth Mikaelsson, and Torunn Selberg. *Myte, magi og mirakel: I möte med det moderne* [Myth, Magic and Miracle: Encounter with Modernity]. Oslo: Pax Forlag, 1999.

Barker, Eileen. "The Church Without and the God Within: Religiosity and/or Spirituality?" In *Religion and Patterns of Social Transformation*, edited by Dinka Marinovi Jerolimov, Siniaa Zrinaak, and Irena Borowik, 23–47. Zagreb: IDIZ, Institute for Social Research in Zagreb, 2004a.

———. "New Religious Movements, Authority and Democracy." A paper given at the conference of New Religious Movements, Authority and Democracy, Högskolan Dalarna, Sweden, June 5, 2004b (unpublished).

Beyer, Peter. *Religion and Globalization*. London: Sage, 1994.

Castells, Manuel. *The Power of Identity*. The Information Age: Economy, Society and Culture, vol. II, 2nd ed. Oxford: Blackwell Publishing, 2004.

Castells, Manuel, and Pekka Himanen. *The Information Society and the Welfare State: The Finnish Model*. Oxford: Oxford University Press, 2004.

Frisk, Liselotte. "Globalization: A Key Factor in Contemporary Religious Change." *Journal of Alternative Spiritualities and New Age Studies, JASANAS* (2009): i–xiv. http://www.asanas.org.uk/files/005Frisk.pdf (accessed December 17, 2011).

———. "Globalization or Westernization? New Age as a Contemporary Transnational Culture." In *New Age Religion and Globalization*, edited by Mikael Rothstein, 21–41. Aarhus: Aarhus University Press, 2001.

———. "New Age Participants in Sweden: Background. Beliefs, Engagement and 'Conversion.'" In *New Religions in a Postmodern World*, edited by Mikael Rothstein and Reender Kranenborg, 241–56. Aarhus: Aarhus University Press, 2003.

————. "New Age-utövare i Sverige: Bakgrund, trosföreställningar, engagemang och 'omvändelse.'" In *Gudars och gudinnors återkomst: Studier i nyreligiositet* [Gods and Goddesses Returning: Studies in New Religiosity], edited by Carl-Gustav Carlsson and Liselotte Frisk, 52–90. Umeå: Institutionen för religionsvetenskap, 2000.

————. *Nyreligiositet i Sverige: ett religionsvetenskapligt perspektiv* [New Religiosity in Sweden: Perspectives from Religious Studies]. Nora: Nya Doxa, 1998.

————. "Religion och medicin inom nyreligiositeten: Deepak Chopra och Stephen Levine som två företrädare." *Chakra* 2 (2004): 33–46.

————. "The Satsang Network: A Growing Post-Osho Phenomenon." *Nova Religio* 6, no. 1 (October 2002): 64–85.

————. "Vad är New Age? Centrala begrepp och historiska rötter." *Svensk religionshistorisk årsskrift* (1997): 87–97.

Geuss, Raymond. *Politics and the Imagination.* Princeton, NJ and Oxford: Princeton University Press, 2010.

Gustafsson, Göran. *Tro, samfund och samhälle: Sociologiska perspektiv* [Faith, Community and Society: Sociological Perspectives]. Örebro: Libris, 1997.

Hammer, Olav. *På spaning efter helheten. New Age – en ny folktro?* [In Search of the Whole. New Age – A New Folklore?] Stockholm: Wahlström & Widstrand, 1997.

Hanegraaff, Wouter. *New Age Religion and Western Culture: Esotericism in the Mirror of Secular Thought.* Leiden, New York, and Köln: Brill, 1996.

————. "Spectral Evidence of New Age Religion: On the Substance of Ghosts and the Use of Concepts." *Journal of Alternative Spiritualities and New Age Studies, JASANAS* 1 (2005): 35–58.

Harvey, David. *A Brief History of Neoliberalism.* Oxford: Oxford University Press, 2005.

Heelas, Paul. *The New Age Movement: The Celebration of the Self and the Sacralization of Modernity.* Oxford: Blackwell Publishers, 1996.

————. "The Spiritual Revolution: From 'Religion' to 'Spirituality.'" In *Religions in the Modern World*, edited by Linda Woodhead, Paul Fletcher, Hiroko Kawanami, and David Smith, 357–78. London and New York: Routledge, 2002.

Heelas, Paul, and Linda Woodhead. *The Spiritual Revolution: Why Religion is Giving Way to Spirituality.* Oxford: Blackwell Publishing, 2005.

Hexham, Irving, and Karla Poewe. *New Religions as Global Cultures: Making the Human Sacred.* Oxford: Westview Press, 1997.

Inglehart, Ronald, and Christian Welzel. *Modernization, Cultural Change, and Democracy: The Human Development Sequence.* Cambridge: Cambridge University Press, 2005.

King, Ursula, ed. *Spirituality and Society in the New Millennium.* Brighton/Portland: Sussex Academic Press, 2001.

Lewis, James R., and Gordon J. Melton. "Introduction." In *Perspectives on the New Age*, edited by James R. Lewis and J. Gordon Melton, ix–xii. Albany: State University of New York Press, 1992.

McGuire, Meredith. *Religion: The Social Context.* 3rd ed. Belmont, CA: Wadsworth Publishing Company, 1992.

Melton, Gordon J. "A History of the New Age Movement." In *Not Necessarily the New Age. Critical Essays*, edited by Robert Basil, 35–53. Buffalo, NY: Prometheus Books, 1988.

Nynäs, Peter. "Människosynen och det kognitiva studiet av religion – en fråga med moraliska implikationer." *Svensk Teologisk Kvartalskrift* 82 (2006): 60–73.

Plant, Raymond. *The Neo-liberal State*. Oxford: Oxford University Press, 2010.

Rajagopal, Arvind. *Politics after Television: Hindu Nationalism and the Reshaping of the Public in India*. Cambridge: Cambridge University Press, 2001.

Roof, Wade Clark, Jackson W. Carroll, and David A. Roozen. *The Post-War Generation and Establishment Religion: Cross-Cultural Perspectives*. Boulder, San Francisco, and Oxford: Westview Press, 1995.

Smith, Christian. *Christian America? What Evangelicals Really Want*. Berkeley, Los Angeles, and London: University of California Press, 2000.

Sutcliffe, Steven J. *Children of the New Age: A History of Spiritual Practices*. London and New York: Routledge, 2003.

Taylor, Charles. *Human Agency and Language: Philosophical Papers I*. Cambridge: Cambridge University Press, 1985.

Woodhead, Linda. "The Turn to Life in Contemporary Religion and Spirituality." In *Spirituality and Society in the New Millennium*, edited by Ursula King and Tina Beattie, 110–23. Brighton/Portland: Sussex Academic Press, 2001.

York, Michael. "Wanting to Have Your New Age Cake and Eat It Too." *Journal of Alternative Spiritualities and New Age Studies, JASANAS* 1 (2005): 15–34.

4

The Global Political Economy, Welfare State Reforms, and the Governance of Religion

Tuomas Martikainen

Introduction

This chapter navigates the muddy waters of contemporary religion by looking at recent transformations of power and rule in late modern societies. It will be argued that we are witnessing changes in the social location of "religion" and thereby questions associated with "religion." The text claims that we are entering a new phase of state–religion relations, which are historically anchored in modernity but affected by neoliberalization and the globalization of society and social life. The first part of this chapter looks at changes and reforms in postwar western welfare states that—it will be asserted—have led to unintended consequences in other areas of life, including religion. These changes have their roots in the global political economy. The second part will look at these developments in three key areas: church–state relations, the mediatization and marketization of religion, and international mobility. The third part will discuss central aspects of these changes and what they might entail for novel forms of "religion" and its governance, and ask what is its relation to the "post-secular." The text will address developments that have taken place in the Nordic countries and western Europe. Similar transformations can also be found in different parts of the world, but they are not in the focus of this chapter. The text is both theoretical and exploratory, and it aims to create a common platform for describing and analyzing changes that are often seen as separate from each other. The chapter concludes that religion is deeply rooted in globalized identity politics, in which it is likely to be a source of provocation and reconciliation in the coming decades.

Religion and Welfare State Reforms

Theoretical discussions of religion and society have been in a highly creative and exploratory state during the first decade of the twenty-first century. Both the previously hegemonic secularization theory and its self-proclaimed successor, the rational choice theory of religion, face constant attacks from many sides. Simultaneously, there is no dominant alternative for them. Illustrative of the situation is *The Oxford Handbook of the Sociology of Religion*,[1] where altogether fifty-seven authors in almost as many chapters discuss the current state of the sociological analysis of religion, and provide a long list of perspectives and theories. The diversity of theoretical views and empirical developments is such that the volume editor Peter Clarke wonders whether "the present age might well be described as an axial age."[2] The reference is a bold one, as Karl Jaspers' notion of "the axial age" originally referred to the formation of the spiritual foundations of humanity which took place from 800 to 200 BCE in the philosophies and religions of many ancient civilizations.

Nevertheless, and irrespective of whether humanity is going through yet another "axial age," there is a growing consensus that the sociological analysis of religion is at least in need of serious rethinking.[3] What aspects of historical theory are still suitable for describing, analyzing, and explaining current developments? Is secularization a mere European projection in the spirit of Enlightenment and modernity? Is rational choice theory anything other than an extension of consumerism and a legitimization of new capitalism? How to understand the apparently complex and contradictory religious changes, where fundamentalism, growing religious markets, and the decline of mainstream churches are part of the same picture? How does increasing globalism and transnational relations challenge the national order of things? The questions are as many as there are the paths one can follow. One of the clues directs us to developments in postwar welfare states in Europe.[4]

Postwar Welfare State Regimes

The post-World War II period was in many western countries accompanied by the growth and development of a welfare state, where the state took, to a greater extent than previously, responsibility for its citizens and created a large institutional structure to support it. In this process the historical role of religious organizations also changed, and it is customary to think that the creation of welfare states has played an important role in the secularization process, understood as the gradual decline in the importance of religion in different spheres of life.[5] The postwar welfare states have again gone through major changes since the 1980s that coincide with the latest phase of globalization. Especially after the fall of the Soviet Union in 1991 and the end of the Cold War, and apparently also following the financial crises of autumn 2008, there has been a major redistribution of power and resources in the global political economy. Global financial and economic actors have been the main beneficiaries of this reshuffling of wealth and the ability to influence, while nation-states and noneconomic actors have fewer opportunities to control external developments.[6] In short, the economy has become stronger relative to politics. The impact of these changes on "religion" is still under scholarly scrutiny.

Gøsta Esping-Andersen in *The Three Worlds of Welfare Capitalism* formulated a widely used categorization of different welfare state regimes. He analyzed how the production of welfare has been distributed between the state, the market, and the family. From his analysis emerged three different welfare regimes which were typical for modern, developed capitalist nations: the liberal, corporatist–statist, and social democratic welfare regimes. The regimes are different from each other in the way they affect *decommodification*, that is, the individual's reliance on the market for welfare, and how different regimes influence *social stratification*. The regimes have also had consequences for religious organizations' positions in society, as churches have historically had an important role in the provision of welfare.[7]

The liberal welfare regime is focused on providing social assistance only to those in most need. The level of decommodification is low and social stratification high. The state both directly and indirectly supports market dependency, and it creates a dualism between the needy and the rest of the population. Differences between social classes are large in this type of society, and people on welfare are easily stigmatized. In social policy, the role of civil society, including religious communities, is to fill in welfare gaps, and, hence, charity combined with service provision plays a significant role for civil society organizations. Religious organizations have a high degree of autonomy as many of their central activities lie outside the interests of the state. Examples of the liberal type include the United States, Canada, and Australia.

The corporatist–statist welfare regime (also *the conservative* or *Bismarckian welfare regime*) is characterized by strong links between state, corporations, and the (Catholic) church. The regime is conservative in the sense that the redistributive role of the state is low, and the continuation of existing class and status structures is embedded in public policy. It is the state rather than markets that are of importance, even though markets may also play a role. Family is a core value, and hence it has traditionally supported a male-breadwinner model and home-centered child rearing. In these countries churches often have various kinds of agreements with the state, or concordats in the case of the Catholic Church, where the churches' and the state's roles in welfare provision and other issues are defined. Minority religions are located at the margins of society. Many central and southern European states are of the corporatist–statist regime, for example, Germany, France, Italy, and Spain.

The social democratic welfare regime is characterized by universal rights, a high level of decommodification and comparatively small differences between social classes, and it "frees" individuals both from the market and the family. The state, or "society" as it is often put, takes care of many child-rearing duties, supports female participation in the labor force, and redistributes welfare among all social classes. The role of religious organizations in welfare provision was not particularly prominent in the postwar welfare state, even though the dominant (Lutheran) churches often had an intimate relationship with the state. Other religions remained on the periphery. The social democratic welfare regime is typical of the Nordic countries.

These three regime types, which are best considered as ideal types, serve as our point of departure in analyzing the very transformations that the various welfare regimes have been going through since the 1980s. On the one hand, the different regimes provide a historical framework that creates *path dependence* for future developments and decisions without which something else might have been more likely to occur. On the other hand, the regimes have all had to cope with similar changes and there seems to be some kind of convergence taking place between the models. As Esping-Andersen notes in his preface to a book that discusses recent changes in the corporatist–statist welfare regime: "I am tempted to conclude that (. . .) the glass seems only half full (or half empty if you prefer); there is a striking convergence in the Bismarckian nations' adaptations profiles; (. . .) almost all nations' reform endeavours look rather incoherent."[8] This quote illustrates a common thread in most commentaries of late twentieth-century societal changes: something important has changed, but it is not at all clear exactly what and to what extent things are different, or where it will lead to. In the following, I will claim that much of the inability to recognize and interpret current transformation lies in the theoretical baggage of modernization theories that do not leave enough room for different path dependencies which cross traditional institutional boundaries.

The Impact of Neoliberalism

While there were and are both internal reasons (for example, the financial feasibility of the welfare state and the emergence of a "risk society") and external ones (for example, the growing role of global interconnectedness in the production of goods) in post-1980s welfare state reforms, ideological matters are also of importance. A central feature of the ideological climate since the 1980s has been the influence of *neoliberalism*, also called by its critics as "market fundamentalism." The roots of contemporary neoliberalism are located in the Chicago School of Economics, including Friedrich von Hayek (1899–1992) and Milton Friedman (1912–2006), who were critical of governments' interventions in most issues and argued that market mechanisms offer the best and most efficient solutions to all economic and social problems. Neoliberals wish for a minimally interventional "night watchman state" that reduces as many obstacles as possible to market operations, but otherwise remains in the shadows. The role of the state is to provide a structure for the economy to function, including societal stability, rule of law, and property rights that are essential for the (capitalist) markets, preventing the state from falling into anarchy.[9] In the words of David Harvey:

> Neoliberalism is in the first instance a theory of political economic practices that proposes that human well-being can best be advanced by liberating individual entrepreneurial freedoms and skills within an institutional framework, characterized by strong private property rights, free markets, and free trade. The role of the state is to create and preserve an institutional framework appropriate to such practices.[10]

Neoliberalism emerged as a globally significant political and economic ideology at the turn of the 1980s. It is associated with the policies of Margaret Thatcher (prime minister of the United Kingdom, 1979–1990) and Ronald Reagan (president of the United States, 1981–1989). Both Thatcher and Reagan emphasized a minimal role for state intervention and played a crucial role in the deregulation of global financial markets and privatization of state-run services. They also questioned the role of the state/society as the caretaker; in the words of Thatcher: "[T]here is no such thing as society. There are individual men and women, and there are families." The emerging neoliberal ideology was later incorporated into the agendas of global institutions such as International Monetary Fund, the World Bank, and the Organisation for Economic Cooperation and Development (OECD), and somewhat later onto the agenda of European Union (EU).[11]

In Europe, the role of the EU is central in understanding the part played by neoliberal or neoliberally inspired policies. According to Christoph Hermann, neoliberal ideology is embedded in the EU through the Single Market Strategy, European competition policy, economic and monetary integration, and the European employment strategy.[12] With the aim of achieving a truly single and globally competitive market, the EU has increasingly entered areas beyond the economic sphere in order to improve its competitiveness. Whereas the above-mentioned core policy areas, initially, related to a very limited degree to social policy (not even to mention religion) and welfare institutions, they form the bedrock of policies that aim to develop European labor markets in ways that should guarantee the availability of workers and the social peace required for economic growth that also has social consequences. This can be described as a move "from welfare to workfare-oriented social policies."[13] Hence, a plethora of policy instruments and practices have been created to improve the existing labor force in order to meet changing economic demands.

Neoliberal ideology has entered religion and minority policy through its concerns for a predictable labor market, a supply of labor and social peace, whereby the notions of "social cohesion," "empowerment," "immigrant integration," and "security" have come to define the contemporary EU's sociocultural ethos for a future, graying, and increasingly multicultural continent. Major instruments in this process have been intergovernmental cooperation in immigrant integration and—to a growing extent—security issues.[14] The general concern for the maximal use of labor reserves is also one motivation for several EU directives and policy recommendations that aim to combat discrimination in the workplace, be it based on gender, disability, ethnicity, or religion.[15] Having this interest, the EU necessarily steps on the toes of existing national minority–majority arrangements. The EU promotes policies that legitimate the role of the economy as the fundamental core of societies in relation to which other areas of life need to be seen. Ever since the growth of the social dimension in European policy, matters related to welfare and other "soft" aspects of integration have become more prominent. For traditional religious institutions, including majority churches, the changes have been less apparent, an issue to which we shall return later.

From Government to Governance

Anne Mette Kjær defines *governance* as "the setting, application and enforcement of the rules of the game,"[16] which is "something broader than government, and it is about steering."[17] In political and social sciences, governance has been one of the most commonly used terms in recent decades in analyzing institutions and institutional change. Kjær sees the roots of these notes in public reforms that have taken place since the 1980s.

> In public administration, the governance debate is about changes that have taken place in the public sector since the 1980s. From a model based on Weberian principles of hierarchy, neutrality and career civil servants, public sector reforms introduced other models of governing: those of markets and networks. The (intended or unintended) outcomes of these reforms have been to reduce the direct 'hands-on' control of service delivery and instead to increase steering through policy networks.[18]

Governance is a popular concept also in other fields of study than public administration, and often its uses are related to changes in the political economy, and reflect global neoliberal trends. In this context, the term *government* acquires a more restricted meaning, referring to the state apparatus only, while public interests are increasingly directed through other means, including networks and markets, or left out altogether. Many of the changes involved in welfare state transformations can be summarized under the banner of *New Public Management* (NPM).

According to Kjær, the following aspects have characterized the most crucial changes: the transfer of private sector management principles to the public sector, privatization, agentification, competition, and decentralization and citizens' empowerment.[19] The transfer of private sector management principles, also called as *managerialism*, to the public sector stresses "Economy, Efficiency and Effectiveness."[20] *Privatization* takes the form of "the selling or transferral of public sector enterprises to private ownership" and contracting-out, whereby various services are paid for, but not produced by the state.[21] *Agentification* is "the establishment of semi-autonomous agencies responsible for the operational management" of particular activities.[22] *Decentralization* of services means empowering lower levels of administration to take more responsibility for their activities. Decentralization takes place by *deconcentration,* where the authority remains at the central level, but policy implementation at the local level, and by *devolution,* where all power is moved to the local level. *Citizens' empowerment* is about the emergent changes of NPM reforms, whereby individual citizens are *more responsible* than before for their choices, but can also demand more from public officials, leading to a *commodification of the citizen–public authority relationships.*

Changes related to NPM have complex and sometimes unintended consequences. First, the role of networks has become more important as bureaucratic hierarchies are less effective in producing the desired results. Hence, network and project management are of increasing importance. According to Pekka Sulkunen, typical features of project governance are contracts, evaluations, programs, external funding, partnerships, and networks.[23] The logic also includes an adoption of a business-based discourse where citizens have become customers, and where an economic vocabulary in general has invaded many areas of life. Second, another result of the decreased ability of bureaucratic control has been a legalization of various relations through legally binding contracts,[24] which is supported by the rise of a *new constitutionalism* that implies the expansion and growing importance of the judicial domain in solving all kinds of social problems. Thereby, a new *juristocracy*[25] is evolving and, hence, it might not be a coincidence that scholars of religion have found a new interest in legal studies.[26]

Challenges to Modern Religion

Welfare state reforms have been under extensive debate in political science, sociology, social policy, and several other disciplines. This has brought politics back onto center stage, and, among others, Håkan Thörn argues for a more general "political turn" in sociology, which is also visible in the sociology of religion.[27] Since the 1990s, a growing number of publications have taken up issues related to the legal regulation of religion, religion in politics, and church–state relations.[28] Only a few, however, have related these changes to the global political economy, neoliberalism, and welfare state reforms. The most notable exceptions are people who study the provision of welfare[29] and faith-based organizations (FBOs).[30] Therefore, what follows are initial attempts to imagine the implications of neoliberalization for the governance of religion, including the consequences of deregulation.

Church–State Relations in a Global Era

In *Secularism or Democracy? Associational Governance of Religious Diversity*, Veit Bader discusses the historical importance of religions in relation to different welfare regimes. He notes (without an explicit reference to Esping-Andersen) that faith-based care is "low in social-democratic welfare systems like Sweden, higher in liberal systems like the UK and the US, and highest in conservative-corporatist systems like Germany, Austria and the Netherlands."[31] Historical churches are also treated favorably in comparison to secular organizations:

> All Western states respect church autonomy in matters of organisation, polity and administration and treat religions favourably compared to most non-religious organisations by exempting them from requirements of internal democratic structure, from the application of labour law and collective agreements, and from equal treatment and nondiscrimination laws.[32]

It is, however, questionable whether Bader's description also holds regarding new trends in state–church relations, as existing state–church relations are being challenged from a number of sources, at least in the EU countries, including on matters of equal treatment and nondiscrimination.

Firstly, the emergence of various instruments of international law focusing on human rights, and through that on religious rights and freedom, are challenging the sovereignty of the nation-state.[33] For instance, the European Court of Human Rights (ECHR) is increasingly questioning existing interpretations of state–church relations, something which it did not do before.[34]

Secondly, the EU has been moving forward to take into account affairs in the social dimension that indirectly influence national models of minority governance, including religion. The main instruments in this endeavor have been the EU directives, recommendations of the EU institutions, and structural funds.[35] Even the influence of intergovernmental cooperation seems to support the coordination of understandings as to how things should and could be run across Europe.

Thirdly, the privatization and outsourcing of state activities since the 1980s has led to an increasing role of nongovernmental organizations (NGOs) and, among them, FBOs in welfare provision and other former state-run activities, even though that development is very uneven in different countries.[36]

Fourthly, the convergence of migration and integration policies with national and global security issues has led to a growth in state interest in controlling minority religions in general. Even though the securitization of religion has in recent memory taken place also regarding new religious movements (NRMs), it has vastly expanded because of fears of Islamic terrorism.[37]

Altogether, the political governance of religious, cultural, and linguistic minorities is now in a state of transformation around Europe and the world. Matthias Koenig and Paul de Guchteneire see this as a result of increasing globalization, where economic, technological, political, migratory, cultural, and social interdependencies are reorganized and the role of nation-states as the main organizing unity of diversities is mutating. This even implies a growing role for interstate and transnational organizations, as well as an emergent global civil society of some kind.[38] In the study of religion, this discussion has taken place with regard to fundamentalism, political religion, immigration, and globalization, and, especially, the place of Islam in Europe.[39] Further topical issues include the politics of recognition and identity, the securitization of migration, state–church relations, democracy and secularism, etc.[40]

Media and the Market

Changes in media technologies have always been important for cultural innovations. The emergence of the printing press, combined with print capitalism, paved the way for new forms of civic action and civil society some centuries ago, as witnessed most notably by the role of the printing press in the Protestant Reformation and print capitalism in the spread of nationalism.[41] Though always regulated in one way or another, the spread of literacy and privately owned media are core elements in the birth of civil society as an autonomous sphere of life. Changes in media technologies have always opened up opportunities for new cultural formations, and these transformations have been vast over the last one hundred years, with the advent of radio, television, and the subsequent digital revolution. Despite the growing role of transnational media corporations, which are in complex ways ties to other market interests, the realm of independent media actors has also significantly grown over the last three decades.[42] The autonomy of the media as well as civil society has, however, always been contested and restricted by power elites.

Mediatization paved the way for the mass media and the modern nation-states. Likewise, new media technologies have allowed novel religious forms to emerge. Television and radio have created their own religious superstars, and paved the way for mega churches in the United States, as privately owned satellite television has also created new openings for religious movements, for instance, in the Islamic world, where the national media is still greatly controlled. The extent of the impact of digital capitalism[43] for religious renewal and entrepreneurs remains an open question at this point of time, but will most likely be of major importance. Digital capitalism, for that matter, appears to be one of the root causes of the success of radical Islamism and Al-Qaida, which have spread as ideologies rooted in cyberspace.[44]

Many western countries have witnessed a deregulation of the media in the early decades of the twentieth century as the "free market" has marched on. As noted already here, on welfare production, the domain in which markets can operate in general has been expanded with the rolling back of the state. At the heart of this issue is the private ownership of a multiform media that challenges and offers alternatives to the different political and cultural claims of hegemony. Resourceful religious groups have also used this to their advantage. For instance, the New Religious Right in the United States, as part of the broader fundamentalist Christian movement, has created parallel media spheres that aim to provide all the media services that its supporters need.[45] This, together with growing individuation, has made the market a more central actor in the general exchange of ideas, goods, and desires, and has weakened the parts that the family, community, and other nearby social formations have played in influencing one's choices and preferences.

The marketization of religion, which can only in part be explained by the secularization theory, enhances "religion's" spillover into domains of life where it had not been prominent for some time. Hence, the growth of "spiritualities"—sometimes in fierce opposition to "religion"—is both enabled and accelerated in the context of the consumer society, where anything can be commodified. While New Age along other modern spiritualities has often been seen as nonpolitical and ultimately harmless examples of contemporary superficiality, it has also had its drawbacks. For instance, in the medical sphere, alternative therapies, often with a spiritual twist, have at times been strongly opposed. These and similar cases show how "religion" as a category is increasingly challenged and mutated in a neoliberalized everyday life. It also means that the mechanisms of the control of religious dissidents may change.

Religion is, as is social life in general, increasingly both mediated and produced outside the direct control of political and religious elites' power. Hence, additional forms of governance are applied as the production of ideas and goods start to threaten existing power formations. The policing of the Internet, expanding rights to monitor suspicious messages in the shady corners of cyberspace and other communication media, have made the search for safety and security an existential fact in even the most loving and peaceful individual's life, at least in the case of air travel. The freedom to consume and communicate has its limits.

International Mobility and Securitization

International migration and mobility are essentially linked to economic globalization and the technological innovations that have made it possible. The presence of large immigrant populations in many countries, together with an increased global interconnectedness, has also become a political concern. As part of the international debate on the governance of religion, we have witnessed the emergence of "religion," as something separate from "culture," "ethnicity," "nationality," and "race," into the discussions of integration and, perhaps foremost, domestic and international security.[46] Even though the Islamic Revolution in Iraq in 1979, the rise of the Christian Right in the United States in the 1980s, and the Salman Rushdie affair in 1988 had made it clear that religion was on its way back onto the international political agenda, it was 9/11 that became the symbolic turning point.[47]

The securitization, which is to say, the means by which things become matters of security,[48] of religion in Europe is intimately tied in with questions of immigrant integration. This general concern also implies that states and other authorities have increasingly needed to identify religious partners for various integration programs. Religion, and most notably Islam, has been identified as a problem among public authorities in Europe. Therefore, various measures have been taken by state authorities in order to normalize or neutralize the threat that "religion" poses to social cohesion and security. The most well-known examples are the creation of Muslim representative councils in Europe, university-based imam education, and religion-sensitive social policy measures.[49]

The current dominant view on the governance of Islam in Europe appears to emphasize the role of historical state–church relationships as the main mechanism through which new Muslim minorities become either attached to, or are denied access to, state structure and the eventual benefits related to official recognition in different domains of life. This historical fact is said to explain the different outcomes around the continent in Islam–state relations.[50] This is in line with the debate about religion and the provision of welfare.[51] Common for both views on state–religion relations is a perception, though with some reservations, of their backward-looking nature in explaining existing religious developments.[52]

But where are the meeting points of public authorities and religious actors? European states have fairly different forms of legislation regarding religion and its position in societies differs, but there are also some parallels.[53] Most often new religions of all kinds organize themselves into some kind of voluntary association. Among the common features of authorities' activities we find financial support, providing meeting places, and networking as tools by which local and national authorities attempt to normalize the newcomers and introduce modes of self-governance.[54] The quest is, hence, to identify the key actors and policies by which public authorities aim at regulating religious behavior so that in the minds of the authorities, it can support the common good and enhance social cohesion. This position is obviously very different from the majority churches' privileged role.

I will nevertheless argue that the formation of new public policies vis-à-vis Muslim communities and other minority religions are embedded in the rise of *Tocquevillean civil society*—in which citizens are perceived as active, moral agents supporting the public order—as a central concept in understanding and describing the more public role of all civil society actors, including both the majority churches and minority religions. It should be in this respect that we see the heightened role of FBOs in general.[55] What about Muslim organizations in Europe? It is clear that there is an increasing public interest in incorporating Islamic organizations into many programs in the areas of immigrant integration, social cohesion, cultural dialogue, and national security.[56] It appears that the main change in this respect has been the appreciation that Muslim organizations can and should be involved in such matters, while the forms this may take are many. It is in this sense that I will argue that the mere inclusion of Muslim organizations strengthens essentialized views of Islam and Muslims, and it is the very inclusion of such organizations into public affairs that supports the Islamification (or otherwise) of migrants. The other side of the coin is that the majority churches are in many places retreating from their privileges and at least in some cases are also redefining themselves as civil society actors.

A New Neoliberal Regime?

The recent changes referred to above can legitimately be seen as minor, if looked at individually. However, if we take the challenge seriously, and look at the broader pattern and direction of change, there seems to be much room to argue for an ongoing regime change. As always, these transformations have a history and context in which they take place. Therefore, one must leave room for path dependency and major variation, and ultimately argue case by case whether the mutations are important enough. Nevertheless, I shall now push the evident minor and major transformations to their limits and sketch out what a neoliberal order of religion could look like, and whether there are cracks in the picture.

If we take Esping-Andersen's welfare regimes as a starting point, we can safely say that they all have experienced similar pressures to adapt to the global economy. The liberal (welfare) regime seems to bear closest affinity to the general direction of change, especially in the case of the United States. In terms of the governance of religion, historical models more or less still hold, but they have to legitimate their position in an increasingly international setting and in increasingly multifaith national environments. Religious institutions are more often framed as actors, participants, and voices in civil society, rather than as inhabiting an institutional sphere of their own. Those at the margins are drawn closer to the center and the mainstream churches are relegated from the premiership a division or two down.

In this new position, as Kjaer notes on public administration, religious organizations also adapt new forms of management strategies and ways to function, in part due to growing competition, but also because of new opportunities. The marketization of religion is related both to the autonomization of individual religious authority, a classical secularization argument, and to the growing impact of the market on everyday life, to which religious actors are not immune.

The state's gradual retreat (that has gone farthest in the United States) from the regulation of religion, has led to a (re-)commodification of religion, so that there is now much more of a real religious economy than earlier in history. As a side note, it can be argued that the whole raison d'être of the rational choice perspective on religion can be seen as a legitimatization of the new capitalism. Hence, we find the same processes of marketization among all kinds of religious actors, or significant traits of them, as elsewhere in recommodified social reality, due to the advancement of the market logic. For instance, Jens Schlamelcher argues for deep neoliberalizing traits among German mainstream churches.[57]

Religions are, however, not mere bystanders, or victims, of the neo-liberalization process. Whereas many feel uncomfortable about the rising power of economic reasoning, others rejoice in it. As Marion Maddox argues, mega churches promoting the prosperity gospel can be seen as successful mutations of religion in late capitalism that not only use novel marketing and media technologies, but also actively contribute to the theological legitimation of a social ethic of individual success.[58] Similar arguments have also been put forward of other contemporary religious movements.[59]

Since the resurgence of "public religion"[60] and a post-secular awakening,[61] there have been loud voices for a "second secularization" of the public sphere, promoted mostly by new atheists and xenophobes. These can be understood as the battle cries of new culture wars, where the politics of identity and claims of recognition by various value-based cultural movements, including religious ones, are the new frontier of identity politics as, among others, Manuel Castells argues.[62] Amidst all this, the national mediascape is much more fragmented than before, and global social movements with varying claims for identities may use transnational resources and legal means in their counterattacks.

Whether the arguments and propositions presented in the chapter hold, or are of some relevance at least, it leads to several theoretical and methodological conclusions. First, it seems necessary to reflect upon the level of analysis necessary to understand the roots of contemporary changes. The claim here is that if we first acknowledge the significance of changes in the global political economy, then we can gain insight into national level changes. This argument is in line with other critiques of methodological nationalism,[63] though the path-dependent role of national histories must be acknowledged. Second, a self-reflexive stance on currently fashionable academic vocabulary (as also used in this text) is necessary, as concepts such as "social capital," "governance," and "transnationalism," are themselves significantly products of this very same change in the global power regime, in the same way as the terms "society," "nation-state," and "religion" have their roots in modernity. Hence, the concepts probably hide as much of their time-boundedness as they are of analytical use in contemporary description. In this sense a metatheoretical stance is useful as it allows one to locate arguments' spatial and temporal boundaries. This is implicit in my critique of the secularization paradigm, which has failed self-reflexivity in the very political location of "religion" in modernity, which has become only evident to many at the very time it is eroding. Whether or not it is "post-secular," remains to be seen.

Acknowledgments

This chapter has been written as part of the Transnational and Local: The Social Integration of Immigrant Communities Project (Academy of Finland, 2010–2013). I would like to thank the editors as well as Peter Beyer, Liselotte Frisk, François Gauthier, Peter Kivisto, and Östen Wahlbeck for their helpful comments in improving this text. The flaws remain mine, though.

Notes

1. Peter Clarke, ed., *The Oxford Handbook of the Sociology of Religion* (Oxford: Oxford University Press, 2009).
2. Peter Clarke, "Introduction: Towards a More Organic Understanding of Religion within a Global Network," in *Oxford Handbook of the Sociology of Religion*, 1–27.
3. E.g., James Beckford, *Social Theory and Religion* (Cambridge: Cambridge University Press, 2003).
4. See Anders Bäckström and Grace Davie, eds., *Welfare and Religion in 21st Century Europe: Volume 1. Configuring the Connections* (Farnham: Ashgate, 2010).
5. E.g., Pippa Norris and Ronald Inglehart, *Sacred and Secular: Religion and Politics Worldwide* (Cambridge: Cambridge University Press, 2004), 16.
6. David Harvey, *A Brief History of Neoliberalism* (Oxford: Oxford University Press, 2005).
7. Gøsta Esping-Andersen, *The Three Worlds of Welfare Capitalism* (Princeton, NJ: Princeton University Press, 1990), 26–27.
8. Gøsta Esping-Andersen, "Prologue: What Does it Mean to Break with Bismarck?" in *A Long Goodbye to Bismarck? The Politics of Welfare Reform in Continental Europe*, ed. Bruno Palier (Amsterdam: Amsterdam University Press, 2010), 11.
9. Andrew Heywood, *Political Ideologies: An Introduction*, 4th ed. (Basingstoke: Palgrave Macmillan, 2007), 52–53.

10. Harvey, *Brief History of Neoliberalism*, 2.
11. Ibid.
12. Christoph Hermann, *Neoliberalism in the European Union* (Wien: Working Life Research Centre, 2005).
13. Ibid., 4.
14. Ariane Chebel d'Apollonia and Simon Reich, eds., *Immigration, Integration, and Security: America and Europe in Comparative Perspective* (Pittsburgh, PA: University of Pittsburgh Press, 2008); Hermann, *Neoliberalism in the European Union.*
15. E.g., Matthias Koenig, "Europeanising the Governance of Religious Diversity: An Institutionalist Account of Muslim Struggles for Public Recognition," *Journal of Ethnic and Migration Studies* 33, no. 6 (2007): 911–32.
16. Anne Mette Kjær, *Governance* (Cambridge: Polity, 2004), 12.
17. Ibid., 7.
18. Ibid., 19.
19. Ibid., 25–31.
20. Ibid., 25.
21. Ibid., 26.
22. Ibid., 27–28.
23. Pekka Sulkunen, "Projektiyhteiskunta ja uusi yhteiskuntasopimus," [The Project Society and a New Social Contract] in *Projektiyhteiskunnan kääntöpuolia* [The Flipside of The Project Society], ed. Kati Rantala and Pekka Sulkunen (Helsinki: Gaudeamus, 2006), 17.
24. Cf. Steven Rathgeb and Judith Smyth, "The Governance of Contracting Relationships: 'Killing the Golden Goose' – A Third Sector Perspective," in *The New Public Governance: Emerging Perspectives on the Theory and Practice of Public Governance*, ed. Stephen P. Osborne (London: Routledge, 2010), 270–300.
25. Ran Hirschl, "The Political Origins of the New Constitutionalism," *Indiana Journal of Global Legal Studies* 11, no. 1 (2004): 71–108.
26. E.g., Paul Bramadat and Matthias Koenig, eds., *International Migration and the Governance of Religious Diversity* (Montreal: McGill-Queen's University Press, 2009).
27. Håkan Thörn, "A 'Political Turn' in Sociology?" *Acta Sociologica* 53, no. 1 (2010): 73–80.
28. For an overview, see Jeffrey Haynes, ed., *Routledge Handbook of Religion and Politics* (London: Routledge, 2009).
29. E.g., Anne Birgitta Pessi and others, "Nordic Majority Churches as Agents in the Welfare State: Critical Voices and/or Complementary Providers?" *Temenos* 45, no. 2 (2009): 207–34; Bäckström and Davie, *Welfare and Religion in 21st Century Europe.*
30. E.g., Adam Dinham, *Faiths, Public Policy and Civil Society: Problems, Policies, Controversies* (Basingstoke: Palgrave Macmillan, 2009).
31. Veit Bader, *Secularism or Democracy? Associational Governance of Religious Diversity* (Amsterdam: University of Amsterdam Press, 2007), 60.
32. Ibid., 57.
33. Mathias Koenig and Paul de Guchteneire, eds., *Democracy and Human Rights in Multicultural Societies* (Aldershot: Ashgate, 2007).

34. James Richardson, "Religion, Law, and Human Rights," in *Religion, Globalization, and Culture*, ed. Peter Beyer and Lori Beaman (Leiden: Brill, 2007), 407–28.

35. Mathias Koenig, "Europeanising the Governance of Religious Diversity: An Institutionalist Account of Muslim Struggles for Public Recognition," *Journal of Ethnic and Migration Studies* 33, no. 6 (2007): 911–32.

36. Dinham, *Faiths, Public Policy and Civil Society*; William Maloney and Jan van Deth, eds., *Civil Society and Governance in Europe: From National to International Linkages* (Cheltenham: Edward Elgar, 2008), 1–2; Jason Hackworth, "Neoliberalism for God's Sake: Sectarian Justifications for Secular Policy Transformation in the United States," in *Exploring the Postsecular*, ed. Arie L. Molendijk, Justin Beaumont, and Christoph Jedan (Leiden: Brill, 2010), 357–79.

37. Jonathan Laurence, "Muslims and the State in Western Europe," in *Immigration, Integration, and Security*, 229–53; Richardson, "Religion, Law, and Human Rights," 407–28.

38. David Herbert, "Religion and Civil Society," in *Routledge Handbook of Religion and Politics*, ed. Jeffrey Haynes (London: Routledge, 2009), 231–45.

39. Timothy A. Byrnes and Peter J. Katzenstein, eds., *Religion in an Expanding Europe* (Cambridge: Cambridge University Press, 2006); Aziz Al-Azmeh and Effie Fokas, eds., *Islam in Europe: Diversity, Identity and Influence* (Cambridge: Cambridge University Press, 2007); Peter Beyer and Lori Beaman, eds., *Religion, Globalization and Culture* (Leiden: Brill, 2007).

40. E.g., Veit Bader, *Secularism or Democracy?*; Thomas Banchoff, ed., *Democracy and the New Religious Pluralism* (Oxford: Oxford University Press, 2007); d'Apollonia and Reich, eds., *Immigration, Integration, and Security*; Charles Taylor, *A Secular Age* (Cambridge: Harvard University Press, 2008).

41. Benedict Anderson, *Imagined Communities: Reflections on the Origin and Spread of Nationalism*, rev. ed. (London: Verso, 1991).

42. David Held and others, *Global Transformations: Politics, Economics and Culture* (Cambridge: Polity, 1999), 342–46.

43. Cf. Dan Schiller, *Digital Capitalism: Networking the Global Market System* (Cambridge: The MIT Press, 1999).

44. Stewart Hoover, "Religion and the Media," in *Oxford Handbook of the Sociology of Religion*, 688–704.

45. Linda Kinz and Julia Lesage, eds., *Media, Culture, and the Religious Right* (Minneapolis: University of Minnesota Press, 1998).

46. E.g., Gerd Baumann, *The Multicultural Riddle: Rethinking National, Ethnic, and Religious Identities* (London: Routledge, 1999); Olivier Roy, *Globalized Islam: The Search for a New Ummah* (New York: Columbia University Press, 2004); Tariq Modood, ed., *Multicultural Politics: Racism, Ethnicity and Muslims in Britain* (Edinburgh: Edinburgh University Press, 2005); Steven Vertovec, *Transnationalism* (London: Routledge, 2009), 143–45.

47. Peter Beyer, *Religions in Global Society* (London: Routledge, 2006).

48. Barry Buzan and others, *Security: A New Framework for Analysis* (London: Lynne Rienner Publishers, 1998), 23–24.

49. Jocelyne Cesari, *The Securitisation of Islam in Europe* (Brussels: CEPS, 2009).

50. E.g., Silvio Ferrari, "The Legal Dimension," in *Muslims in the Enlarged Europe*, ed. Brigitte Maréchal and others (Leiden: Brill, 2003), 219–54; Joel Fetzer and Christopher Soper, *Muslims and the State in Britain, France, and Germany* (Cambridge: Cambridge University Press, 2005); José Casanova, "Immigrants and the New Religious Pluralism: A European Union/United States Comparison," in *Democracy and the New Religious Pluralism*, ed. Thomas Banchoff (Oxford: Oxford University Press, 2007), 59–83; Nancy Foner and Richard Alba, "Immigrant Religion in the U.S. and Western Europe: Bridge or Barrier to Inclusion?" *International Migration Review* 42, no. 2 (2008): 360–92.

51. Grace Davie, *The Sociology of Religion* (London: Sage, 2007), 225–28.

52. E.g., Eva Jeppsson Grassman, "Welfare in Europe: New Trends and Old Regimes," in *Welfare, Church and Gender in Eight European Countries*, ed. Ninna Edgardh Beckman (Uppsala: Uppsala Institute for Diaconical and Social Studies, 2004), 11–25.

53. Gerhard Robbers, ed., *State and Church in the European Union*, 2nd ed. (Baden-Baden: Nomos, 2005); Timothy A. Byrnes and Peter J. Katzenstein, eds., *Religion in an Expanding Europe* (Cambridge: Cambridge University Press, 2006); Veit Bader, *Secularism or Democracy?*, 49–56.

54. Brigitte Maréchal, "Institutionalisation of Islam and Representative Organisations for dealing with European States," in *Muslims in the Enlarged Europe*, 151–82.

55. Cf. Robert Wuthnow, *Saving America? Faith-based Services and the Future of Civil Society* (Princeton, NJ: Princeton University Press, 2004); Gerard Clarke and Michael Jennings, eds., *Development, Civil Society and Faith-based Organizations: Bridging the Sacred and the Secular* (Basingstoke: Palgrave Macmillan, 2008); Dinham, *Faiths, Public Policy and Civil Society: Problems, Policies, Controversies*.

56. Levent Tezcan, "Interreligiöser Dialog und politische Religionen" [Inter-religious Dialogue and Political Religion], *Aus Politik und Zeitgeschichte* 28–29 (2006): 26–32; Levent Tezcan, "Kultur, Gouvernementalität der Religion und der Integrationsdiskurs" [Culture, Governmentality of Religion and the Discourse on Integration], in *Konfliktfeld Islam in Europa* [The Conflictual Field of Islam in Europe], ed. Monika Wohlrab-Sahr and Levent Tezcan (Baden-Baden: Nomos, 2007); Tuomas Martikainen, "The Governance of Islam in Finland," *Temenos* 43 (2007): 243–65; Cesari, *Securitisation of Islam in Europe*.

57. Jens Schlamelcher, "Ökonomisierung der Kirchen?" [Inter-religious Dialogue and Political Religion], in *Paradoxien kirchlicher Organisation: Niklas Luhmanns frühe Kirchensoziologie und die aktuelle Reform der evangelischen Kirche* [Paradoxes of Church Organisation: The Early Sociology of Church of Niklas Luhmann and Current Reforms of the Evangelical Church], ed. Gerhard Wegner and Jan Hermelink (Würzburg: Ergon, 2008), 145–78.

58. Marion Maddox, "'It's Like I'm in the Goofy Parking Lot': Growth Churches as the Cultic Expression of Late Capitalism," paper presented at the 31st ISSR Conference, Aix-en-Provence, France, July 2011.

59. E.g., François Gauthier and others, eds., "Religion in Consumer Society," *Social Compass* 58, no. 3 (2011): 291–352.

60. José Casanova, *Public Religions in the Modern World* (Chicago, IL: The University of Chicago Press, 1994).
61. Jürgen Habermas, "Religion in the Public Sphere," *European Journal of Philosophy* 12, no. 1 (2006): 1–25; "Notes on a Post-Secular Society," *New Perspectives Quarterly* 25 (2008): 17–29.
62. Manuel Castells, *The Power of Identity*, 2nd ed. (Oxford: Blackwell, 2004).
63. Andreas Wimmer and Nina Glick-Schiller, "Methodological Nationalism and Beyond: Nation–state Building, Migration and the Social Sciences," *Global Networks* 2, no. 4 (2002): 301–34.

Bibliography

Al-Azmeh, Aziz, and Effie Fokas, eds. *Islam in Europe: Diversity, Identity and Influence.* Cambridge: Cambridge University Press, 2007.

Anderson, Benedict. *Imagined Communities: Reflections on the Origin and Spread of Nationalism.* Rev. ed. London: Verso, 1991.

Bäckström, Anders, and Grace Davie, eds. *Welfare and Religion in 21st Century Europe: Volume 1. Configuring the Connections.* Farnham: Ashgate, 2010.

Bader, Veit. *Secularism or Democracy? Associational Governance of Religious Diversity.* Amsterdam: University of Amsterdam Press, 2007.

Banchoff, Thomas, ed. *Democracy and the New Religious Pluralism.* Oxford: Oxford University Press, 2007.

Baumann, Gerd. *The Multicultural Riddle: Rethinking National, Ethnic, and Religious Identities.* London: Routledge, 1999.

Beckford, James. *Social Theory and Religion.* Cambridge: Cambridge University Press, 2003.

Beyer, Peter. *Religions in Global Society.* London: Routledge, 2006.

Beyer, Peter, and Lori Beaman, eds. *Religion, Globalization and Culture.* Leiden: Brill, 2007.

Bramadat, Paul, and Matthias Koenig, eds. *International Migration and the Governance of Religious Diversity.* Montreal: McGill-Queen's University Press, 2009.

Buzan, Barry, Ole Wæver, and Jaap de Wilde. *Security: A New Framework for Analysis.* London: Lynne Rienner Publishers, 1998.

Byrnes, Timothy A., and Peter J. Katzenstein, eds. *Religion in an Expanding Europe.* Cambridge: Cambridge University Press, 2006.

Casanova, José. "Immigrants and the New Religious Pluralism: A European Union/United States Comparison." In *Democracy and the New Religious Pluralism,* edited by Thomas Banchoff, 59–83. Oxford: Oxford University Press, 2007.

———. *Public Religions in the Modern World.* Chicago, IL: The University of Chicago Press, 1994.

Castells, Manuel. *The Power of Identity.* 2nd ed. Oxford: Blackwell, 2004.

Cesari, Jocelyne. *The Securitisation of Islam in Europe.* Brussels: CEPS, 2009.

Clarke, Gerard, and Michael Jennings, eds. *Development, Civil Society and Faith-based Organizations: Bridging the Sacred and the Secular.* Basingstoke: Palgrave Macmillan, 2008.

Clarke, Peter. "Introduction: Towards a More Organic Understanding of Religion within a Global Network." In *The Oxford Handbook of the Sociology of Religion,* edited by Peter Clarke, 1–27. Oxford: Oxford University Press, 2009.

------. *The Oxford Handbook of the Sociology of Religion*. Oxford: Oxford University Press, 2009.

d'Apollonia, Ariane Chebel, and Simon Reich, eds. *Immigration, Integration, and Security: America and Europe in Comparative Perspective*. Pittsburgh, PA: University of Pittsburgh Press, 2008.

Davie, Grace. *The Sociology of Religion*. London: Sage, 2007.

Dinham, Adam. *Faiths, Public Policy and Civil Society: Problems, Policies, Controversies*. Basingstoke: Palgrave Macmillan, 2009.

Esping-Andersen, Gøsta. "Prologue: What Does it Mean to Break with Bismarck?" In *A Long Goodbye to Bismarck? The Politics of Welfare Reform in Continental Europe*, edited by Bruno Palier, 11–18. Amsterdam: Amsterdam University Press, 2010.

------. *The Three Worlds of Welfare Capitalism*. Princeton, NJ: Princeton University Press, 1990.

Ferrari, Silvio. "The Legal Dimension." In *Muslims in the Enlarged Europe*, edited by Brigitte Maréchal, Stefano Allievi, Felice Dassetto, and Jørgen Nielsen, 219–54. Leiden: Brill, 2003.

Fetzer, Joel, and Christopher Soper. *Muslims and the State in Britain, France, and Germany*. Cambridge: Cambridge University Press, 2005.

Foner, Nancy, and Richard Alba. "Immigrant Religion in the U.S. and Western Europe: Bridge or Barrier to Inclusion?" *International Migration Review* 42, no. 2 (2008): 360–92.

Gauthier, François, Tuomas Martikainen, and Linda Woodhead, eds. "Religion in Consumer Society." Special issue, *Social Compass* 58, no. 3 (2011): 291–352.

Grassman, Eva Jeppsson. "Welfare in Europe: New Trends and Old Regimes." In *Welfare, Church and Gender in Eight European Countries*, edited by Ninna Edgardh Beckman, 11–25. Uppsala: Uppsala Institute for Diaconical and Social Studies, 2004.

Habermas, Jürgen. "Notes on a Post-Secular Society." *New Perspectives Quarterly* 25 (2008): 17–29.

------. "Religion in the Public Sphere." *European Journal of Philosophy* 12, no. 1 (2006): 1–25.

Hackworth, Jason. "Neoliberalism for God's Sake: Sectarian Justifications for Secular Policy Transformation in the United States." In *Exploring the Postsecular*, edited by Arie L. Molendijk, Justin Beaumont, and Christoph Jedan, 357–79. Leiden: Brill, 2010.

Harvey, David. *A Brief History of Neoliberalism*. Oxford: Oxford University Press, 2005.

Haynes, Jeffrey, ed. *Routledge Handbook of Religion and Politics*. London: Routledge, 2009.

Held, David, Anthony McGrew, David Goldblatt, and Jonathan Perraton. *Global Transformations: Politics, Economics and Culture*. Cambridge: Polity, 1999.

Herbert, David. "Religion and Civil Society." In *Routledge Handbook of Religion and Politics*, edited by Jeffrey Haynes, 231–45. London: Routledge, 2009.

Hermann, Christoph. *Neoliberalism in the European Union*. Thematic paper. Wien: Working Life Research Centre, 2005.

Heywood, Andrew. *Political Ideologies: An Introduction*. 4th ed. Basingstoke: Palgrave Macmillan, 2007.

Hirschl, Ran. "The Political Origins of the New Constitutionalism." *Indiana Journal of Global Legal Studies* 11, no. 1 (2004): 71–108.

Hoover, Stewart. "Religion and the Media." In *The Oxford Handbook of the Sociology of Religion*, edited by Peter Clarke, 688–704. Oxford: Oxford University Press, 2009.

Kintz, Linda, and Julia Lesage, eds. *Media, Culture, and the Religious Right.* Minneapolis: University of Minnesota Press, 1998.

Kjær, Anne Mette. *Governance.* Cambridge: Polity, 2004.

Koenig, Matthias. "Europeanising the Governance of Religious Diversity: An Institutionalist Account of Muslim Struggles for Public Recognition." *Journal of Ethnic and Migration Studies* 33, no. 6 (2007): 911–32.

Koenig, Matthias, and Paul de Guchteneire, eds. *Democracy and Human Rights in Multicultural Societies.* Aldershot: Ashgate, 2007.

Laurence, Jonathan. "Muslims and the State in Western Europe." In *Immigration, Integration, and Security: America and Europe in Comparative Perspective*, edited by Ariane Chebel d'Apollonia and Simon Reich, 229–53. Pittsburgh, PA: University of Pittsburgh Press, 2008.

Maddox, Marion. "'It's Like I'm in the Goofy Parking Lot': Growth Churches as the Cultic Expression of Late Capitalism." Paper presented at the 31st ISSR Conference, Aix-en-Provence, France, July 2011.

Maloney, William, and Jan van Deth, eds. *Civil Society and Governance in Europe: From National to International Linkages.* Cheltenham: Edward Elgar, 2008.

Maréchal, Brigitte. "Institutionalisation of Islam and Representative Organisations for Dealing with European States." In *Muslims in the Enlarged Europe*, edited by Brigitte Maréchal, Stefano Allievi, Felice Dassetto, and Jørgen Nielsen, 151–82. Leiden: Brill, 2003.

Martikainen, Tuomas. "The Governance of Islam in Finland." *Temenos* 43 (2007): 243–65.

Modood, Tariq, ed. *Multicultural Politics: Racism, Ethnicity and Muslims in Britain.* Edinburgh: Edinburgh University Press, 2005.

Norris, Pippa, and Ronald Inglehart. *Sacred and Secular: Religion and Politics Worldwide.* Cambridge: Cambridge University Press, 2004.

Pessi, Anne Birgitta, Olav Helge Angell, and Per Pettersson. "Nordic Majority Churches as Agents in the Welfare State: Critical Voices and/or Complementary Providers?" *Temenos* 45, no. 2 (2009): 207–34.

Rathgeb, Steven, and Judith Smyth. "The Governance of Contracting Relationships: 'Killing the Golden Goose' – A Third Sector Perspective." In *The New Public Governance: Emerging Perspectives on the Theory and Practice of Public Governance*, edited by Stephen P. Osborne, 270–300. London: Routledge, 2010.

Richardson, James. "Religion, Law, and Human Rights." In *Religion, Globalization, and Culture*, edited by Peter Beyer and Lori Beaman, 407–28. Leiden: Brill, 2007.

Robbers, Gerhard, ed. *State and Church in the European Union.* 2nd ed. Baden-Baden: Nomos, 2005.

Roy, Olivier. *Globalized Islam: The Search for a New Ummah.* New York: Columbia University Press, 2004.

Schiller, Dan. *Digital Capitalism: Networking the Global Market System.* Cambridge: The MIT Press, 1999.

Schlamelcher, Jens. "Ökonomisierung der Kirchen?" [Inter-religious Dialogue and Political Religion]. In *Paradoxien kirchlicher Organisation: Niklas Luhmanns frühe Kirchensoziologie und die aktuelle Reform der evangelischen Kirche* [Paradoxes of Church Organisation: The Early Sociology of Church of Niklas Luhmann and Current Reforms of the Evangelical Church], edited by Gerhard Wegner and Jan Hermelink, 145–78. Würzburg, 2008.

Sulkunen, Pekka. "Projektiyhteiskunta ja uusi yhteiskuntasopimus" [The Project Society and a New Social Contract]. In *Projektiyhteiskunnan kääntöpuolia* [The Flipside of The Project Society], edited by Kati Rantala and Pekka Sulkunen, 17–38. Helsinki: Gaudeamus, 2006.

Taylor, Charles. *A Secular Age.* Cambridge: Harvard University Press, 2008.

Tezcan, Levent. "Interreligiöser Dialog und politische Religionen" [Inter-religious Dialogue and Political Religion]. *Aus Politik und Zeitgeschichte* 28–29 (2006): 26–32.

———. "Kultur, Gouvernementalität der Religion und der Integrationsdiskurs" [Culture, Governmentality of Religion and the Discourse on Integration]. In *Konfliktfeld Islam in Europa* [The Conflictual Field of Islam in Europe], edited by Monika Wohlrab-Sahr and Levent Tezcan, 51–74. Baden-Baden: Nomos, 2007.

Thörn, Håkan. "A 'Political Turn' in Sociology?" *Acta Sociologica* 53, no. 1 (2010): 73–80.

Vertovec, Steven. *Transnationalism.* London: Routledge, 2009.

Wimmer, Andreas, and Nina Glick-Schiller. "Methodological Nationalism and Beyond: Nation–state Building, Migration and the Social Sciences." *Global Networks* 2, no. 4 (2002): 301–34.

Wuthnow, Robert. *Saving America? Faith-based Services and the Future of Civil Society.* Princeton, NJ: Princeton University Press, 2004.

5

The Concept of the Post-Secular and the Contemporary Nexus of Religion, Media, Popular Culture, and Consumer Culture

Marcus Moberg and Kennet Granholm

Introduction

The current general state of the sociological study of the changing societal and cultural role and place of religion in the Western world can well be described as being simultaneously marked by both a substantial degree of theoretical innovation and of disarray.[1] The past couple of decades have seen the emergence of reformulated versions of the secularization thesis,[2] further developed variants of rational choice and supply-side approaches to religion,[3] new theoretical perspectives on "desecularization"[4] and the "deprivatization" of religion,[5] as well as new theorizing on (re)sacralization[6] and religious subjectivization.[7]

In spite of these different macro-theoretical approaches and perspectives each having offered quite different, and sometimes sharply contrasting, renderings of contemporary and likely future developments and transformations in the Western religious landscape, a growing number of sociologists of religion nevertheless appear to agree with the notion that the *public visibility* of religious actors and discourses is on the rise across many Western societies.[8] This notion is also central to the more recently developed concept of the "post-secular."[9]

In this chapter we explore how a more empirically and context-oriented understanding of the concept of the post-secular would benefit considerably from paying particular attention to how the contemporary nexus of religion, media, popular culture, and consumer culture has come to contribute greatly to the increased general public visibility of religion today. We conclude by offering some suggestive observations on how the concept of the post-secular could be afforded more substance and be better differentiated from other related current theoretical concepts within the wider sociological study of religion, were it to be developed in a direction that allows for a more sustained engagement with these areas.

The Concept of the Post-Secular

Like many other macro-level concepts aimed at providing a broader framework for describing and conceptualizing the changing general significance and locations of religion and religious actors across contemporary late modern, multicultural, and religiously pluralistic Western societies, the concept of the post-secular has appeared in many different guises and types of scholarly writing (e.g., social philosophy, social theory, theology, and sociology).[10] Consequently, as is discussed in more detail in the introduction to this volume, there have also developed a multitude of rather different understandings of what the concept actually can be taken to signify, or refer to.[11] As is also noted in the introduction, thus far, wider debates on the concept have primarily been social–philosophical and social–theoretical in character and have mainly been concerned with challenging received understandings of "the secular" in light of "ongoing tensions between religious cultures and civic political life."[12]

In this chapter, we take the version of the concept of the post-secular as outlined by Habermas,[13] and particularly as it has been further critically elaborated upon in the introduction to this volume, as our main starting point. It is worth reiterating here, though, that Habermas' version of the concept of the post-secular is based on the (thus far sociologically unsubstantiated) premise that there has occurred a more recent and widespread general rise in "public consciousness" regarding religion and religion-related issues across many Western liberal democratic societies (with the exception of the United States). As noted in the introduction, Habermas regards the increasing coupling of religion with global conflicts, the proliferation of religious discourses in connection with various types of value-laden national civil debates, and an increasing level of immigration of people "with traditional cultural backgrounds" as having played a particularly crucial role in this regard.[14]

Habermas goes on to argue that the above developments have necessitated a more thoroughgoing rethinking of received secularist ideologies and traditional monolithic theories of secularization.[15] However, as also noted in the introduction, from the perspective of the sociological study of religion more generally, this comes as no news, and Habermas' notion of post-secularity clearly also needs to be further developed in a direction that would allow for it to become more firmly empirically substantiated. Moreover, Habermas' notion of the post-secular also contains an expressed normative social–philosophical element that can be differentiated from the more sociologically oriented side of his argument. Our focus in this chapter lies firmly on the latter.

However, it is worth emphasizing once again that, in the concept's current state of development, it would be premature to simply talk about "examples" or "instances" of post-secularity. Before reaching that stage, there needs to be more clarity, not only with regard to the boundaries of the concept as such, but also with regard to exactly in relation to *which types or kinds* of phenomena "signs" or "characteristics" of post-secularity might be empirically observed and investigated. Indeed, one primary aim of this volume as a whole is to suggest avenues for further reflection to that effect. This is to say, then, that although the concept of the post-secular may carry much descriptive, or at least evocative, potential, it does not yet possess much analytical value. Hence the need for it to become further developed and differentiated from other related concepts within the broader study of contemporary religion, and the sociology of religion in particular.

Building on the understanding of the concept of the post-secular as outlined in the introduction to this volume, our main argument in this chapter is that when developing a concept that is inherently based on the (ultimately sociologically testable) assumption that religion is gaining increased public visibility across many Western democratic societies, leading to an increased general public awareness of religion and religious actors, it becomes of crucial importance to pay due attention to the ways in which the general character and locations of religion and religious life and practice on the whole have undergone significant transformations in late modern times. For example, as Knott points out when exploring the "post-secular city" in a British context, although there are clear "signs that religion has re-entered the public domain," it is equally clear that it has "had to adapt in order to do so."[16]

The concept of the post-secular, she suggests, could therefore not merely be taken to refer to a situation in which "religion" has simply reentered public life and debate in a way that has brought traditional interpretive frameworks of accelerating secularization and irreversible religious decline into question. In addition to this, she argues, we might also take the concept to "signify *a new kind of religion that is informed and changed* by its historical experience of exclusion and changing relationship with the modern nation state and the condition of the secular."[17]

Although we concur with Knott, it is important to recognize that the above observations also largely remain to be empirically substantiated across different Western social and cultural contexts. Nonetheless, if the concept of the post-secular is understood in this broader sense, some potentially very fruitful, and perhaps even vital, connections could be made to a range of other notable streams of thought in the broader scholarship on contemporary religion, which have highlighted the ways in which the location and general character of religion and religious life and practice have undergone considerable transformations in late modern times, following more recent changes in the relationships of religion to states, structures of authority, media, and the marketplace of culture.[18] Consequently, we regard the scholarship on the intersection of religion, media, popular culture, and consumer culture as offering particularly constructive avenues for further reflection in this regard.

Lastly, it is also worth noting that while the impact of media on contemporary religious life has become ever more widely recognized within the wider scholarship on contemporary religion, the scholarship on religion and popular culture and religion and consumer culture is still experiencing some difficulties in establishing sufficiently common ground with current macro-level theorizing in the sociology of religion in particular. If further developed with a clearer focus on the areas suggested above, the concept of the post-secular could possibly also prove useful in bridging this gap.

Post-Secularity, Religion, and Media

Generally speaking, if the concept of post-secularity is taken to refer to a social and cultural condition marked by the resurgence and growing public visibility and awareness of religion, coupled with the changing character and locations of religion and religious life in general, then it would appear to be safe to say that developments in modern communications media have played an absolutely pivotal role in bringing about this situation or state of affairs.[19]Although the relationship between religion and media has always been a close one, a more consolidated scholarship focusing on this area did not emerge until the mid-1980s.[20] Today, however, there exists an extensive and fast-growing scholarly literature on the subject that covers a plethora of different approaches, perspectives, and more particular areas of focus.[21]

Scholarship on media and religion has also experienced a gradual shift from its earlier principal focus on so-called "media effects" toward a more multi-way focus on media reception, use, interaction, and interpretation among media audiences themselves. Writing from a primarily North American perspective, Hoover describes this move in terms of a gradual shift of focus "from medium to meaning."[22] This approach, he writes, "sees media in terms of their *integration into daily life* rather than in terms of their *effects on it.*"[23] Hoover summarizes this shift as having brought about a more sustained focus on the following interrelated issues in particular:

> First is the question of what symbols or scripts are available in the media environment, what we might call the "symbolic inventory" out of which individuals make religious or spiritual meaning. Second is the practices of consumption, interaction, and articulation through which those meanings are accessed, understood, and used. And third is the centering of this in the experiences of the individuals who are doing the consuming and meaning-making.[24]

Indeed, the view that our contemporary and increasingly media-saturated social and cultural environment constitutes a "symbolic inventory" that is continuously being tapped into by individuals in a myriad of different ways highlights how the very character and locations of religion and religious life and practice have changed and diversified in late modern times. Furthermore, as these observations also should remind us, it is important to recognize that religion has always constituted a *mediated* phenomenon, i.e., a phenomenon that necessarily needs to be understood in intimate relation to the different forms or types of media that it interacts with and through which it is communicated, expressed, disseminated, and experienced.[25] As Meyer and Verrips state: "The very assumption of a divide between religion and media stems from a dematerialized and disembodied understanding of religion /.../ Pondering the nexus of religion and media has yielded an understanding of religion as a practice of mediation /. . ./ to which media are intrinsic."[26]

While remaining wary of the pitfalls of technological determinism and simplistic media effects approaches, exploring the present-day relationship between media and religion still entails examining the ways in which media have come to *affect* and *shape* how contemporary religion is organized, practiced, experienced, and lived. As Hoover points out, "On a more pervasive level /. . ./ the 'common culture' represented by the media has today become determinative of the contexts, extents, limits, languages, and symbols available to religious and spiritual discourse."[27] In order to gain an adequate understanding of the general character of contemporary religious life and practice, it is thus crucial that we pay sufficient attention to how the explosive increase in different media outlets and technologies during the latter part of the twentieth century (and especially during the past two decades with the rise of digital technologies) has affected the ways in which religious communities of virtually all strands *themselves* interact, express, and communicate (and even construct) their message (both outward and inward) in ways unknown to previous generations.

Focusing on issues of the above type, more recently, a growing number of scholars have also started to reexamine the impact of media on contemporary religious life at a structural meso or institutional level in relation to the concept of *mediatization*. In this context, "media" are conceptualized broadly as "technologies, institutional arrangements, circulatory systems, and shifting modalities of reception."[28] Basically, the concept of mediatization denotes the process whereby the influence of media—as technology, means of communication, organization, and commercial enterprise—has extended into and proliferated within virtually all spheres of society and culture (e.g., politics, economy, and religion) and social and cultural everyday life.[29] As outlined by Hjarvard, mediatization denotes a *dual* process whereby the various forms of media have become (and are continually *becoming*) ever more "*integrated* into the operations" of modern social and cultural institutions, while simultaneously having also attained the position of independent social and cultural institutions in themselves.[30]

It should be emphasized here that the impact of mediatization on religion continues to be the subject of much debate. Generally speaking, when applied to religion, the concept aims to draw our attention to how media have developed into a virtually inescapable aspect of daily life in modern societies on the whole and consequently also into an ever more integrated and *shaping* component of contemporary religious life and practice as well. But as noted, religion and media scholars disagree on the impact and possible consequences of processes of mediatization on religion.[31]

Irrespective of how one chooses to understand the effects and outcomes of processes of mediatization on contemporary religious life, one nevertheless needs to remain attentive to the many ways in which developments in media technologies have greatly increased the opportunities for religious groups and communities to swiftly and easily communicate their messages to people all over the globe. These developments are thus continually expanding the environments and parameters of religious communication, practice, and agency.[32] In addition, it seems safe to say that these developments also have brought heightened pressures to bear on religious groups and communities to keep up with today's increasingly pervasive media environment, including the development of new media technologies, in order to be able to keep their voices heard in the din.[33] Notably, all of this equally applies to actors critical of religion, such as free-thinker activists, or proponents of the so-called New Atheism. As Stolow points out:

> More than just instruments used by religious, non-religious, or even anti-religious actors, media constitute an environment that makes it possible for religion to sustain a presence in both public and private life. It is within and through mediated environments that so-called religious folk increasingly carry out their business of seeking knowledge, performing rituals, proclaiming faith, proselytizing to others, embarking on moral campaigns, or engaging in holy wars.[34]

As hinted at by Stolow, and in addition to the observations presented above, when attempting to make sense of the apparent general resurgence and growing public visibility of religion today, sufficient attention, no doubt, also needs to be paid to the profound influence that "the media"—conceptualized more narrowly as referring to media corporations and mass media in particular—exercise in forming and framing our conceptions of the world and the social and cultural environments in which we find ourselves.[35]

Would it be an exaggeration to say that, in late-modern times, the media, and various types of mass media in particular, have taken on the role as *the* most significant facilitator of the public sphere as a whole?[36] Indeed, as has been already argued by Habermas (among others) in the mid-1960s, the general commercialization of the mass media and the resulting gradually increasing concentration of media power and ownership has brought about a situation where the mass media has not only come to function as a principal facilitator of the public sphere, but as a principal *shaper* and *organizer* of it as well.[37] As such, the mass media has certainly come to function as a hugely influential agenda-setter and shaper of public discourse on religion-related issues and topics.[38]

Among the plethora of various types and genres of media that exist today, various types of news or "public affairs media" certainly count among those which have taken on particular significance in this regard.[39] For example, for most people except those directly, personally, and physically involved, globally mediated and extensively reported religion-related events such as the 9/11 attacks and their aftermath, the Danish Muhammad cartoon controversy,[40] and the child abuse scandals within the Roman Catholic church, were all events principally acted out via and through the news media in particular. Indeed, it has become difficult to imagine any given contemporary religion-related issue or event becoming the subject of wider public awareness and discussion separately from news media constructions and representations of that event.

When examining these issues we also need to keep in mind that the construction and reporting of news is, to a significant degree, driven by specific notions of newsworthiness, or so-called "news values."[41] As Hodkinson reminds us, "as well as determining what will make a good story in the first place, news values influence the particular version of events that is constructed."[42] This, of course, has obvious implications for *how* certain religions, religious groups, or religion-related issues and events become represented and constructed through news media. Consider, for example, how the long-standing news value of *negativity*,[43] i.e., that negative stories (e.g., of disasters, tragedies, conflicts, and wars) make better (i.e., more compelling and profitable) news than positive ones, affect the news media's coverage of religion and religion-related issues. Indeed, such coverage tends to be overwhelmingly dominated by negative stories, such as religious extremism (and nowadays Islamic extremism and terrorism in particular), or scandals and controversies within large and globally spread religious institutions such as the Anglican or Roman Catholic churches.

Any adequate analysis of the contemporary resurgence, increased public visibility, or growing public consciousness of religion needs to examine empirically the central role played by the mass media.

For example, relating the impact of the news media to Habermas' argument about the primary characteristics of post-secular societies, they obviously play a central role in forming and shaping wider public opinion about the relationship between religion and global conflicts through the particular ways in which they frame and represent the role played by religion in those contexts. Moreover, across different national contexts (as well as beyond them), the role that news and public affairs media play in facilitating, framing, and shaping public discussions of value-laden, controversial social and political issues is just as evident, not least since such discussions tend to become largely orchestrated by and carried out via and through such media (and with such media often serving to provoke or tease out such debates in the first place).[44] As an example of this we might generally consider the ways in which the European public affairs media has come to display an ever stronger interest in issues related to Muslim immigration, especially when such issues can be connected to social tension and disorder, public controversies, or acts or threats of violence of some sort. More recent instances include the extensive coverage, both nationally and internationally, of events such as the assassination of the Dutch film director Theo van Gogh by a Muslim man in 2004, the Swiss national referendum on the prohibition of building new minarets in 2009, and the French signing into law of the ban on wearing full-length Islamic veils such as niqābs and burquas in public in 2010. When it comes to Muslim immigrants in Europe, therefore, the public affairs media play a hugely influential role in determining both what types of issues become highlighted as well as in what light they are discussed.

In reality, of course, these are highly complex issues, since media messages and representations are continuously the subject of multiple forms of reinterpretation and contestation. For example, the increasing accessibility of media technologies has entailed a considerable expansion and diversification of news providers and different types of news (for example, through the emergence of specific target audiences, citizen journalism, independent online providers, etc.).[45] Even so, it nevertheless remains the case that mainstream news and public affairs media still not only function as primary facilitators, agenda-setters, and shapers of public debate on religion-related issues, but that they also continue to provide the principal contemporary *arena* through which such public debates largely tend to unfold.

With the above observations in mind, future developments of the concept of post-secularity would no doubt benefit considerably from incorporating insights provided by both the extensive scholarship that has developed on the relationship between religion and mass media, as well as the more recently developed and closely related scholarship focusing more directly on how individuals themselves make use of and interpret media messages in the context of their everyday lives.[46] If we accept that media (in both its broader and narrower sense) have come to constitute an ever-present and inescapable aspect of contemporary social and cultural life, then we must also recognize the profound implications this has for how we approach and attempt to understand both the contemporary resurgence and growing public visibility of religion, as well as the changing character and locations of religion and religious life in general.

The types of religion-related issues that come to be most conspicuously covered in the news and other types of public affairs media also gradually tend to be filtered through into various types of entertainment media such as cinema and television series.[47] But in addition to this, the realm of mass-mediated popular culture has clearly also evolved into an ever more important arena for the exploration and dissemination of a much wider variety of religious, spiritual, and existential themes, teachings, and ideas. It is to this area that we now turn.

The Visibility of Religion within Contemporary Mass-Mediated Popular Culture

Although the public visibility of religion appears to be growing across many Western societies, as is suggested by the concept of the post-secular, there is wide agreement among sociologists of religion that much of the Western religious landscape still remains marked by a general decline in institutional forms of religion, accompanied by increasing religious privatization and progressively weakening mechanisms of institutional and traditional religious socialization. While generally concurring with this view, an increasing number of scholars have more recently started highlighting how a vast array of different religious teachings, themes, and ideas continue to be conspicuously explored within the realm of mass and communications media-based popular culture.

Explicitly, religious themes have been central to some of the most successful works/products/forms of popular culture during the last four or so decades and, arguably, have also considerably contributed to their success and enduring appeal. Examples include top-grossing films such as the *Star Wars* series (1977, 1980, 1982, 1999, 2002, 2005) and *Avatar* (2009); popular television series such as *Touched by an Angel* (1994–2003), *The X-Files* (1993–2002), and the reenvisioned *Battlestar Galactica* (2003, 2004–2009); more mainstream fantasy and science-fiction novels, such as Phillip Pullman's *His Dark Materials* trilogy (1995, 1997, 2000), as well as other works such as Paolo Coelho's *The Alchemist* (1988) and Dan Brown's *The Da Vinci Code* (2003); comic book series such as *The Mighty Thor* (1962–), *Sandman* (1989–1996), and *Hellblazer* (1988–); as well as various types of popular music cultures such as electronic dance music, reggae, and heavy metal.[48]

In short, various types of religious themes, ideas, teachings, symbols, imagery, language, etc. abound in contemporary Western mass-mediated popular culture. As is commonly emphasized by scholars focusing on this field, the wider cultural/popular cultural realm has developed into an increasingly important source of religious inspiration for growing numbers of people today.[49] Contemporary mass-mediated popular culture reaches vast, transnational audiences and does so with increasing rapidity. In this broader context, it becomes quite feasible to argue that for increasing numbers of people, traditional religious institutions no longer constitute the main providers of religious/spiritual/existential meaning and interpretation. In such a situation, the aliens of a TV series such as *The X-Files*, the Greek mythology of Rick Riordan's *Percy Jackson & the Olympians* books (2005–2009), or the magic of J. K. Rowling's *Harry Potter* books (1997–2007) may well appear to be and feel just as, if not more, familiar to people today than the teachings and practices found in conventional and institutional mainline religions. One might equally plausibly argue that people's knowledge and views of institutional forms of religion, and indeed of the very category of religion as such, is ever more often derived from representations and narratives found in mass-mediated popular culture.

Popular culture must therefore be viewed as constituting an important area of investigation when aiming to make sense of how contemporary religion is experienced, practiced, and lived.[50] This principal focus on the "contemporary" should not, however, distract us from acknowledging the historically close relationship that has always existed between religion and broader particular cultural climates at different points in time.[51] The close relationship between religion and popular culture in general is thus not appropriately understood as something "new." But this does not detract from the fact that late modern mass-mediated popular culture has had, and continues to have, a major impact on the transformation of religion and religious life today in ways that are not directly comparable to the relationship between religion and popular culture in earlier history.[52]

At the risk of simplifying matters somewhat, researchers of religion and popular culture tend to employ broad understandings of popular culture and to reject binary or "arbitrary and ideologically enforced" hierarchical–typological understandings of culture which differentiate between "high," "low," "folk," "popular," or "mass" culture.[53] For example, in contrast to such approaches, as argued by Lynch, it is more useful to regard popular culture "as the shared environment, practices, and resources of everyday life in a given society."[54] Exploring the present-day relationship between religion and popular culture therefore entails directing particular attention at the changing locations and changing general character of religion, as well as at the various ways in which individuals encounter and engage with religious/spiritual subject matter through their everyday cultural practices, both collectively and privately.[55] As Lynch points out, looking at the ways in which religion appears and is explored in relation to contemporary popular culture "is illuminating both in terms of what people are attempting to do and say about their cultural practices /. . ./ as well as suggesting what people imagine religion to be."[56]

Indeed, some more detailed studies aimed at developing more unified approaches and interpretive frameworks for studying these issues have also been produced in recent years.[57] Among these, the perhaps most thought-provoking argument presented so far has been provided by Partridge in his two-volume work on the "re-enchantment" of the West.[58] Partridge argues that "the West" (broadly understood) has witnessed a general shift from an earlier dominant Christian "religio-cultural milieu" to one which is occult in character.[59] This new religio-cultural milieu, which Partridge terms *occulture*, "includes those often *hidden, rejected* and *oppositional* beliefs and practices associated with esotericism, theosophy, mysticism, New Age, Paganism, and a range of other subcultural beliefs and practices."[60] This occultural milieu, he argues, has developed into a widely tapped "reservoir of ideas, beliefs, practices, and symbols."[61] As such, for increasing numbers of people, it has come to provide the "unpredictable raw materials" for religious inspiration and the construction of religious identities.[62] Mass-mediated popular culture, argues Partridge, plays a pivotal role in supporting this occultural, or religio-cultural milieu, through having developed into "a key sacralizing factor which has a far more influential role in the shaping and dissemination of contemporary occultural thought than is often acknowledged."[63] For example, through being surrounded by, consuming, and engaging with popular culture during the course of our daily lives, we also repeatedly come across and become ever more familiar with the diverse religious and spiritual themes, teachings, and ideas that we encounter through it.[64] In this way, mass-mediated popular culture also significantly contributes to the "de-exotification" of such themes, teachings, and ideas, so aiding their integration into the broader Western cultural consciousness and thereby further adding to the increased general visibility of religion throughout contemporary Western culture.[65]

The growing general visibility and awareness of religion should thus by no means be regarded as being limited to organized and institutional religions such as Christianity and Islam. Within the realm of mass-mediated popular culture we instead encounter a much richer variety of religious themes, teachings, and ideas than we would normally come across in other types of media, such as mainstream news and public affairs media. There is, however, as already noted, also a clearly noticeable connection between news and popular cultural representations of religion. For example, the religion-related topics that become most widely circulated and represented through the news media also tend to become reenacted on the silver screen. One example of this would be the growing number of action films dealing with Islamic extremism and terrorism. Another example would be how contemporary filmic portrayals of Catholic clergy typically cast them as corrupt child abusers. As argued by Forbes, "because popular culture surrounds us, it seems reasonable to assume that its messages and subtle themes influence us as well as reflect us."[66] If we accept this argument, we might certainly ask ourselves what a popular cultural milieu littered with religious subject matter (as our present-day popular cultural environment no doubt is) says more generally about the place and significance of religion in the contemporary West.

Above all, the pervasiveness of religious subject matter in popular culture should draw our attention to how the present-day apparent resurgence and growing public visibility of religion can be observed not only in relation to issues relating more directly to politics and public civil debate, but also throughout a number of different areas of contemporary social and cultural life. Moreover, the various ways in which religion has come to figure within popular culture should also alert us to how the very category of religion is undergoing significant changes in late modern times. We are suggesting, therefore, that if we were to look more closely at the role of mass-mediated popular culture when developing the concept of post-secularity, this could ideally bring some valuable expansions to the horizons of the concept as a whole.

Post-Secularity, Consumer Capitalism, and Consumer Culture

In addition to taking the increasingly close relationship between religion, media, and popular culture into account, researchers interested in exploring the growing public visibility of religion and the changing general character of contemporary religious life and practice also have much to gain from looking more closely at the present-day relationship between religion, general socioeconomic arrangements, consumer capitalism, and consumer culture. Indeed, and as has become increasingly recognized in the wider study of contemporary religion, it has become virtually impossible to adequately account for almost any present-day social and cultural phenomena without paying close attention to the wider socioeconomic environment in which they are embedded, how they interact with that environment, as well as how they become affected and shaped by it.

As a basic starting point we should keep in mind that, as a social and cultural phenomenon that (for better or worse) is often regarded as constituting a central element of the very fabric of society and culture as we know it, religion has always been deeply intertwined with the economic arrangements of the day in any given society. At a general level, therefore, as Passas observes, "it appears that there is no clear-cut distinction separating religious organizations from commercial ones and the two are best conceived as the ideal-type ends of a continuum."[67] As such, we need to recognize that the general character of religion and religious life and practice in any given society changes and evolves in tandem with broader developments in the general socioeconomic makeup of that society, although this often happens in highly complex and varied ways.

In modern times, such developments have become ever more intimately connected to a range of overarching macro-level transformations of the global political economy following accelerating globalization in recent decades and the resulting increasing global interconnectedness of national societies with regard to the economy, politics, culture, media, and populations. As a central element of these developments, over the past three or so decades, the proliferation and implementation of neoliberal policies across different national and local levels have also entailed significant restructurings of earlier state arrangements through processes of decentralization, marketization, and the outsourcing and privatization of public services. Moreover, as these developments have brought significant changes to the power relations between religious groups and other societal institutions, they have also made possible a range of new and innovative forms of both collective and individual religious agency. It is important, therefore, to recognize on a more general level how these processes have brought about a range of profound changes in the general socioeconomic makeup of Western societies on the whole—changes that religious communities of virtually all strands, both old and new, have been forced to adapt to.

It would no doubt also prove fruitful to bring these macro-level transformations of modern Western societies into clearer focus when attempting to further develop and refine a theoretical concept such as that of the post-secular, which places particular emphasis on the growing role and visibility of religion in the public sphere. In addition to the types of macro-level processes briefly discussed above, we would argue that the following, more specific issues (among many other conceivable ones) would also be worthy of closer consideration.

Firstly, it may be argued that the economic and financial activities and transactions of religious/spiritual groups increasingly often have come to directly pertain to issues concerning the broader governance and management of religious diversity in contemporary Western societies. For instance, the financial activities of religious groups have increasingly come to affect the attitudes of both legal authorities as well as wider public opinion about what religious groups are "supposed" to be doing in their function as religious groups, as opposed to, for example, commercial firms or political organizations. Such issues may, among other things, affect wider public opinion about what "counts" as "genuine," "authentic," or "acceptable" religion, thereby serving as a basis on which the religious status of particular groups and communities may come to be questioned and contested.[68] New religious movements such as Scientology, proponents of prosperity gospel Christianity, or various immigrant religions constitute but a few examples of religious groups for whom these issues at times may, and indeed have, become especially pressing.[69] Arguably, however, these days the financial activities of immigrant religions have become the subject of particularly close wider scrutiny. A primary present-day example of this would be the increasingly close monitoring by authorities of the financial activities of many Muslim groups in Europe (especially in countries with large Muslim populations such as Britain and France) because of their suspected or alleged support for the spreading of extremist teachings. It is, of course, principally through the media that information about such things becomes (or does not become) disseminated to the wider public.

Secondly, in addition to issues of the above type, the present-day relationship between religion and economic arrangements in modern societies necessarily also needs to be viewed in more direct relation to the general impact of consumer capitalism, consumer culture, and the ideology of consumerism on contemporary religious life and practice.[70] We need to acknowledge that, although historically there has always existed a close relationship between religion and economic arrangements, and although the selling, marketing, and commodification of religious goods and services is not appropriately understood as something "new," in the media-centered consumerist marketplace of late modern societies, religious communities of all kinds have become increasingly both inclined and compelled to communicate and package their messages in ways that correspond to market imperatives and the consumption-oriented sensibilities and practices of modern populations.[71]

As noted above, the exponential expansion and diversification of various media outlets in recent decades has both greatly increased the availability of information about virtually any form of religion and also increasingly forced religious communities and groups of all kinds to become ever more marketing savvy and consumer oriented.[72] For example, in *Brands of Faith: Marketing Religion in a Commercial Age*, Einstein contends that consumer capitalism and consumer culture have had a profound effect on the very character of the Western religious landscape and led to a rapid proliferation and increase in the marketing and branding of religion in general.[73] Indeed, the present-day general commodification of religion takes a huge variety of different forms, ranging from the marketing and branding of individual religious personas such as evangelical preachers and Indian gurus to the utilization of elements of Indian religions and "New Age" religiosity in the marketing of everyday commodities such as tea and soap (e.g., ayurvedic tea and aromatherapy shower gel promising to revitalize our "body, mind, and soul").

The contemporary general commodification of religion and religious teachings, practices, and goods, therefore, needs to be approached as a multifaceted phenomenon that is difficult to pin down because of the large variety of different forms that it may take. For example, within the context of more traditional forms of religion, these days it is not difficult to discern the impact of consumer culture when looking at the contemporary practices and activities of many evangelical communities,[74] or even many institutional mainline churches.[75] However, at a time when religion and religious life and practice in general have become ever more detached from traditional religious institutions and have increasingly taken on the character of a complex, varyingly tapped, and individualistically utilized cultural resource, the contemporary commodification of religion extends much further into virtually every sector of everyday social and cultural life, including, for example, the spheres of healthcare and work.[76]

Even though historical and contemporary relationships between religion and wider socioeconomic arrangements have remained a perhaps somewhat underresearched area within the study of religion in general, scholarly interest in the topic nevertheless stretches a long way back in time.[77] For example, Weber's classic *The Protestant Ethic and the Spirit of Capitalism* highlighted the importance of the study of religion to pay close attention to how particular religious sensibilities give rise to and shape particular economic regimes.[78] It needs to be noted, however, that whereas the study of religion and media and, to some extent, the study of religion and popular culture both have developed into more clearly delineated and consolidated fields of study, a more cohesive and unified scholarship of religion and consumer culture has yet to develop. Even so, a substantial, albeit quite fragmented, body of literature has nevertheless emerged on the subject. This scholarship includes studies of the historical relationship between markets, economic arrangements, and some particular forms of religion or religious institution[79]; the general commodification of religious teachings and practices in consumer-capitalist societies of today[80]; the utilization of religious themes in the marketing and advertising of everyday commodities[81]; the marketing of particular religious communities, products, and their associated niche markets[82]; the relationship between religion and tourism[83]; and the shaping impact of consumer culture on the actual religious life and practice of various types of religious communities and groups themselves.[84]

The bulk of this research has been carried out within a North American context and has been particularly focused on exploring the contemporary relationship between religion and consumer culture in more direct relation to the increasingly privatized, personal choice driven, and entrepreneurial character of the religious landscape of the United States.[85] It needs to be noted here, however, that research into the relationship between religion and economics/capitalism/consumer culture/consumerism should not be directly equated with more general uses of economic metaphorical concepts figuring within broader so-called "new paradigm" debates on religious change (and in relation to the United States in particular) such as "spiritual marketplace," "rational choice," or "supply-side model." This is not to say, however, that such metaphors would not be able to carry much explanatory potential.

Notably, a significant portion of this scholarship has raised the question of whether the increasingly close relationship between religion and consumer culture in modern times has been instrumental in bringing about a general *trivialization* of religion and religious life and practice on the whole. The argument here is not primarily that religions or religious traditions in themselves have been radically changed or altered in consumer-capitalist/consumerist culture but, rather, that people have come to engage with them, and indeed have become increasingly socialized and predisposed into engaging with them, in a way that is generally concomitant with consumer culture behavior and "the interpretive habits and dispositions it instills."[86] This notion has probably most frequently appeared in the scholarship focusing more specifically on the rise and proliferation of "alternative"[87] spiritualities in the West.[88] For example, as Heelas reflects: "Of all the controversies surrounding contemporary inner-life spiritualities, by far and away the most significant within the academy and beyond revolves around the criticism that the great majority (or virtually all) of provisions and activities serve as consumer products."[89]

Irrespective of what weight we choose to afford such critical perspectives, it nevertheless appears clear that the increasing general commodification of religion/spirituality no doubt needs to be taken into account when exploring the contemporary resurgence and growing public visibility of religion. For example, as discussed above, religion constitutes a highly visible element of the contemporary media and popular cultural environment as a whole. And, we must keep in mind that this is an environment that is deeply intertwined with contemporary consumer capitalism and consumer culture in a range of complex ways. As Hoover maintains, "as spiritual seekers turn in part to the marketplace of commodity culture for purposes of religious exploration, that marketplace (which is, after all, a media marketplace) provides more and more such material."[90]

Above all, the contemporary relationship between religion, consumer capitalism, and consumer culture further highlights how the locations and very category of religion are undergoing significant transformations in late modern times. Admittedly, it is quite difficult to more concretely connect the contemporary commodification of religion to the concept of post-secularity as it has been developed thus far. Even so, it nevertheless appears clear that the present-day relationship between religion and consumer culture can be seen as contributing to an increased general visibility of religion throughout Western social and cultural life in general.

Concluding Remarks

To conclude this chapter, let us now again ask ourselves why it would be important to look more closely at the present-day nexus of religion, media, popular culture, and consumer culture when (and if) striving to refine and develop the concept of the post-secular into a broader interpretive framework for the study of religious change in contemporary Western societies and Western European societies in particular.

As discussed above, the wider debates on post-secularity have so far primarily been social–philosophical and social–theoretical in character. As also noted above, the concept has so far largely been developed on the premise that many contemporary Western societies have witnessed a more recent general increase in the public visibility and awareness of religion, religious actors, and religious discourses. As such, the concept of post-secularity obviously connects more closely to certain contemporary theoretical debates and perspectives on religious change than it does to others. For example, through its emphasis on the visibility, role, and continued significance of religion in the *public* domain, the concept has so far remained firmly embedded in debates on "public religion," the contemporary governance of religious diversity in multicultural (primarily Western) societies, and both earlier and current theorizing on "desecularization"[91] and the "de-privatization" of religion in particular.[92]

As such, in the largely normative philosophical directions in which it has been developed thus far, the concept of post-secularity connects much *less* to other notable, more recently developed theoretical perspectives in the study of contemporary religion, which direct particular focus at the re-enchantment and resacralization of culture and everyday life.[93] One could argue, therefore, that the concept of post-secularity so far has remained firmly linked to some particular types of debates, largely governed by a particular set of established "mainstream" perspectives within the wider sociological study of religion, which tend to emphasize the contemporary resurgence and growing public visibility of religion through focusing on such things as the increasingly prominent role played by (certain forms of) religion in the context of global conflicts, the sphere of national and international politics, or in relation to immigration and the many challenges brought by increasing multiculturalism, while typically paying insufficient attention to the impact of factors such as media, popular culture, and consumer culture. Moreover, and perhaps largely due to their philosophical character, wider debates on post-secularity have so far almost solely concentrated on conventional, institutional, and established religions (mostly Christian and Muslim), while "unconventional" religious expressions, as well as the lived religious realities of increasing numbers of people today—the perspective of most recent scholarship on religion and media and religion and popular culture, as previously discussed—has received only a very limited amount of attention indeed.[94] We do, however, recognize that every particular perspective inevitably has to concentrate on some set of aspects or factors at the expense of others.

Even so, we learn most about ongoing transformations of the contemporary Western religious landscape, as well as about changes in people's perceptions of the very category of religion, when we allow the insights offered by different perspectives to be combined and strive to develop broader interpretive frameworks with sufficiently broad applicability.[95] It is therefore worth pointing out that, since the general current social–philosophical debates in which the term "post-secular" remains most commonly employed tend to operate with understandings of religion which are based on the formal theologies of established and conventional religious institutions, they are undoubtedly rather skewed and ill-equipped for addressing the wide variety of religious representations that figure on the broader contemporary Western cultural scene.

Indeed, if the increasingly sustained focus on the visibility of religion in the public sphere that characterizes current debates on post-secularity and the sociology of religion more broadly were to be coupled with an equally sustained focus on the impact of the media (in the forms of both technologies and institutions), popular culture, and consumer culture, then scholars might well arrive at drastically different interpretations of the actual composition and general character of the religious landscape of the West today than most established mainstream perspectives so far have allowed for. But, again, in the form in which it has principally been discussed so far, the concept of post-secularity has not yet taken us very far in this regard. Hence the more pressing need for it to be further developed in a direction that allows for it to become more attentive to the insights provided by a broader scope of present-day perspectives and interpretive frameworks on the changing face of religion in the West.

Finally, on a more general note, debates on the concept of the post-secular may also be discussed in relation to currently prevalent broader academic discourses on religious change. Looked at in this way, scholarly talk and theorizing about the post-secular could be conceived of as discourses critical of earlier hegemonic secularist discourses that presented religion as a negative social force, and which no doubt also played an important role in informing and underpinning various earlier monolithic theories of secularization which projected the gradual but ultimately inevitable demise of religion.[96] Post-secular discourses could then be taken to represent new ways of looking at the role of religion in late modern Western societies, and even as informing rethought conceptions about what "counts" as religion, what the function of religion is, what the various arenas and locations of religion are, and so forth.

As the scope of the category of religion itself is broadened, a natural outcome of post-secular and related discourses is that perceived instances of religion and religiosity (often conceptualized through the somewhat problematic term "spirituality") in the public sphere are greatly increased—something which scholars are in no way immune to, and which arguably also factors into the various theories of re-enchantment, resacralization, desecularization, and de-privatization of religion that have become more and more common within the broader sociological study of religion today.[97] Lastly, looking at things from a discursive perspective also entails that we as scholars keep wary of simply uncritically accepting "post-secular" outlooks and remain attentive to the role that we ourselves play in creating the religious landscape we perceive in front of us and subsequently purport to describe and explain.

Acknowledgments

We are thankful to Jan Svanberg, Sofia Sjö, Tuomas Martikainen, Gordon Lynch, and Mia Lövheim for their helpful and constructive remarks on earlier drafts of this chapter.

Notes

1. E.g., James V. Spickard, "Narrative Versus Theory in the Sociology of Religion: Five Stories of Religion's Place in the Late Modern World," in *Theorising Religion: Classical and Contemporary Debates*, ed. James A. Beckford and John Walliss (Hampshire: Ashgate, 2006), 169–81; Linda Woodhead, "Old, New, and Emerging Paradigms in the Sociological Study of Religion," *Nordic Journal of Religion and Society* 22 (2009): 103–21.
2. E.g., Steve Bruce, *God is Dead: Secularization in the West* (Oxford: Blackwell, 2002).
3. E.g., Rodney Stark and Richard Finke, *Acts of Faith: Exploring the Human Side of Religion* (Berkeley, CA: University of California Press, 2000).
4. E.g., Peter L. Berger, ed., *The Desecularization of the World: Resurgent Religion and World Politics* (Washington, DC: The Ethics and Public Policy Center, 1999).
5. E.g., José Casanova, *Public Religions in the Modern World* (London: The University of Chicago Press, 1994).
6. E.g., Christopher Partridge, *The Re-enchantment of the West (vol. 1): Alternative Spiritualities, Sacralization, Popular Culture and Occulture* (London: Continuum, 2004); Grace Davie, "Resacralization," in *The New Blackwell Companion to the Sociology of Religion*, ed. Bryan S. Turner (Chichester: Blackwell, 2010), 160–77.
7. E.g., Paul Heelas and Linda Woodhead (with Benjamin Seel, Bronislaw Szerszynski, and Karin Tusting), *The Spiritual Revolution: Why Religion is Giving Way to Spirituality* (Oxford: Blackwell, 2005).
8. E.g., José Casanova, *Public Religions*; "Religion, European Secular Identities, and European Integration," in *Religion in an Expanding Europe*, ed. Timothy A. Byrnes and Peter J. Katzenstein (Cambridge: Cambridge University Press, 2006), 65–92; Berger, ed., *Desecularization of the World*; Davie, "Resacralization"; Bryan S. Turner, *Religion and Modern Society: Citizenship, Secularisation and the State* (Cambridge: Cambridge University Press, 2011), x.
9. We use "post-secular" and "post-secularity" as interchangeable terms.
10. See, for example, Victoria Barker, "After the Death of God: Postsecularity?" *Journal of Religious History* 1 (2009): 82–95; Gregor McLennan, "Spaces of Postsecularism," in *Exploring the Postsecular: The Religious, the Political and the Urban*, ed. Arie L. Molendijk, Justin Beaumont, and Christopher Jedan (Leiden: Brill, 2010), 41–62; Bernice Martin, "Contrasting Modernities: 'Postsecular' Europe and Enspirited Latin America," in *Exploring the Postsecular*, 63–89.
11. E.g., Gregor McLennan, "Towards a Postsecular Sociology?" *Sociology* 41 (2007): 857–70; "Spaces of Postsecularism"; Kim Knott, "Cutting Through the Postsecular City: A Spatial Interrogation," in *Exploring the Postsecular*, 20.

12. Michele Dillon, "Can Post-Secular Society Tolerate Religious Differences?" *Sociology of Religion* 71 (2010): 141.

13. Jürgen Habermas, "Religion in the Public Sphere," *European Journal of Philosophy* 14 (2006): 1–25; "Notes on Post-Secular Society," *New Perspectives Quarterly* 25 (Fall 2008): 17–29.

14. Habermas, "Notes on Post-Secular Society," 20.

15. Ibid., 18.

16. Knott, "Cutting Through the Postsecular," 34; cf. Turner, *Religion and Modern Society*, 202–7.

17. Knott, "Cutting Through the Postsecular," 34, our emphasis.

18. E.g., Birgit Meyer, "Introduction: From Imagined Communities to Aesthetic Formations: Religious Mediations, Sensational Forms, and Styles of Binding," in *Aesthetic Formations: Media, Religion, and the Senses*, ed. Birgit Meyer (New York: Palgrave Macmillan, 2011), 2; Partridge, *Re-enchantment of the West (vol. 1)*; Colin Campbell, *The Easternization of the West: A Thematic Account of Cultural Change in the Modern Era* (Boulder, CO: Paradigm Publishers, 2007).

19. E.g., Jeremy Stolow, "Religion, Media, and Globalization," in *The New Blackwell Companion to the Sociology of Religion*, ed. Bryan S. Turner (Chichester: Blackwell, 2010), 544–62; Gordon Lynch, "Religion, Media and Cultures of Everyday Life," in *The Routledge Companion to the Study of Religion*, ed. John R. Hinnells, 2nd ed. (Oxon: Routledge, 2010), 543.

20. E.g., Stewart M. Hoover, *Mass Media Religion: The Social Sources of the Electronic Church* (London: Sage, 1988); Lynch, "Religion, Media and Cultures of Everyday Life," 546.

21. E.g., Nick Couldry, *Media Rituals: A Critical Approach* (London: Routledge, 2003); Jolyon Mitchell and Sophia Marriage, eds., *Mediating Religion: Conversations in Media, Religion and Culture* (London: T&T Clark, 2003); Morten T. Højsgaard and Margit Warburg, eds., *Religion and Cyberspace* (London: Routledge, 2005); Stewart M. Hoover, *Religion in the Media Age* (New York: Routledge, 2006); David Morgan, ed., *Key Words in Religion, Media and Culture* (New York: Routledge, 2008); Heidi Campbell, *When Religion Meets New Media* (New York: Routledge, 2010).

22. Hoover, *Religion in the Media Age*, 35–38, 55–56.

23. Ibid., 41.

24. Ibid., 55–56.

25. Stewart M. Hoover and Knut Lundby, "Summary Remarks: Mediated Religion," in *Rethinking Media, Religion, and Culture*, ed. Stewart M. Hoover and Knut Lundby (London: Sage, 1997), 305; cf. Lynn Schofield Clark, "At the Intersection of Media, Culture, and Religion: A Bibliographic Essay," in *Rethinking Media, Religion, and Culture*, 17.

26. Birgit Meyer and Jojada Verrips, "Aesthetics," in *Key Words in Religion, Media and Culture*, ed. David Morgan (New York: Routledge, 2008), 25; cf. Stolow, "Religion, Media, and Globalization," 549.

27. Hoover, *Religion in the Media Age*, 284.

28. Stolow, "Religion, Media, and Globalization," 544.

29. E.g., Knut Lundby, "Introduction: 'Mediatization' as Key," in *Mediatization: Concept, Changes, Consequences*, ed. Knut Lundby (New York: Peter Lang, 2009).

30. Stig Hjarvard, "The Mediatization of Religion: A Theory of the Media as Agents of Religious Change," *Northern Lights* 6 (2008): 9–26; *The Mediatization of Religion: Enchantment, Media and Popular Culture, Northern Lights 2008* (Bristol: Intellect, 2008); cf. Stewart M. Hoover, "Complexities: The Case of Religious Studies," in *Mediatization: Concept, Changes, Consequences*, 123–38.

31. E.g., Lundby, "Introduction," 4; *Culture and Religion* 12 (2011), *Special Issue: The Mediatisation of Religion*.

32. Cf. Hent de Vries, "Introduction: Before, Around, and Beyond the Theologico-Political," in *Political Theologies: Public Religions in a Post-Secular World*, ed. Hent de Vries and Lawrence E. Sullivan (New York: Fordham University Press, 2006), 8.

33. E.g., Mara Einstein, *Brands of Faith: Marketing Religion in a Commercial Age* (New York: Routledge, 2008), 35–36.

34. Stolow, "Religion, Media, and Globalization," 544.

35. Paul Hodkinson, *Media, Culture and Society* (London: Sage, 2011).

36. Ibid., 174–75.

37. Habermas, *Structural Transformation*, 188; Hodkinson, *Media*, 180–81.

38. E.g., Stewart M. Hoover and Nadia Kaneva, "Fundamental Mediations: Religion, Meaning and Identity in Global Context," in *Fundamentalisms and the Media*, ed. Stewart M. Hoover and Nadia Kaneva (London: Continuum, 2009), 1.

39. Norman Fairclough, *Media Discourse* (London: Bloomsbury, 1995), 3.

40. E.g., Hoover and Kaneva, "Fundamental Mediations," 2; e.g., Stolow, "Religion, Media, and Globalization," 553–56; Edward Michael Lenert, "Are Free Expression and Fundamentalism Two Colliding Principles?" in *Fundamentalisms and the Media*, 39–55.

41. E.g., Hodkinson, *Media*, 127–34.

42. Ibid., 135.

43. Ibid., 134–35.

44. Cf. Lynch, "Religion, Media and Cultures of Everyday Life," 553; Fairclough, *Media Discourse*.

45. Hodkinson, *Media*, 146.

46. E.g., Daniel A. Stout and Judith M. Buddenbaum, *Religion and Mass Media: Audiences and Adaptations* (London: Sage, 1996); Lynn Schofield Clark, *From Angels to Aliens: Teenagers, the Media, and the Supernatural* (New York: Oxford University Press US, 2003); Hoover, *Religion in the Media Age*.

47. Hodkinson, *Media*, 203.

48. Cf. Lynch, "The Role of Popular Music in the Construction of Alternative Spiritual Identities and Ideologies," *Journal for the Scientific Study of Religion* 45 (2006): 482–83.

49. E.g., Partridge, *Re-enchantment of the West (vol. 1)*, 121; Lynch, "The Role of Popular Music," 482.

50. E.g., David Lyon, *Jesus in Disneyland: Religion in Postmodern Times* (Cambridge: Polity Press, 2000), 56–64; Daniel A. Stout, "Beyond Culture Wars: An Introduction to the Study of Religion and Popular Culture," in *Religion and Popular Culture: Studies on the Interaction of Worldviews*, ed. Daniel A. Stout and Judith M. Buddenbaum (Ames: Iowa State University Press, 2001), 3–17; Hoover, *Religion in the Media Age*, 290.

51. E.g., Stout, "Beyond Culture Wars," 8; Jeffrey H. Mahan, "Reflections on the Past and Future of the Study of Religion and Popular Culture," in *Between Sacred and Profane Researching Religion and Popular Culture*, ed. Gordon Lynch (London. I.B. Tauris, 2007), 48.

52. Cf. Partridge, *Re-enchantment of the West (vol. 1)*, 119.

53. David Morgan, "Studying Religion and Popular Culture: Prospects, Presuppositions Procedures," in *Between Sacred and Profane*, 24; John Storey, *Inventing Popular Culture: From Folklore to Globalization* (Oxford: Blackwell, 2003).

54. Gordon Lynch, *Understanding Theology and Popular Culture* (Oxford: Blackwell, 2005), 14; cf. Lynn Schofield Clark, "Why Study Popular Culture? Or, How to Build a Case for your Thesis in a Religious Studies or Theology Department," in *Between Sacred and Profane*, 8–9.

55. Cf. Lynch, "Religion, Media and Cultures of Everyday Life," 548.

56. Ibid., 553.

57. E.g., Clark, *From Angels*; Partridge, *Re-enchantment of the West (vol. 1)*; *The Re-enchantment of the West (vol. 2): Alternative Spiritualities, Sacralization, Popular Culture and Occulture* (London: Continuum, 2005); Richard W. Santana and Gregory Erickson, *Religion and Popular Culture: Rescripting the Sacred* (Jefferson, NC: McFarland Publishers, 2008).

58. Partridge, *Re-enchantment of the West (vol. 1)*; *Re-enchantment of the West (vol. 2)*.

59. Partridge, *Re-enchantment of the West (vol. 1)*, 3–4.

60. Ibid., 68.

61. Ibid., 84.

62. Ibid., 85.

63. Ibid., 119.

64. Ibid., 53; cf. Hoover, *Religion in the Media Age*, 28.

65. Partridge, *Re-enchantment of the West (vol. 1)*, 53.

66. Bruce D. Forbes, "Introduction: Finding Religion in Unexpected Places," in *Religion and Popular Culture in America*, ed. Bruce D. Forbes and Jeffrey H. Mahan, rev. ed. (Berkeley: University of California Press, 2005), 5.

67. Nikos Passas, "The Market for Gods and Services: Religion, Commerce, and Deviance," in *Between Sacred and Secular: Research and Theory on Quasi-Religion*, Religion and the Social Order, vol. 4, ed. Arthur L. Greil and Thomas Robbins (London: Jai Press, 1994), 225.

68. James A. Beckford, *Social Theory and Religion* (Cambridge: Cambridge University Press, 2003), 197–98; cf. Turner, *Religion and Modern Society*, 176–78.

69. Passas, "Market for Gods," 224–25.

70. E.g., Mike Featherstone, *Consumer Culture and Postmodernism*, 2nd ed. (London: Sage, 2007).

71. Cf. Turner, *Religion and Modern Society*, xii, 149–50; Justin Beaumont, "Transcending the Particular in Postsecular Cities," in *Exploring the Postsecular*, 11.

72. E.g., Einstein, *Brands of Faith*, 35–36.

73. Ibid.

74. E.g., Ibid., 120–22.

75. Erik Sengers, "Marketing in Dutch Mainline Congregations: What Religious

Organizations Offer and How They Do It," *Journal of Contemporary Religion* 25 (2010): 21–35.

76. E.g., Anne-Christine Hornborg, "Designing Rites to Reenchant Secularized Society: New Varieties of Spiritualized Therapy in Contemporary Sweden," *Journal of Religion and Health* (May 2010), http://www.springerlink.com/content/x1qp028pq0542443/fulltext.pdf (accessed January 18, 2011); Tom Heller and Geraldine Lee Treweek, *Perspectives on Complementary and Alternative Medicine* (Abingdon: Routledge, 2005).

77. E.g., Linda Woodhead and Paul Heelas, *Religion in Modern Times: An Interpretive Anthology* (Oxford: Blackwell, 2000), 173–213; Lyon, *Jesus in Disneyland*, 73–96; Tuomas Martikainen, "Religion and Consumer Culture," *Tidskrift for kirke, religion og samfunn* 14 (2001): 111–25; Robert Burton Ekelund and others, *The Marketplace of Christianity* (Cambridge, MA: MIT Press, 2006).

78. Max Weber, *The Protestant Ethic and the Spirit of Capitalism* (1905; repr., Mineola, NY: Courier Dover Publications, 2003).

79. E.g., Laurence R. Moore, *Selling God: American Religion in the Marketplace of Culture* (Bridgewater, NJ: Replica Books, 2001); Mark A. Noll, ed., *God and Mammon: Protestants, Money, and the Market, 1790-1860* (Oxford: Oxford University Press, 2001); John Michael Giggie and Diane H. Winston, *Faith in the Market: Religion and the Rise of Urban Commercial Culture* (Piscataway, NJ: Rutgers University Press, 2002); Ekelund and others, *Marketplace*.

80. E.g., Passas, "Market for Gods"; Martyn Percy, "The Church in the Market Place: Advertising and Religion in a Secular Age," *Journal of Contemporary Religion* 15 (2000): 97–119; Martikainen, "Religion and Consumer Culture"; "Consuming a Cathedral: Commodification of Religious Places in Late Modernity," *Fieldwork in Religion* 2 (2006): 126–144; James B. Twitchell, *Branded Nation: The Marketing of Megachurch, College Inc., and Museumworld* (New York: Simon & Schuster, 2004); *Shopping for God. How Christianity Went from In Your Heart to In Your Face* (New York: Simon & Schuster, 2007); Hillary Warren, *There's Never Been a Show Like Veggie Tales: Sacred Messages in a Secular Market* (Lanham, MD: AltaMira Press, 2005); Einstein, *Brands of Faith*; Sandra Mottner, "Marketing and Religion," in *The Routledge Companion to Nonprofit Marketing*, ed. Adrian Sargeant and Walter W. Wymer (Abingdon: Routledge, 2008), 97–113; Pattana Kitiarsa, "Towards a Sociology of Religious Commodification," in *The New Blackwell Companion*, 563–83.

81. E.g., Carlton Johnstone, "Marketing God and Hell: Strategies, Tactics and Textual Poaching," in *Exploring Religion and the Sacred in a Media Age*, ed. Christopher Deacy and Elisabeth Arweck (Hampshire: Ashgate, 2009), 105–21; Galit Marmor-Lavie and others, "Spirituality in Advertising: A New Theoretical Approach," *Journal of Media and Religion* 8 (2009): 1–23.

82. E.g., Razelle Frankl, *Televangelism: The Marketing of Popular Religion* (Carbondale, IL: Southern Illinois University Press, 1987); Percy, "Church in the Market Place"; Kevin L. Keenan and Sultana Yeni, "Ramadan Advertising in Egypt: A Content Analysis with Elaboration on Select Items," *Journal of Media and Religion* 2 (2003): 109–17. Hillary Warren, "'Jewish Space Aliens are Lucky to be Free!': Religious Distinctiveness, Media, and Markets

in Jewish Children's Culture," in *Religion, Media and the Marketplace*, ed. Lynn Schofield Clark (Toronto: Rutgers University Press, 2007), 90–104; Lynn Schofield Clark, "Introduction. Identity, Belonging, and Religious Lifestyle Branding (Fashion Bibles, Bhangra Parties and Muslim Pop)," in *Religion, Media and the Marketplace*, 1–33; Sengers, "Marketing in Dutch Mainline Congregations."

83. E.g., Michael Stausberg, *Religion and Tourism: Crossroads, Destinations and Encounters* (New York: Routledge, 2010).

84. E.g., Colleen McDannell, *Material Christianity: Religion and Popular Culture in America* (New Haven, CT: Yale University Press, 1995); Jay R. Howard and John M. Streck, *Apostles of Rock: The Splintered World of Contemporary Christian Music* (Lexington: Kentucky University Press, 1999); Heather Hendershot, *Shaking the World for Jesus: Media and Conservative Evangelical Culture* (Chicago, IL: University of Chicago Press, 2004); Eileen Luhr, *Witnessing Suburbia: Conservatives and Christian Youth Culture* (Berkeley: University of California Press, 2009).

85. E.g., Einstein, *Brands of Faith*.

86. Vincent J. Miller, *Consuming Religion: Christian Faith and Practice in a Consumer Culture* (New York: Continuum, 2008), 30; cf. Turner, *Religion and Modern Society*, 204–6.

87. It should be noted that the term "alternative spirituality" is problematic. It posits that certain types of religiosity (in specific institutional expressions of Christianity) are normative and casts types of religiosity that diverge from the model as in some way "deviant." See Marion Bowman and Steven J. Sutcliffe, "Introduction," in *Beyond the New Age: Exploring Alternative Spirituality*, ed. Marion Bowman and Steven Sutcliffe (Edinburgh: Edinburgh University Press, 2000), 10–11.

88. E.g., Kimberly Lau, *New Age Capitalism: Making Money East of Eden* (Philadelphia, PA: University of Pennsylvania Press, 2000); Michael York, "New Age Commodification and Appropriation of Spirituality," *Journal of Contemporary Religion* 16 (2001): 361–72; Jeremy Carette and Richard King, *Selling Spirituality: The Silent Takeover of Religion* (London: Routledge, 2005); for a critical assessment of such arguments see Teemu Taira, "The Problem of Capitalism in the Scholarship on Contemporary Spirituality," in *Postmodern Spirituality*, ed. Tore Ahlbäck (Åbo: The Donner Institute for Religious and Cultural History, 2008), 230–44.

89. Paul Heelas, *Spiritualities of Life: New Age Romanticism and Consumptive Capitalism* (Oxford: Blackwell, 2008), 6.

90. Stewart M. Hoover, "The Culturalist Turn in Scholarship on Media and Religion," *Journal of Media and Religion* 1 (2002): 28.

91. E.g., Berger, *Desecularization of the World*.

92. E.g., Casanova, *Public Religions*; "Public Religions Revisited," in *Religion: Beyond a Concept*, ed. Hent de Vries (New York: Fordham University Press, 2008); Turner, *Religion and Modern Society*, 175–82.

93. E.g., Partridge, *Re-Enchantment of the West (vol. 1)*.

94. Turner, *Religion and Modern Society*, 147.

95. Cf. Davie, "Resacralization," 168.

96. Cf. Ibid., 162–63.

97. Cf. Murphy, "Discourse," 404–7; Davie, "Resacralization," 160.

Bibliography

Beaumont, Justin. "Transcending the Particular in Postsecular Cities." In *Exploring the Postsecular: The Religious, the Political and the Urban*, edited by Arie L. Molendijk, Justin Beaumont, and Christopher Jedan, 3–17. Leiden: Brill, 2010.

Beckford, James A. *Social Theory and Religion*. Cambridge: Cambridge University Press, 2003.

Berger, Peter L., ed. *The Desecularization of the World: Resurgent Religion and World Politics*. Washington, DC: The Ethics and Public Policy Center, 1999.

Bowman, Marion, and Steven Sutcliffe. "Introduction." In *Beyond the New Age; Exploring Alternative Spirituality*, edited by Marion Bowman and Steven Sutcliffe, 1–13. Edinburgh: Edinburgh University Press, 2000.

Bruce, Steve. *God is Dead: Secularization in the West*. Oxford: Blackwell, 2002.

Campbell, Colin. *The Easternization of the West: A Thematic Account of Cultural Change in the Modern Era*. Boulder, CO: Paradigm Publishers, 2007.

Campbell, Heidi. *When Religion Meets New Media*. New York: Routledge, 2010.

Carette, Jeremy, and Richard King. *Selling Spirituality: The Silent Takeover of Religion*. London: Routledge, 2005.

Casanova, José. *Public Religions in the Modern World*. London: The University of Chicago Press, 1994.

———. "Public Religions Revisited." In *Religion: Beyond a Concept*, edited by Hent de Vries, 101–19. New York: Fordham University Press, 2008.

———. "Religion, European Secular Identities, and European Integration." In *Religion in an Expanding Europe*, edited by Timothy A. Byrnes and Peter J. Katzenstein, 65–92. Cambridge: Cambridge University Press, 2006.

Clark, Lynn Schofield. "At the Intersection of Media, Culture, and Religion: A Bibliographic Essay." In *Rethinking Media, Religion, and Culture*, edited by Stewart M. Hoover and Knut Lundby, 15–36. London: Sage, 1997.

———. *From Angels to Aliens: Teenagers, the Media, and the Supernatural*. New York: Oxford University Press, 2003.

———. "Introduction. Identity, Belonging, and Religious Lifestyle Branding (Fashion Bibles, Bhangra Parties and Muslim Pop)." In *Religion, Media and the Marketplace*, edited by Lynn Schofield Clark, 1–33. Toronto: Rutgers University Press, 2007a.

———."Why Study Popular Culture? Or, How to Build a Case for your Thesis in a Religious Studies or Theology Department." In *Between Sacred and Profane: Researching Religion and Popular Culture*, edited by Gordon Lynch, 5–20. London. I.B. Tauris, 2007b.

Couldry, Nick. *Media Rituals: A Critical Approach*. London: Routledge, 2003.

Davie, Grace. "Resacralization." In *The New Blackwell Companion to the Sociology of Religion*, edited by Bryan S. Turner, 160–77. Chichester: Blackwell, 2010.

Dillon, Michele. "Can Post-Secular Society Tolerate Religious Differences?" *Sociology of Religion* 71 (2010): 139–56.

Einstein, Mara. *Brands of Faith: Marketing Religion in a Commercial Age*. New York: Routledge, 2008.

Ekelund, Robert Burton, Robert F. Hébert, and Robert D. Tollison. *The Marketplace of Christianity*. Cambridge, MA: MIT Press, 2006.

Fairclough, Norman. *Media Discourse*. London: Bloomsbury, 1995.

Featherstone, Mike. *Consumer Culture and Postmodernism*. 2nd ed. London: Sage, 2007.

Forbes, Bruce D. "Introduction: Finding Religion in Unexpected Places." In *Religion and Popular Culture in America*, edited by Bruce D. Forbes and Jeffrey H. Mahan, rev. ed., 1–20. Berkeley: University of California Press, 2005.

Frankl, Razelle. *Televangelism: The Marketing of Popular Religion*. Carbondale, IL: Southern Illinois University Press, 1987.

Giggie, John Michael, and Diane H. Winston, ed. *Faith in the Market: Religion and the Rise of Urban Commercial Culture*. Piscataway, NJ: Rutgers University Press, 2002.

Habermas, Jürgen. "Notes on Post-Secular Society." *New Perspectives Quarterly* 25 (Fall 2008): 17–29.

———. "Religion in the Public Sphere." *European Journal of Philosophy* 14 (2006): 1–25.

———. *The Structural Transformation of the Public Sphere*. 1964. Reprint, Cambridge: Polity Press, 1992.

Heelas, Paul. *Spiritualities of Life: New Age Romanticism and Consumptive Capitalism*. Oxford: Blackwell, 2008.

Heelas, Paul, Linda Woodhead, Benjamin Seel, Bronislaw Szerszynski, and Karin Tusting. *The Spiritual Revolution: Why Religion is Giving Way to Spirituality*. Oxford: Blackwell, 2005.

Heller, Tom, and Geraldine Lee Treweek. *Perspectives on Complementary and Alternative Medicine*. Abingdon: Routledge, 2005.

Hendershot, Heather. *Shaking the World for Jesus: Media and Conservative Evangelical Culture*. Chicago, IL: University of Chicago Press, 2004.

Hjarvard, Stig. "The Mediatization of Religion. A Theory of the Media as Agents of Religious Change." *Northern Lights* 6 (2008a): 9–26.

———, ed. *The Mediatization of Religion: Enchantment, Media and Popular Culture*. Special issue, *Northern Lights* 6 (2008b).

Hodkinson, Paul. *Media, Culture and Society*. London: Sage, 2011.

Højsgaard, Morten T., and Margit Warburg, eds. *Religion and Cyberspace*. London: Routledge, 2005.

Hoover, Stewart M. "Complexities: The Case of Religious Studies." In *Mediatization: Concept, Changes, Consequences*, edited by Knut Lundby, 123–38. New York: Peter Lang, 2009.

———. "The Culturalist Turn in Scholarship on Media and Religion." *Journal of Media and Religion* 1 (2002): 25–36.

———. *Mass Media Religion: The Social Sources of the Electronic Church*. London: Sage, 1988.

———. *Religion in the Media Age*. New York: Routledge, 2006.

Hoover, Stewart M., and Knut Lundby. "Summary Remarks: Mediated Religion." In *Rethinking Media, Religion, and Culture*, edited by Stewart M. Hoover and Knut Lundby, 298–309. London: Sage, 1997.

Hoover, Stewart M., and Nadia Kaneva. "Fundamental Mediations: Religion, Meaning and Identity in Global Context." In *Fundamentalisms and the Media*, edited by Stewart M. Hoover and Nadia Kaneva, 1–21. London: Continuum, 2009.

Hornborg, Anne-Christine. "Designing Rites to Reenchant Secularized Society: New Varieties of Spiritualized Therapy in Contemporary Sweden." *Journal of Religion and Health* (May 2010): http://www.springerlink.com/content/x1qp028pq0542443/fulltext.pdf (accessed January 18, 2011).

Howard, Jay R., and John M. Streck. *Apostles of Rock: The Splintered World of Contemporary Christian Music.* Lexington: Kentucky University Press, 1999.

Johnstone, Carlton. "Marketing God and Hell: Strategies, Tactics and Textual Poaching." In *Exploring Religion and the Sacred in a Media Age,* edited by Christopher Deacy and Elisabeth Arweck, 105–21. Hampshire: Ashgate, 2009.

Keenan, Kevin L., and Sultana Yeni. "Ramadan Advertising in Egypt: A Content Analysis with Elaboration on Select Items." *Journal of Media and Religion* 2 (2003): 109–17.

Kitiarsa, Pattana. "Towards a Sociology of Religious Commodification." In *The New Blackwell Companion to the Sociology of Religion,* ed. Bryan S. Turner, 563–83. Chichester: Blackwell, 2010.

Knott, Kim. "Cutting Through the Postsecular City: A Spatial Interrogation." In *Exploring the Postsecular: The Religious, the Political and the Urban,* edited by Arie L. Molendijk, Justin Beaumont, and Christopher Jedan, 19–38. Leiden: Brill, 2010.

Lau, Kimberly. *New Age Capitalism: Making Money East of Eden.* Philadelphia: University of Pennsylvania Press, 2000.

Lenert, Edward Michael. "Are Free Expression and Fundamentalism Two Colliding Principles?" *In Fundamentalisms and the Media,* edited by Stewart M. Hoover and Nadia Kaneva, 39–55. London: Continuum, 2009.

Luhr, Eileen. *Witnessing Suburbia: Conservatives and Christian Youth Culture.* Berkeley: University of California Press, 2009.

Lundby, Knut. "Introduction: 'Mediatization' as Key." In *Mediatization: Concept, Changes, Consequences,* ed. Knut Lundby, 1–18. New York: Peter Lang, 2009.

Lynch, Gordon. "Religion, Media and Cultures of Everyday Life." In *The Routledge Companion to the Study of Religion,* edited by John R. Hinnells, 2nd ed., 543–57. Oxon: Routledge, 2010.

———. "The Role of Popular Music in the Construction of Alternative Spiritual Identities and Ideologies." *Journal for the Scientific Study of Religion* 45 (2006): 481–88.

———. *Understanding Theology and Popular Culture.* Oxford: Blackwell, 2005.

Lynch, Gordon, and Mia Lövheim, eds. "The Mediatisation of Religion." Special issue, *Culture and Religion* 12 (2011).

Lyon, David. *Jesus in Disneyland: Religion in Postmodern Times.* Cambridge: Polity Press, 2000.

Mahan, Jeffrey H. "Reflections on the Past and Future of the Study of Religion and Popular Culture." In *Between Sacred and Profane: Researching Religion and Popular Culture,* edited by Gordon Lynch, 47–62. London. I.B. Tauris, 2007.

Marmor-Lavie, Galit, Patricia A. Stout, and Wei-Na Lee. "Spirituality in Advertising: A New Theoretical Approach." *Journal of Media and Religion* 8 (2009): 1–23.

Martikainen, Tuomas. "Consuming a Cathedral: Commodification of Religious Places in Late Modernity." *Fieldwork in Religion* 2 (2006): 126–44.

———. "Religion and Consumer Culture." *Tidskrift for kirke, religion og samfunn* 14 (2001): 111–25.

Martin, Bernice. "Contrasting Modernities: 'Postsecular Europe and Enspirited Latin America." In *Exploring the Postsecular: The Religious, the Political and the Urban*, edited by Arie L. Molendijk, Justin Beaumont, and Christopher Jedan, 63–89. Leiden: Brill, 2010.

McDannell, Colleen. *Material Christianity: Religion and Popular Culture in America*. New Haven, CT: Yale University Press, 1995.

McLennan, Gregor. "Spaces of Postsecularism." In *Exploring the Postsecular: The Religious, the Political and the Urban*, edited by Arie L. Molendijk, Justin Beaumont, and Christopher Jedan, 41–62. Leiden: Brill, 2010.

———. "Towards a Postsecular Sociology?" *Sociology* 41 (2007): 857–70.

Meyer, Birgit. "Introduction: From Imagined Communities to Aesthetic Formations: Religious Mediations, Sensational Forms, and Styles of Binding." In *Aesthetic Formations: Media, Religion, and the Senses*, edited by Birgit Meyer, 1–28. New York: Palgrave Macmillan, 2011.

Meyer, Birgit, and Jojada Verrips. "Aesthetics." In *Key Words in Religion, Media and Culture*, edited by David Morgan, 20–30. New York: Routledge, 2008.

Miller, Vincent J. *Consuming Religion: Christian Faith and Practice in a Consumer Culture*. New York: Continuum, 2008.

Mitchell, Jolyon, and Sophia Marriage, eds. *Mediating Religion: Conversations in Media, Religion and Culture*. London: T&T Clark, 2003.

Moore, Laurence R. *Selling God: American Religion in the Marketplace of Culture*. Bridgewater, NJ: Replica Books, 2001.

Morgan, David. "Introduction. Religion, Media, Culture: The Shape of the Field." In *Key Words in Religion, Media and Culture*, edited by David Morgan, 1–19. New York: Routledge, 2008a.

———, ed. *Key Words in Religion, Media and Culture*. New York: Routledge, 2008b.

———. "Studying Religion and Popular Culture: Prospects, Presuppositions Procedures." In *Between Sacred and Profane: Researching Religion and Popular Culture*, edited by Gordon Lynch, 21–33. London. I.B. Tauris, 2007.

Mottner, Sandra. "Marketing and Religion." In *The Routledge Companion to Nonprofit Marketing*, edited by Adrian Sargeant and Walter W. Wymer, 97–113. Abingdon: Routledge, 2008.

Murphy, Tim. "Discourse." In *Guide to the Study of Religion*, edited by Willi Braun and Russell T. McCutcheon, 396–408. London: Cassell, 2000.

Noll, Mark A., ed. *God and Mammon: Protestants, Money, and the Market, 1790-1860*. Oxford: Oxford University Press, 2001.

Partridge, Christopher. *The Re-enchantment of the West (vol. 1): Alternative Spiritualities, Sacralization, Popular Culture and Occulture*. London: Continuum, 2004.

———. *The Re-enchantment of the West (vol. 2): Alternative Spiritualities, Sacralization, Popular Culture and Occulture*. London: Continuum, 2005.

Passas, Nikos. "The Market for Gods and Services: Religion, Commerce, and Deviance." In *Between Sacred and Secular: Research and Theory on*

Quasi-Religion. Religion and the Social Order, vol. 4, edited by Arthur L. Greil and Thomas Robbins, 217–40. London: Jai Press, 1994.

Percy, Martyn. "The Church in the Market Place: Advertising and Religion in a Secular Age." *Journal of Contemporary Religion* 15 (2000): 97–119.

Santana, Richard W., and Gregory Erickson. *Religion and Popular Culture: Rescripting the Sacred*. Jefferson, NC: McFarland Publishers, 2008.

Sengers, Erik. "Marketing in Dutch Mainline Congregations: What Religious Organizations Offer and How They Do It." *Journal of Contemporary Religion* 25 (2010): 21–35.

Spickard, James V. "Narrative Versus Theory in the Sociology of Religion: Five Stories of Religion's Place in the Late Modern World." In *Theorising Religion: Classical and Contemporary Debates*, edited by James A. Beckford and John Walliss, 169–81. Hampshire: Ashgate, 2006.

Stark, Rodney, and Richard Finke. *Acts of Faith: Exploring the Human Side of Religion*. Berkeley, CA: University of California Press, 2000.

Stausberg, Michael. *Religion and Tourism: Crossroads, Destinations and Encounters*. New York: Routledge, 2010.

Stolow, Jeremy. "Religion, Media, and Globalization." In *The New Blackwell Companion to the Sociology of Religion*, edited by Bryan S. Turner, 544–62. Chichester: Blackwell, 2010.

Storey, John. *Inventing Popular Culture: From Folklore to Globalization*. Oxford: Blackwell, 2003.

Stout, Daniel A. "Beyond Culture Wars: An Introduction to the Study of Religion and Popular Culture." In *Religion and Popular Culture: Studies on the Interaction of Worldviews*, edited by Daniel A. Stout and Judith M. Buddenbaum, 3–17. Ames: Iowa State University Press, 2001.

Stout, Daniel A., and Judith M. Buddenbaum. *Religion and Mass Media: Audiences and Adaptations*. London: Sage, 1996.

Taira, Teemu. "The Problem of Capitalism in the Scholarship on Contemporary Spirituality." In *Postmodern Spirituality*, edited by Tore Ahlbäck, 230–44. Åbo: The Donner Institute for Religious and Cultural History, 2008.

Turner, Bryan S. *Religion and Modern Society: Citizenship, Secularisation and the State*. Cambridge: Cambridge University Press, 2011.

Twitchell, James B. *Branded Nation: The Marketing of Megachurch, College Inc., and Museumworld*. New York: Simon & Schuster, 2004.

———. *Shopping for God. How Christianity Went from In Your Heart to In Your Face*. New York: Simon & Schuster, 2007.

de Vries, Hent. "Introduction: Before, Around, and Beyond the Theologico-Political." In *Political Theologies: Public Religions in a Post-Secular World*, edited by Hent de Vries and Lawrence E. Sullivan, 1–88. New York: Fordham University Press, 2006.

Warren, Hillary. "'Jewish Space Aliens are Lucky to be Free!': Religious Distinctiveness, Media, and Markets in Jewish Children's Culture." In *Religion, Media and the Marketplace*, edited by Lynn Schofield Clark, 90–104. Toronto: Rutgers University Press, 2007.

———. *There's Never Been a Show Like Veggie Tales: Sacred Messages in a Secular Market*. Lanham, MD: AltaMira Press, 2005.

Weber, Max. *The Protestant Ethic and the Spirit of Capitalism*. 1905. Reprint, Mineola, NY: Courier Dover Publications, 2003.

Woodhead, Linda. "Old, New, and Emerging Paradigms in the Sociological Study of Religion." *Nordic Journal of Religion and Society* 22 (2009): 103–21.

Woodhead, Linda, and Paul Heelas. *Religion in Modern Times: An Interpretive Anthology.* Oxford: Blackwell, 2000.

York, Michael. "New Age Commodification and Appropriation of Spirituality." *Journal of Contemporary Religion* 16 (2001): 361–72.

6

Dimensions of Innovationism

Katja Valaskivi

Somewhere in some activity or condition lies a fullness and richness. In that place (activity or condition) life is fuller, richer, deeper, more worthwhile, more admirable, more what it should be.[1]

Innovation is a contemporary buzzword, used in a great number of situations. The concept has been circulated from economics to the media, and is used in contexts ranging from national competitiveness strategies to R&D. It appears in business prospectuses and academic textbooks, strategy documents and funding applications, and local industry policy statements and guidelines for cultural enhancement. In each context the concept gains new meanings—gradually becoming almost a blanket term, all-encompassing and inevitable in discussions about the future, science, society, education, development, the economy, and so on. Thus, when one listens to politicians, consultants, academics, and journalists, it can appear that purely through innovations one can achieve a life that is fuller, richer, deeper, and more worthwhile. In this way innovations appear to form a whole worldview or belief system. I refer to this belief system as *innovationism*.

According to Beyer, a central structural feature of secularized societies is the differentiation of institutional subsystems, such as culture, politics, and the economy. These subsystems are relatively independent of religious norms, values, and justifications, and thus we are led into a situation in which the religious area of operations continually becomes narrower.[2] However, in order to understand the role of the religious in the contemporary world, it will be necessary to widen the perspective. The way in which I wish to discuss the post-secular is connected to the ways in which the religious domain is present in subsystems that might appear to be secular. The apparent invisibility of an explicitly religious domain in a subsystem does not imply an absence of aspects, dimensions, or patterns of action that function in religious ways. Thus, in this chapter I shall attempt to identify how, in this faith called innovationism, practices of faith with religious implications have developed within frames that are not perceived as religious at all—or could even be perceived as totally opposed to religion.

One of the main propositions of the post-secularity debate states that because of the growing public visibility of religion and religious phenomena, theories of secularization are no longer able to explain social conditions in contemporary developed societies. However, in this chapter I wish to look beyond the conventional definitions of religion. Given the pervasiveness of innovationism, it is imperative to understand the ways in which it communicates a belief system that manages power, flows of funding, and social relationships.[3]

In discussions of secularity and the post-secular society, the question of a search for meaning appears frequently. Charles Taylor acknowledges that even in societies that have rid themselves of God there is nevertheless an aspiration for something better: the issue is an example of what Habermas[4] describes as "an awareness of what is missing." Taylor[5] borrows Luc Ferry's concept of the "meaning of meaning" ("*sens du sens*") in explicating the notion that "somewhere there is a fullness or richness which transcends the ordinary." In this sense, the question indeed concerns "meaning of life." Why are we here? What is the purpose of all this? The question of (collective) meaning is intertwined with feelings of insecurity and a desire for security in (globalized) times.

In this chapter I shall describe the dimensions[6] of innovationism and the ways in which it is used in a collective search for meaning, or quest for certainty, in three national settings, the United States, Finland, and Japan. The research has been conducted via a combination of content analysis and discourse analysis[7]; it involves interviews with journalists and innovation systems specialists[8] in the three countries, focusing particularly on two countries, Finland and Japan.

It is obvious that innovationism could be analyzed in numerous ways, for instance, as a hegemonic ideology. In this chapter, however, innovationism (based on the interviews I conducted) is perceived as a rationalized symbolic universe with religious features. Thus, what I wish to do here is to test the conceptualization of innovationism as a transnational[9] symbolic universe and social imaginary—one which is apparently used in a rational and secular sense, but which nevertheless has religious usages and implications. In discussing the dimensions of innovationism as a worldview,[10] I wish to elucidate how innovationism works, first of all, in organizing and maintaining core values, and secondly, in managing hope and threat in those post-secular societies in which religion is a matter of choice.

The renowned "theologian of hope," Paul Tillich, defines religion as being about the ultimate concerns of humankind. Thus, religion provides in the first place a meaningful set of ultimate values on which the morality of a society can be based. When these values are institutionalized, they can be spoken of as central values of a society.[11] Secondly, religion provides an adequate explanation for the "ultimate frustrations" which are inherent to the human situation, and which are not manageable or morally meaningful. Death is the type case of (individual) ultimate frustrations, while environmental concerns and climate change are current issues that appear to threaten the whole of humankind.

Ultimate values should be greater than ultimate frustrations, and religion should provide an adequate explanation for ultimate frustrations, so that the individual or the group can accept them without having their core values rendered meaningless.[12] In a similar way, Tillich emphasizes the necessity of hope for human beings and for the collective: hope should exist as the driving force for a human being "as long as he lives."[13]

In religious studies, Tillich's view on ultimate concerns has for some time been considered "rather empty and too wide-ranging" to facilitate an understanding of religions. Ninian Smart advocates a comparative perspective, with the study of "dimensions of worldviews." According to Smart, there are seven dimensions that need to be taken into account: (1) the ritual or practical, (2) the philosophical, (3) the mythic or narrative, (4) the experiential or emotional, (5) the ethical or legal, (6) the organizational or social, and (7) the material or artistic dimension.[14]

In understanding innovationism as a belief system or worldview, it appears that the approaches of Tillich and Smart may complement each other. Innovationism is strongly based on certain shared values. The circulation of these values not only contributes to the construction of an imagined (global) community,[15] but is also the basis on which the more practical dimensions are constructed.

Thus, the tentative conclusion would be that innovationism provides for contemporary developed societies both a set of ultimate values and a way of controlling the ultimate frustrations. In this way innovationism can be perceived of as religious. The set of values is institutionalized through the constant circulation of innovationism in different contexts and conjunctures.

In what follows, I will first explore innovationism as it appears in my empirical material from the point of view of ultimate values at the individual, corporate, national, and global levels, and in relation to dimensions of worldviews. Secondly, I will discuss the ultimate frustrations and how innovationism appears to manage them in its various dimensions. Thirdly, I will study the actors taking part in the institutionalization of innovationism, as demonstrated in the interviews. Finally, I will discuss the mechanisms of innovationism that contribute to the contemporary, collective search for meaning and the quest for certainty.

Before that, however, it will be necessary to take a look at the definitions and usages of the concept of innovation; these can also be analyzed through the *doctrinal dimension* of innovationism.[16]

Innovation

The current use of the word *innovation* is generally acknowledged to have derived from the economist Joseph A. Schumpeter. His perception of innovation can be summed up in the following four themes:

1. Innovations are changes in production functions which cannot be decomposed into infinitesimal steps. In other words, innovation involves putting productive resources to uses which have hitherto been untried in practice. At the same time, resources are withdrawn from the uses that they have served so far.[17]
2. Innovation should be distinguished from invention or experimentation. It is not invention that matters, but the adoption and actual working of something. In themselves, inventions do not exert any influence on business life at all. In other words: "Innovation, unless it consists in producing, and forcing upon the public a new commodity, means producing at a smaller cost per unit, breaking off the old supply schedule and starting a new one. It is quite immaterial whether this is done by making use of a new invention or not."[18]
3. Innovations appear in clusters at certain times because "as soon as the various kinds of social resistance to something that is fundamentally new and untried have been overcome, it is much easier not only to do the same thing again but also to do similar things in different directions, so that a first success will always produce a cluster (e.g., the emergence of the motorcar industry)."[19]

4. In competitive capitalism innovations are the mechanism which creates disturbance, mainly through the foundation of new firms. In the short term, innovations require large investments and "supernormal energy and courage." In the long term they will—in successful cases—produce progress and profit.[20]

In the empirical material comprising the interviews with journalists and innovation system specialists in Japan, Finland, and the United States, the interviewees produce various explanations when asked to define the concept of "innovation." However, it is apparent that the Schumpeterian definition is to a large extent internalized and adopted as a doctrinal starting point, since most emphasized that innovation is more than just a new thing. For the interviewees, innovation means a new invention or product which can be, or has already been commercialized and which brings in money to a company or individual who is in possession of the innovation. However, although the fourth characteristic of innovations as creating disturbance is often stated, and might even be referred to directly as "creative destruction," the point that innovations require risk-taking and a lot of time in order for a profit to be gained is often discarded.

Furthermore, the usage of the word *innovation* (or of the term translated in this way) varies greatly in different languages. For instance, in Japanese there is strong emphasis on new technology and gadgets. Interviewees also use notions such as "service innovation" and "social innovation," which further blurs the picture. Service innovations and social innovations can be made by public actors as well as private companies, and no cash flow is necessary. The uncertainty in the term has been resolved by some interviewees by referring to the concept of "surplus value." Thus, innovations would be "new commercialized inventions that bring surplus value to the users and the producer." In practice, during the interviews the word is used in ways that have a very vague connection with the definitions given by the interviewees at the start of each interview. This demonstrates the doctrinal aspect of the concept: the word *innovation* is used in such a wide range of contexts that its implications are supposed to be known to all.

Thus, it is necessary to make a conceptual distinction between talk about specific cases of innovation and individual innovations (*the technical dimension*), talk about the innovation system and the innovation environment (*the social dimension*), and the wider discursive web of conjunctures where national competitiveness in fear-provoking global circumstances appears to require innovation as a means for national survival (*a blend of the ritual, mythical, and doctrinal dimensions*). In the interviews these distinctions are often blurred and talked of simultaneously.

The Value System of Innovationism

Myths can be defined as authoritative stories belonging to certain groups or traditions. Myths are recited in the community, and these kinds of stories are foundational for the group in question. The shared values of the community are narrated in circulated and repeated mythic tales. This practice is linked to the *mythic, or narrative dimension* of a worldview.[21]

The narrative dimension appears in the definitions of innovations used by the interviewees. By analyzing this dimension it is possible to begin to draft the set of ultimate values on which innovationism relies, and to describe how the values appear in the interviews.[22] Here, values are perceived as aims, as aspirations toward which the actors strive. In the narratives which circulate in the interviews the core values cut across individual, corporate, national, and global levels; moreover, to a certain extent all of the values are present on all the levels, and thus they create a whole circulatory system of innovationism. However, it appears that certain values pertain to particular levels more than others.

Based on the interviews, the following values would appear to lie at the core: success, growth, competiveness, and progress. These values appear in stories that recur within the interviews.

The values appear on four levels within the narratives: firstly, at the individual level, innovation becomes a means for success for the interviewees, in the United States in particular. The myth of the American dream of the individual entrepreneur is frequently repeated in the U.S. interviews. The success of individual entrepreneurs can also involve new start-up companies, which can generate growth. At the individual level, the narrative dimension seems to have a particular connection with *the ethical dimension*. The innovation system specialists emphasized how the behavior of individuals should become suitable for creating innovations: more mobility, flexibility, creativity, language proficiency, and openness, plus a risk-taking mentality, are qualities required of the citizens of an innovative nation.

At the corporate level, innovation first and foremost provides a means for productivity and the possibility for growth. Innovations can also mark the beginnings of new corporations, which is one of the aspirations of competing nations: to get more start-up companies. It is at the corporate level that the *material dimension* of innovationism appears most visibly: enterprises create new technology, new services, and new markets though innovations.

The competitiveness of the nation-state is the third value appearing in the interviews.

The global setting in which nation-states compete with each other is a myth that is hardly ever questioned. Through innovativeness, the basic starting point of economic competition is widened to include competition in general. National competitiveness is then more than economic; it is about being useful for the global community, becoming visible and important—being meaningful—for others in the global setting.

At the national level, innovationism is also a part of the political discourse on national competitiveness, a discourse that was introduced during the 1980s throughout the industrialized world. In the narrative of innovationism, the globalizing economy poses a threat to nation-states.[23] Thus, national actors became worried about their survival and success. At the same time, Schumpeterian technology-driven ideas on innovation became influential in economics. It is important to note that although the discourse on competitiveness is a global one, the consequences and actions are taken at a national level. Thus, competitiveness becomes an aim primarily at the national level, although it is a value also at the corporate level.

Fourthly and finally, at the global level, the narrative of innovationism appears in the emphasis on progress. This could be considered the *philosophical level* of innovationism. The reliance on constant progress remains even when, occasionally, growth is questioned. Innovations then become a means for the further enhancement of humankind, providing hope during times of global environmental threat. The values of progress and competitiveness are constantly intertwined when the national and the global circulate in the interviews:

> [. . .] in Asia relations between Japan, China, and Korea are complicated and difficult. We have been competing for hundreds of years. During the last twenty years Japan has been the underdog and has suffered severe mental [spiritual] damage. Should we progress [purely] with style or charm? With the arts? [referring to the Cool Japan phenomenon and the global growth of sales in Japanese popular culture] Our citizens are wondering about this as well. That is why we compete in science and want to compete for who is

best in developing solutions for the [environmental] threats facing humanity. Our current prime minister has set a target to cut down carbon dioxide emissions by 25 per cent. This is a truly idealistic goal, and a significant one. It is something China and Korea cannot do. We no longer compete in food, fashion, or cars, but we want to be a presence and to be important in the world in other ways. We are looking for these ways now.[24]

This excerpt from the interview with a Japanese journalist also exemplifies the fear of failure in reaching what is aimed at. A nation that fails in competition will be damaged and will need to seek out new areas in which to become competitive. The possibility of innovation brings determination and hope: "We will be meaningful in the world of tomorrow."

Affective Resonance: Threat and Hope

"The emphasis in religion is today on this world, not the world to come," writes Liselotte Frisk in her discussion of Linda Woodhead's concept, the "turn to life." The turn to life refers to the focus on gaining desirable results in this world, in other words in the immanent frame. According to Woodhead, themes of punishment, hell, damnation, and demonology have been losing their importance as societies have become more "this-worldly."[25] Innovationism can be seen as following this trend in its focus on human capabilities and abilities. However, innovationism can also be seen as narrating something of a substitute for "hell," in foreseeing the failure of humankind to solve global threats, of which global warming is the most threatening.

At every level, the management of threat and hope in innovationism can be analyzed through the emotional dimension: innovationism creates a sense of threat by narrating the ultimate frustrations and also attempts to manage these threats through positing innovations as solutions to the threats it narrates—thus giving hope for the future.

The ultimate frustrations appear in the interviews in expressions of a sense of threat and fear. The sense of threat is concentrated within issues of global warming and environmental change, phenomena that intensify an awareness of the limitedness of natural resources. To some extent, the talk about the environment and demographics is invited by the framework of the interviews, in which innovations are discussed in the context of global warming and aging. Nevertheless, the interviewees frequently list threats and challenges which correspond to multiple features of the risk society.[26] The world is dangerous at every level: the global level, the national level, the level of (the media) industry, and at the individual level. Exacerbated by the global economic recession and the development of an aging society (in Japan in particular) the ultimate frustrations are concentrated into the issue of sustaining the nation. However, at the core of global threats is the competition.

In *The Birth of Biopolitics*, Michel Foucault points out that within neoliberalism, it is not the market mechanism that is new. What *is* new is the idea of constant competition and the aim of continuous growth.[27] At this point, taking up Foucault's identification of competition as the novel feature, I wish to set out one of my central claims: *that through innovationism, competition is transformed into the central generator of the sense of threat.* The operational environment of nation-states and corporations is one of constant competition for resources, for "top" workers, and for foreign investment. And similarly, individuals compete against each other: for jobs, for visibility, for fame.

The outcome of possible failure was hardly ever explicated in the interviews, but it can be read between the lines. In fact, the ultimate frustrations derivable from the interviews involve *death, waning, chaos,* and *extinction.*

The following table (Table 1) illustrates how innovationism manages hope and threat at different levels in relation to the ultimate values. The table also lists the most relevant corresponding dimensions for each level. It should, however, be noted that all the dimensions and values cut across all the levels. In fact, two other dimensions, the *narrative* and the *emotional* dimension permeate all the levels and values to such a degree that it would be unreasonable to mark them in the table.

Table 1
How Innovationism Manages Hope and Threat at Different Levels

Level	Value (Aim)	Hope	Outcome of Failure	Threat	Dimension
Individual	Success	Memory	Unemployment	Death	Ethical
Corporate	Growth	Expansion	Takeover	Merger or bankruptcy	Material
National	Competitiveness	Sustaining the nation	Competitive ineptness	Waning, oblivion	Social/ritual
Global	Progress	Continuity	Climate change	Chaos, extinction	Philosophical

In the manner of a religion, innovationism offers a way to counter ultimate frustrations. The sense of threat is used to create an affective resonance[28] for particular institutional demands, and as a justification for political practices and funding decisions. The interviewees repeated the Porterian[29] thesis, that in order to survive and prosper amid global competition, the nation has to have a high level of competitiveness.[30]

In the definitions of innovation proposed by Schumpeter (see above), innovation is a means to create growth and productivity and thus competitiveness. However, in innovationism, innovations are loaded with much more significance. Innovations and innovativeness become the aim itself, and the creation of a good environment for innovation becomes the goal of nations. Because of the threat of losing out in competition, the focus is shifted onto innovations as an apparent means of controlling uncontrollable circumstances. In this way innovations emerge not only as an instrument of hope, but also as a chance to shift the focus away from the looming threat of competition and onto innovations per se.

The Power and Social Dimension of Innovationism

I shall now move to the *organizational and social dimensions* of innovationism, focusing on the actors and roles present in the production and circulation of innovationism.

The most important actors in the circulation of innovationism are the national elites. Among the interviewees there are innovation systems specialists and journalists, both of whom can be regarded as the elites of innovationism. Some members of the elite play advocational roles such as "preachers," gurus, theologians, and prophets. Others take more neutral or even skeptical roles. For "ordinary people" the interviewees provide two possible role positions: they are either the audience, which should be educated or informed, or those who have the potential for creating innovations that the system is not yet able to tap into. I shall return to these actors and roles after considering the *national* frame of innovationism.

Benedict Anderson uses the concept of imagined communities in discussing the development of nationalism. For him, the imagined community is the nation. Many others take a similar view, arguing that the nation holds the position in society that religion used to occupy before the development of modernization.[31]

Anderson sees the nation as the idea upon which communities can create a secular transformation, from fatality into continuity, and contingency into meaning. "With the ebbing of religious belief, the suffering which belief in part composed did not disappear. Disintegration of paradise: nothing makes fatality more arbitrary. Absurdity of salvation: nothing makes another style of continuity more necessary."[32]

For Charles Taylor, imagined communities are a particular kind of social imaginary, socially shared in ways in which social spaces are imagined.[33] An essential part in the conjuncture of global competition is the reproduction of a social imaginary in which the imagined communities perceived as nations take part. Innovationism can be seen as a complementary element in sustaining the imaginary community of the nation within this conjuncture. The imaginary structure of the world in innovationism is based on two contradictory logics: on the one hand, there is the conforming, global logic of innovations and the emphasis on the global setting, including the idea of the global, imagined center of Silicon Valley. On the other hand, there is the strong emphasis on the nation-state, which in fact has the role of a mediator in the circulation of ideas. (Trans)national elites circulate innovationism to the national level, while doing this they apply the national framework and make use of the imagined community within the nation. The nation and the national political system is the frame within which resources are distributed, and elites with symbolic power themselves possess an interest in this distribution. The affective nature of these processes is significant. The power struggle is conjunctured with questions of national survival and a sense of threat and hope.

The imagined center of Silicon Valley appears in the interviews as the "center" but also as the "peak" of innovativeness. Smart describes the various ways in which height has symbolic value in most cultures and notes how height, size, and centrality are often connected.[34] Interviewees, not only in Japan and Finland, but also on the East Coast of the United States refer to the Silicon Valley, not just as a source of innovative new solutions, but also as an ideal innovation environment: a place with a highly competitive atmosphere, plus a creative buzz—both desired characteristics. In Silicon Valley one sees a reversal of the norm: interviewees emphasize that there is no need to travel to see the world, since "everybody comes here." This mentality can be understood through social practices belonging to the *ritual dimension*. One of these is *pilgrimage*. Groups and individuals traveling to the Silicon Valley and to Stanford University to learn innovativeness

139

can be seen as pilgrims traveling to the center of innovationism. In pilgrimage, travelers go to "high sacral bumps in space, learn and gain from its merit, and convey it back to the periphery."[35] Within the periphery there is a desire to become like the center, or at least to overcome the spatial and mental distance between the center and the periphery.

The strength of the imagined center is underlined in the interviews with the Japanese and Finnish elite experts, who are almost in despair over a national lack of innovativeness, mobility, or openness, and express the desire to reach the level of innovation in Silicon Valley. The sense of inadequacy cannot be assuaged by international comparisons that emphasize the innovativeness of Japan or Finland.[36] Nevertheless, journalists, who act as mediators between the elites and ordinary citizens, are not as certain of the circumstances: *In Finland politicians appear to have taken on this [idea of developing innovations]. [They are] creating—I'"m not sure if it is an illusion—but at least I have a perception of Finland being innovative.*[37]

The framework of national competitiveness leads the Japanese and Finnish interviewees into circulating the idea that there needs to be a national solution—an innovation system or innovation environment—that will help in reaching the level of Silicon Valley. The irony is that in Silicon Valley itself the interviewees emphasize the anarchic and unstructured nature of the innovation environment as being the source of its innovativeness.[38] Nevertheless, in Finland and Japan the interviewees perceive the orientation first and foremost as a national one: innovations are a means to maintain (national) competitiveness and to help in solving problems on a (national and) global scale. In the United States in general, but particularly in Silicon Valley, interviewees focus more on innovations as means for the success of the individual.

Within the interviews the nation-states become actors in a literal sense. The global community is a stage on which the nation-state wishes to play a major role. Nation-states compete to achieve these roles and hope to become visible on the stage. Nation-states also worry about being overtaken by new actors with superior competitiveness and more innovative ability:

> Well, I think that in general world powers are shifting. And the rise of the BRIC[39] countries and other places outside of the United States as powerful centres of business with much potential for growth has shifted some of our entrepreneurial energy to places like India, China

and Brazil, I mean, certainly I would say, I myself have done a bunch of reporting in India around telecom and have been amazed, blown away by the entrepreneurial spirit and the good ideas that are coming out of India and migrating to the US when in fact always in decades before you would see innovation go the other way. Ideas would rise up in the US and they would migrate to India. Now I think you are seeing it happen [the other way around].[40]

The national narrative in the United States, as illustrated in this citation, is centered around the supposed essentially innovative nature of the United States. The United States is perceived as having "always" been the source of innovations, as compared to China, India, or Brazil, but now the roles are reversing for the first time. The nation-state as the leading actor is now under threat of being replaced by younger and more flexible players. Important here is the portrayal of a sense of threat within the imagined order of nations. (The obvious historical distortedness of the perceptions is of less importance.)

I shall now return to the individual actors and role positions in the circulation of innovationism. As noted above, it is possible to make a division between elites and ordinary people. The difference between these groups is in their access to transnational sources of information and opportunities to take part in the circulation of information—in other words, the differences lie at the level of symbolic power that they possess.[41]

The actors exercise "pastoral power" through the "effects of words." Foucault emphasizes that power of the pastoral type has spread from religious institutions and has entered the entire social body. The aim of pastoral power, as Foucault sees it, is to take part in "the development of knowledge of man," both in a globalizing frame and in relation to the individual.[42]

In his discussion of pastoral power, Foucault refers to "the power exercised by private ventures, welfare societies, benefactors, and [. . .] philanthropists."[43] In a similar manner, innovationism has figures who exercise pastoral power while taking a variety of roles within innovationism. As manifested in the interviews, some of the pastoral figures are academics, consultants, some work for think tanks, and others for multinational corporations. Usually they are not politicians, though they may have had a political career previously. At the present time they tend to be in a managerial position in relation to politics.[44] Their role can be one of a preacher or sometimes a theologian, who "formulates the doctrines or teachings of a tradition or sub-tradition."[45] The role of the theologian often appears to be played by the consultants.

Some of the pastoral figures act as prophets who describe what a future with better innovations will be like. Alternatively, they may issue predictions of a terrible future if national systems are not developed into a functioning innovation system/if new technology is not commercialized effectively/if the social media are not made use of innovatively, and so on. As often as not they are speakers at seminars or workshops and called "Social Media Gurus." There are even people with the title of "evangelist" working in technology parks, aiming to achieve "innovation development" or "innovation transfer."

These pastoral figures constitute the authorities of innovationism; they are the ones who describe the kinds of measures to be taken in order to enhance national innovativeness and to develop the national innovation system. In the case of Finland, these figures include Pekka Himanen, who during the 1990s[46] was the youngest scholar ever to defend a dissertation in philosophy, and Jorma Ollila, the former CEO of Nokia. The younger generation of these preachers may well be self-made entrepreneurs who have made fortunes through ICT-related innovations. Pastoral power is also exercised by the directors and employees of national funding apparatuses, such as Tekes in Finland or JST in Japan. Consultants and researchers working in think tanks and universities can also fall into this category.

The people mentioned above appear frequently in the media, where they describe and define how the innovation system should be organized in order to maximize the production of innovations. Indeed, some of the people in this category were interviewees for this study. An equally important function of these figures is to "preach" at seminars, symposiums, and workshops; these are the arenas in which they spread enthusiasm, propagate innovationism as a faith, and emphasize the relevance of related values to officials, decision makers, journalists, academics, and entrepreneurs. They are, as it were, performing in such a way as to generate affective resonance, so that institutional structures and funding decisions may be legitimized.

The actors taking part in the circulation of innovationism are predominantly male, and so too (almost exclusively) are the pastoral figures appearing in the media. The overall picture is one of men predominating in discussions concerning innovations, innovation policies, and the measures that need to be taken. Overtly, the world of innovations is gender neutral, and it is true that women are not explicitly excluded, however, they are not actively included either. In practice, this means that the women who are actually visible in this field are exceptions.[47] The point here is that in both Finland and in Japan, innovation discourse exists as part of a continuum of science and technology policy discourses, and that women have been sidelined for decades in national discourses related to technological development.[48] Similar restrictions apply in discourses related to a number of areas of technology—ICT in particular.[49]

The belief that innovations can raise a nation's competitiveness is obviously strongest among specialists in innovation systems. These interviewees emerge not only as "believers" but also as "theologians," or as the kinds of "preachers" mentioned above. For these people, innovations are self-evidently phenomena to be supported. The repeated argument is that we need methods to develop more innovativeness: the innovation system or innovation environment should be made more fertile so that innovations can increase.[50] The comparisons with the Silicon Valley ideal are frequent and admiring. The people in question see many kinds of problems in the innovation system, in the national mentality, in the general mood of the times, and in the attitude of the "ordinary people." Criticism is also directed at the quality of scientists and journalists.[51]

The symbolic, pastoral power that is represented and reproduced by elites through the circulation of innovationism is connected to economic and political power. Symbolic power in general differs from other forms of power in the sense that it affects "not just what we do, but our ability to *describe* the social itself; it affects the perception of the inequalities in the social world, including the unequal distribution of those very symbolic resources themselves."[52]

The elite interviewees saw society first and foremost as an environment for innovation—one whose purpose is to provide good circumstances for more innovative activities and competitiveness. The question is predominantly one of flows of public funding. Innovationism has meant that the flood of public money to the private sector has been plentiful and rapid. Among other things, it has meant that health care institutions, schools, and universities are seen as deserving of investment, insofar as they are basic elements of the innovation environment.

One of the contradictions of innovationism lies in the relationship between the transnational and the nation. The processes to which innovationism is attached—namely, the free flow of capital, economic growth, and competition—are transnational, and could in fact lead to the dissolution and erosion of the nation-state. However, the particular actors and elites with symbolic power in the circulation of innovationism are always national, although they have access to the transnational mechanisms by which innovationism is circulated. Consequently, national elites, while preaching innovationism within the nation, in fact use their symbolic power in a contradictory manner, to advance the globalizing processes that are tightly bound up with their faith in innovation. The nation-state is a necessary vehicle for globalization. And at the same time, global trends constitute the vehicle through which the elites attempt to sustain their power. This happens through twin endeavors—the summoning up of threatening images of globalization and the preaching of innovationism.

The Consecrating Role of the Journalist and Journalism

Pierre Bourdieu describes the way in which the art-businessman has the power to *consecrate* works of art and to create value for works and artists.[53] In a similar way, journalists have symbolic power in the process of consecrating individual innovations, and in the recycling and reproduction of innovationism. This consecrating role is recognized both by specialists and by journalists themselves, but the perspectives of the parties are different. The pastoral specialists would like to have journalists employ their consecrating power and take part in the national project of supporting innovations. The specialists see the role of journalism and the media as focal in creating a more innovation-friendly mental environment within society. "It is the media through which we construct the world of technology and innovations," was how one of the Finnish specialists put it.[54] But (as indicated above) it is clear that journalists, too, recognize the potential influence of journalism[55]:

> The Japanese in general have a relative mentality; they watch people or society and then adopt their standpoints, judging what to do. This is a national feature, because Japan is so closed. In that sense, the media in Japan play a more important role than in other countries. I think that it is not bad to be balanced in writing, but sometimes I think that the established media prioritise consensus.[56]

Within the interviews, "ordinary journalists" might repeat slogans on innovation that are similar to those used by specialists. However, it is less likely that journalists will be able to explain the entire structure of the innovation system. It was notable that those interviewees who had a deeper knowledge of the innovation environment seemed also to be more committed to innovationism. Generally, specialists would like journalists to take on a "consecrating" role. The journalists in the interviews were, in some cases, explicit in resisting such wishes. Thus, there were interviewees who subscribed to the idea of global competition and who believed in innovations, but who were nevertheless opposed to the position offered to them by "the state"—a position equivalent to the national, official stance toward innovations:

> These days you very seldom encounter this thing that journalists are supposed to commit themselves to promoting good things. And here, suddenly, they've dug this idea out of its grave, I feel, that we all have a shared agenda here. This idea that we've been sent to Stanford and it's assumed that we understand that this is important, important for the future of the nation. [. . .] The way those in the top echelon of society talk about innovation as a subject [. . .] they have this idea of the survival of the nation. And then, it seems so easy to extend [the idea to journalism] and to say that journalism should commit itself to this objective, too. But [we] should just be able to separate [ourselves] from this. [The task of journalism then] is to put these matters on the agenda [. . .] to that extent we have a common project. After that, journalism and journalists should continue in an independent and self-contained manner.[57]

Even though interviewees might be critical of the demands placed on them to further the innovation system and promote innovations, they nevertheless do believe that innovations are good and necessary: innovations can help to solve social problems and contribute to economic growth; they can also help the nation to gain and or/maintain its status among other nations.[58]

Looking for Security in a Dangerous World

In this section, I shall describe how questions of collective meaning (in the sense of meaning in life) were bound up with innovationism in the interviews. For this purpose, I shall make a brief detour via John Dewey, who noted that human beings living in a dangerous world have to look for safety and certainty. According to Dewey, humans have historically done this in two ways: either by trying to conciliate the surrounding environmental forces through prayer, rites, and magic, or by developing skills to use natural forces for human advantage. The second of these methods changes the world through action, while the first changes human thoughts and feelings.[59]

In the search for meaning and certainty, innovations combine action and feeling in at least three ways. First of all, innovations appear to be the only means for survival in the "risk society" and in a world full of threats. Producing more innovations provides a way of changing the world through action. Thus, I would suggest that within innovationism these two aspects—action and feeling (or affect)—are merged: innovationism aims at changing human thoughts and feelings concerning the world, since it suggests that the world is there first and foremost for utilization.

Secondly, innovations provide a way of changing human feelings and thoughts related to certain looming threats. Innovations give hope for a better future at the national level (we can become visible on the global stage) and at the individual level (what I do can have meaning, and I can become rich).

Thirdly, innovationism has an exhilarating aspect, containing within it enthusiasm for creating a better future. Innovations appear to achieve something more than reliance on economic growth; they contain the possibility for a nation to become visible on the global stage even when it is about to shift involuntarily into an era of degrowth because of an aging population. By being innovative as a nation, the country (Japan) can become a notable model for other nations in demonstrating controllable degrowth.

"There is a limit to which economic growth can answer the question of the meaning of life. We are like the sorcerer's apprentice: What we have unleashed is out of control. Nowhere is this more true than in Japan."[60] An interviewee puts this in other words:

> [. . .] Our success at present is based on economic success. However, the natural resources, such as oil, which made that success possible, will run out sooner or later, and we can't think of the economy alone. The five billion people in the world suddenly have to face difficulties. I think we have to make efforts to solve the problems. Since there is no way we can get out of this reality, we should try to think how to mitigate the damage or how to alleviate it. We need to find a balance and find a way to downgrade our standards of living. From that perspective, the decrease in the population of Japan might not be so bad after all. [. . .] But we need to maintain some basic level of economy. We need bread first, and we can't let the economy come crashing down. The downgrading should be controlled, and we need overall planning for that. In Japan the population is decreasing. When this

development becomes visible, and if we can manage the downgrading here, we can give examples to other countries as well.[61]

By these means, through innovations, nations can prove that they are original and authentic. This includes being useful for the global community and for humanity, amid the worrisome, threatening issues of global warming and aging. Some of the interviewees believed that if innovative thinking became sufficiently advanced, it could find ways toward a better future in which economic growth would no longer be the necessary framework.

> Competition is part of the today's world, and I think there are two parts that we should think of, today and the future. These two often contradict each other. At present, if we put a higher priority on the former, say, selling goods more and ruining natural resources, we will end up ruining the future, too. I think we should make rules like in boxing matches; in the course of the match, people compete with one another, but keep to certain rules of sportsmanship. Of course, politicians can make rules, but they have to think mainly about today, in order to survive an election, so ideally, the intelligent citizens or NGOs should form groups for discussion. These kinds of ideal groups can't be brought about by the UN, unfortunately. It can't be the OECD or a world economy forum or anything like that. It should be something unrelated to the economy, because the point of view of the economy belongs to today, not to the future.[62]

This perception is nevertheless very different from the ideology of what has been termed the degrowth movement. The degrowth movement calls for the dissolving of the global financial system and a return to local economies, in which consumption and needs would be in balance with natural resources. It criticizes the concept of sustainable development on the grounds that it continues the exploitation of the natural environment by virtue of the ideology of growth. In fact, such critical notions in respect of growth and global competition did not appear in the interviews.

Innovationism is attractive because it provides a hope for a better collective future, and hope for security during times that appear to be full of insecurities. By circulating a belief in innovations, late modern societies have created a transnational, yet nationally applicable belief system which appears to be rational and intelligible. Here we have a way of managing prevailing fears and insecurities—and holding to a utopian view of a better future. In line with this, and taking an

147

optimistic view, Hautamäki offers the possibility of "sustainable innovation," or "creating products and services promoting sustainable economic growth without undermining quality of life and equilibrium with nature"[63]—hence a mechanism for creating a sense of certainty. Thus, innovationism rises above the mundanities of politics and the economy: it becomes a promise that we will find tools not only for economic survival, but also for physical survival in an age of environmental dangers.

To Conclude: A Quest for Certainty in the Immanent Frame

If the idea of a God is ruled out, the answer to the issue of the meaning of life can be sought from two directions: either by denying the question itself or by saying that one of our present purposes already has the fullness or richness that we seek.[64] The discourse on innovations can then be seen in conjunction with the latter. It provides a means of avoiding the underlying, deeper question about a collective and individual meaning for life by appearing to provide one. The belief in innovations is based on rationality and has no (apparent) connection with divinity, however, it is strongly oriented toward the future. There is no doubt that innovationism is a this-worldly belief system: its focus is on continuous growth through innovations. Yet, innovationism also has its utopian side, since it forms a collective way of imagining a better future.

Socially, innovationism creates a sense of "us," connected to an imagined (global) community, and it offers a chance to contribute to this community, in creating solutions for problems that threaten the very existence of that community (including, preeminently, global warming). In this worldview, innovations themselves build a bridge to a better future and to saving the world.

Charles Taylor describes different ways of perceiving secularity. He describes how secularity refers to a condition in which "public spaces have been emptied of God" and belief in God is declining. Taylor wishes to move further, and to discuss the conditions of belief in a society where God is one alternative among others rather than unchallenged and unproblematic as was the case in previous centuries.[65]

Berger calls this pluralism. In his article *Protestantism and the Quest for Certainty*, he admits to having made one big mistake in his career: thinking that modernity would lead necessarily to the decline of religion. This, of course, has been documented as contrary to fact by many others as well.[66] The insight that Berger says he has had during his career is that modernity leads to pluralism. And in pluralism, certainty is hard to find:

> People may still hold the same beliefs and values that were held by their predecessors in more uniform situations, but they will hold them in a different manner: what before was given through the accident of birth now becomes a matter of *choice*. Pluralism brings on an era of many choices, and by the same token, an era of *uncertainty*.[67]

This citation can be reflected on from two sides in relation to the empirical findings of this study. On the one hand, modernity, undoubtedly, did bring plurality in a certain sense. However, considering the strength of the ideology of national competitiveness and the belief in the beneficial nature of innovations manifested in the interviews, I might provocatively ask whether or not there is any pluralism in these beliefs. Has believing in innovations perhaps taken on the position of a "consensus on the nature of reality and on the norms by which one should lead one's life"[68]—at least in large parts of the three societies where the persons interviewed in this study live? (And if this is the case, are they living in conditions that can no longer be called modernity?) On the other hand, we can interpret a belief in innovations as an attempt to control the *uncertainty* brought on by the conditions of pluralism.

Relying on innovations would thus be a "quest for certainty" and a quest for knowledge, an effort to transcend belief. As Dewey points out, belief is often assumed to be a mode of thinking about a realm of uncertainty.[69] The future, including innovations, belongs to the realm of uncertainty, as one of the interviewees agonises: "Innovation is fundamentally unpredictable [. . .] it's hard to put a narrative on a process which is fundamentally unpredictable. [. . .] it was just not easy to predict beforehand."[70] Thus, relying on uncertain innovations as the way to a seemingly certain future becomes a contemporary, mundane version of religion. There is a strong parallel here with Noble's argument about the religion of technology, by which human engagement with technology provides a means to regain the (supposedly) lost sense of divinity, meaning, and control over the world.[71]

Innovationism is a secular belief in the sense that it does not belong to the realm of institutional and historic religions. It can be regarded as belonging more to the secular subsystem of the economy, politics, or science.[72] Thus, it is not practised in the "religious" sphere and is not perceived as religious. Because of this, innovationism provides an important case in our understanding of changes in society. Post-secularity might thus mean not only more instances of institutional religion in the public space, but also understanding and identifying features of belief systems and worldviews across what used to be understood as separate subsystems of society.

Innovationism is public. Its narratives appear to invoke the rational *homo economicus*. I would argue that this is the particular allure of belief in innovation. It appears to belong to the rational, scientific, public sphere: it is collectively acceptable to be ecstatic about new gadgets, future prospects, and economic growth. Like any ideology, innovationism is invisible and naturalized: the shared faith in it is transparent and seems self-evident. There is nothing mystical about innovationism, and thus it is more than acceptable to be enthusiastic about innovations, to go on pilgrimages to Stanford, to take part in revival meetings where canonized preachers profess their faith.

In a pluralist society, where life is complicated and values are created by individuals themselves, believing in innovations provides an accepted, self-evident, future-oriented—and collective—way of imagining a better future.

Acknowledgments

I would like to thank professor Risto Kunelius from University of Tampere and adjunct professor Johanna Sumiala for their comments and encouragement in different phases of writing this article.

Notes

1. Charles Taylor, *A Secular Age* (London: The Belknap Press of Harvard University, 2007), 5.
2. See Peter Beyer, *Religion and Globalization* (London: Sage, 1994), 75.
3. "[. . .] religion is a type of communication based on the immanent/transcendent polarity, which functions to lend meaning to the root indeterminability of all meaningful human communication, and which offers ways of overcoming or at least managing this indeterminability and its consequences." Beyer, *Religion and Globalization*, 6.
4. Habermas appears to be referring to solidarity as the thing missing, but that is not completely explicit in his text. Jürgen Habermas, "An Awareness of What is Missing," in *An Awareness of What is Missing. Faith and Reason in a Post-Secular Age*, ed. Jürgen Habermas and others (Cambridge: Polity Press, 2007), 15–23.
5. Taylor, *Secular Age*, 676.
6. Ninian Smart, *Dimensions of the Sacred. An Anatomy of the World's Beliefs* (Berkeley: University of California Press, 1996), 8–14.

7. The interviews were first thematically coded to a computerized qualitative analysis program (Atlas.ti). Thereafter, a close discourse analysis was conducted on particular thematic sections relevant for this chapter.

8. The research material was collected within a research project that studied the conditions and consequences of "innovation journalism." The project was funded by the Finnish Funding Agency for Technology and Innovation and headed by Professor Risto Kunelius. The material (eighty interviews in total) included sixty-nine interviews with journalists and eleven with innovation systems specialists. I interviewed journalists in three different countries, Finland ($n=34$), the United States ($n=21$), and Japan ($n=14$). The interviewees also represent three different thematic groups: business/technology reporters (those who typically write about innovation topics, $n=34$), journalists who focus on environmental issues including climate change ($n=18$), and journalists who have written on issues related to aging ($n=16$). The Finnish focus group consisted of journalists writing for daily newspapers and magazines (print/online). The U.S. journalists are employed by newspapers, magazines, and online publications. The Japanese journalists represent journalists writing for the most substantial and oldest-established newspapers. The gender split for the journalists was thirty-nine males and thirty females. The interviewees are identified in this study by national codes FI1 . . . FI34, US1 . . . US21, and JP1 . . . JP14. The interviewees within a given national group are categorized alphabetically. The interviews were conducted by four different interviewers in several locations in Finland, Japan, and the United States. Some of the Finnish interviews were conducted on the phone or by e-mail, whereas all the interviews in Japan and the United States were conducted face-to-face.

    In addition to the interviews with journalists, eleven innovation system specialists were interviewed, six in Finland, one in the United States, and four in Japan. All of them were male, except for one female interviewee in Japan. These interviews are coded with the "A" prefix, hence AFI1 . . . AFI6, AUS1, and AJP1 . . . AJP4.

    All the interviews were conducted between August 2009 and March 2010.

9. Transnational phenomena occur across nations and cultures, but are nevertheless connected with the concept and framework of the nation. That is why I have chosen to perceive innovationism as transnational rather than a global phenomenon. In this paper, "global" and "globalized" are seen as belonging to the discourse of innovationism rather than as analytical concepts.

10. Smart, *Dimensions of the Sacred*, 8–14.

11. Paul Tillich, *Systematic Theology I* (Chicago: University of Chicago Press, 1950), see also Robert Bellah, *Tokugawa Religion. The Cultural Roots of Modern Japan* (New York: The Free Press, 1957; repr. New York: The Free Press, 1985).

12. Bellah, *Tokugawa Religion*, 6–7.

13. Paul Tillich, "The Right to Hope," in *Theology of Peace*, ed. Ronald H. Stone (Westminster/John Knox, 1990), 182–93.

14. Smart, *Dimensions of the Sacred*, 9.

15. On the concept of imagined communities, see Benedict Anderson, *Imagined Communities. Reflections on the Origin and Spread of Nationalism* (London: Verso, 1991; rev. and ext. repr., London: Verso, 2003), 9–36, 37–46.

16. Smart, *Dimensions of the Sacred*, 27–69.

17. Joseph A. Schumpeter, "The Analysis of Economic Change," *The Review of Economics and Statistics* 17, no. 4 (1935): 4; "The Instability of Capitalism," *The Economic Journal* 38, no. 151 (1928): 378.

18. Joseph A. Schumpeter, "The Explanation of Business Cycle," *Economica* 21 (December 1927): 297; "Analysis of Economic Change," 6; "Instability of Capitalism," 378.

19. Schumpeter, "Analysis of Economic Change," 6.

20. Schumpeter, "Instability of Capitalism," 384.

21. Smart, *Dimensions of the Sacred*, 136.

22. It is important to remember that Schumpeter himself emphasized that he was talking *only* of the economic system and that he explicitly attempted to mark out "external" influences. Thus, he did not talk of society as a whole, or of developing societal models. Despite this, his work is constantly used in ways that are bound up with the development of society in different national settings. Indeed, his work implicitly supports this. For example, in his "Instability of Capitalism," Schumpeter juxtaposes competitive and "trustified" capitalism.

23. Anu Kantola and Hannele Seeck, "Dissemination of Management into Politics: Michael Porter and the Political Uses of Management Consulting," *Management Learning* 41, no. 4 (2010): 1–23.

24. JP9.

25. Liselotte Frisk, "Globalization: A Key Factor in Contemporary Religious Change," *Journal of Alternative Spiritualities and New Age Studies* 5 (2009–2011): i–xiv; Linda Woodhead, "The Turn to Life in Contemporary Religion and Spirituality," in *Spirituality and Society in the New Millennium*, ed. Ursula King and Tina Beattie (Portland: Sussex Academic Press, 2001), 110–23.

26. Cf. Anthony Giddens, *Consequences of Modernity* (Cambridge: Polity Press, 1990); Ulrich Beck, *Risk Society: Towards a New Modernity* (New Delhi: Sage, 1992); see also Pat Caplan, "Introduction: Risk Revisited," in *Risk Revisited*, ed. Pat Caplan (London: Pluto Press, 2000), 1–29.

27. Michel Foucault, *The Birth of Biopolitics. Lectures at the Colléége de France 1978-1979*, ed. Michel Senellart (London: Palgrave Macmillan, 2008), x–xx.

28. William Mazzarella, "Affect: What is it Good for?" in *Enchantments of Modernity. Empire, Nation, Globalization*, ed. Saurab Dube (London: Routledge, 2008), 292–309.

29. Harvard professor Michael Porter is the leading theoretician on national competitiveness. He has analyzed the competitive advantage of more than fifty nations (Kantola and Seeck 2010).

30. Kantola and Seeck, "Dissemination of Management into Politics," 1–23.

31. Benedict Anderson, *Imagined Communities: Reflections on the Origin and Spread of Nationalism* (London: Verso, 1991; rev. and ext. repr., London: Verso, 2003), 1–8; Smart, *Dimensions of the Sacred*, 1–25.

32. Anderson, *Imagined Communities*, 11–12.

33. Taylor, *Secular Age*, 713.
34. Smart, *Dimensions of the Sacred*, 138–40.
35. Ibid., 86–87.
36. Cf. e.g., Richard Florida and Tim Gulden, "The World Is Spiky," *The Atlantic Monthly*, October 2005.
37. FI17.
38. E.g., AUS1, US3.
39. Brazil, Russia, India, and China.
40. US8.
41. For the concept of symbolic power, see Pierre Bourdieu, *Language and Symbolic Power* (Cambridge: CUP, 1991), 105–37; Stuart Hall, *Representation: Cultural Representations and Signifying Practices* (London and Thousand Oaks: Sage, 2003), 12–74.
42. Michel Foucault, "The Subject and Power," *Critical Inquiry* 8, no. 4 (1982): 783–85, 792.
43. Ibid.
44. Cf. Kantola and Seeck, "Dissemination of Management into Politics," 1–23.
45. Smart, *Dimensions of the Sacred*, 215–25.
46. http://www.pekkahimanen.org/ (accessed December 19, 2011).
47. It was difficult to find female interviewees for the project. Among the specialists, only one of the interviewees was female. The journalists specializing in science and innovations were predominantly male, while the journalists focusing on aging were almost exclusively female in all three countries.
48. Marja Vehviläinen, "Teknologinen nationalismi," in *Suomineitonen hei! Kansallisuuden sukupuoli* [Hello Maiden of Finland. Nationality of Gender], ed. Tuula Gordon, Katri Komulainen, and Kirsti Lempiäinen (Tampere: Vastapaino, 2002), 211–29; "Gendered Agency in Information Society: On Located Politics of Technology," in *Women & Everyday Uses of the Internet. Agency & Identity*, ed. Mia Consalvo and Susanna Paasonen (Oxford: Peter Lang Publishing, 2002), 275–91.
49. William A. Stahl, *God and the Chip: Religion and the Culture of Technology* (Waterloo, ON: Wifred Laurier University Press, 1999), 54.
50. E.g., AJP2, AFI1, AFI2, AUS1.
51. AFI1, AFI2, AJP1, AJP3.
52. Nick Couldry, *Media Rituals. A Critical Approach* (London: Routledge, 2003), 39, original italics.
53. Bourdieu, Pierre, "The Production of Belief: Contribution to an Economy of Symbolic Goods," in *Media, Culture and Society. A Critical Reader*, ed. Richard Collins, James Curran, Nicholas Garnham, Paddy Scannell, Philip Schlesinger, and Colin Sparks (London: Sage, 1986), 134.
54. AFI2.
55. However, this does not apply to the United States, where both specialists and journalists see the role and power of journalism as much smaller. This corresponds to the fact that the national framework in relation to the innovation environment is weaker in the United States.
56. JP5.
57. FI4.

58. US13, JP6, FI14.
59. John Dewey, *The Quest for Certainty* (New York: Minton Balch, 1929, repr., New York: Capricorn Books, 1960), 11.
60. Robert Bellah, *Tokugawa Religion*, xx. The theme is analyzed empirically in Gavan McGormack, *The Emptiness of Japanese Affluence* (London: M.E. Sharpe, 1996), 287–98.
61. JP12.
62. Ibid.
63. Antti Hautamäki, "Sustainable Innovation: A New Age of Innovation and Finland's Innovation Policy," *Sitra Reports Series* 87 (2010).
64. Taylor, *Secular Age*, 677.
65. Ibid., 3–5
66. E.g., José Casanova, *Public Religions in the Modern World* (Chicago, IL: University of Chicago Press, 1994).
67. Peter Berger, "Protestantism and the Quest for Certainty," *The Christian Century* (August 26–September 2, 1998): 783, his italics.
68. Ibid.
69. Dewey, *Quest for Certainty*, 7.
70. US13.
71. David F. Noble, *The Religion of Technology: The Divinity of Man and the Spirit of Invention* (New York: Penguin, 1999), 199, 201; see also Heidi A. Campbell and Antonio C. La Pastina, "How the iPod Became Divine: New Media, Religion and the Intertextual Circulation of Meaning," *New Media & Society* 12, no. 7 (2010): 1193.
72. Beyer, *Religion and Globalization*, 75–76.

Bibliography

Anderson, Benedict. *Imagined Communities: Reflections on the Origin and Spread of Nationalism*, 1991. Rev. and ext. reprint. London: Verso, 2003.

Beck, Ulrich. *Risk Society: Towards a New Modernity*. New Delhi: Sage, 1992.

Bellah, Robert. *Tokugawa Religion. The Cultural Roots of Modern Japan.* New York: The Free Press, 1957. Reprint, New York: The Free Press, 1985.

Berger, Peter. "Protestantism and the Quest for Certainty." *The Christian Century* (August 26–September 2, 1998): 782–96.

———. *Religion and Globalization.* London: Sage, 1994.

Bourdieu, Pierre. *Language and Symbolic Power.* Cambridge: CUP, 1991.

———. "The Production of Belief: Contribution to an Economy of Symbolic Goods." In *Media, Culture and Society. A Critical Reader*, edited by Richard Collins, James Curran, Nicholas Garnham, Paddy Scannell, Philip Schlesinger, and Colin Sparks, 131–63. London: Sage, 1986.

Campbell, Heidi A., and Antonio C. La Pastina. "How the iPod Became Divine: New Media, Religion and the Intertextual Circulation of Meaning." *New Media & Society* 12, no. 7 (2010): 1191–207.

Caplan, Pat. "Introduction: Risk Revisited." In *Risk Revisited*, edited by Pat Caplan, 1–29. London: Pluto Press, 2000.

Casanova, José. *Public Religions in the Modern World.* Chicago, IL: University of Chicago Press, 1994.

Couldry, Nick. *Media Rituals. A Critical Approach.* London: Routledge, 2003.

Dewey, John. *The Quest for Certainty.* 1929. Reprint, New York: Capricorn books, 1960.

Foucault, Michel. *The Birth of Biopolitics. Lectures at the Colléége de France 1978-1979.* Edited by Michel Senellart. London: Palgrave Macmillan, 2008.

———. "The Subject and Power." *Critical Inquiry* 8, no. 4 (1982): 777–95.

Florida, Richard, and Tim Gulden. "The World Is Spiky." *The Atlantic Monthly,* October 2005.

Frisk, Liselotte. "Globalization: A Key Factor in Contemporary Religious Change." *Journal of Alternative Spiritualities and New Age Studies* 5 (2009–2011): i–xiv.

Giddens, Anthony. *Consequences of Modernity.* Cambridge: Polity Press, 1990.

Habermas, Jürgen. "An Awareness of What is Missing." In *An Awareness of What is Missing. Faith and Reason in a Post-Secular Age,* edited by Habermas et al., 15–23. Cambridge: Polity Press, 2007.

Hall, Stuart. *Representation: Cultural Representations and Signifying Practices.* London and Thousand Oaks: Sage, 2003.

Hautamäki, Antti. "Sustainable Innovation: A New Age of Innovation and Finland's Innovation Policy." *Sitra Reports Series* 87 (2010).

Kantola, Anu, and Hannele Seeck. "Dissemination of Management into Politics: Michael Porter and the Political Uses of Management Consulting." *Management Learning* 41, no. 4 (2010): 1–23.

Mazzarella, William. "Affect: What is it Good for?" In *Enchantments of Modernity. Empire, Nation, Globalization,* edited by Saurab Dube. London: Routledge, 2008, 291–305.

McGormack, Gavan. *The Emptiness of Japanese Affluence.* London: M.E. Sharpe, 1996.

Noble, David F. *The Religion of Technology: The Divinity of Man and the Spirit of Invention.* New York: Penguin, 1999.

Schumpeter, Joseph A. "The Analysis of Economic Change." *The Review of Economics and Statistics* 17, no. 4 (1935): 2–10.

———. "The Explanation of Business Cycle." *Economica* 21 (December 1927): 286–311.

———. "The Instability of Capitalism." *The Economic Journal* 38, no. 151 (1928): 361–86.

Smart, Ninian. *Dimensions of the Sacred. An Anatomy of the World''s Beliefs.* Berkeley: University of California Press, 1996.

Stahl, William A. *God and the Chip: Religion and the Culture of Technology.* Waterloo, ON: Wifred Laurier University Press, 1999.

Taylor, Charles. *A Secular Age.* London: The Belknap Press of Harvard University, 2007.

Tillich, Paul. "The Right to Hope." In *Theology of Peace,* edited by Ronald H. Stone. Louisville, KY: Westminster/John Knox Press, 1990, 182–95.

———. *Systematic Theology I.* Chicago, IL: University of Chicago Press, 1950.

Vehviläinen, Marja. "Gendered Agency in Information Society: On Located Politics of Technology." In *Women & Everyday Uses of the Internet. Agency & Identity,* edited by Mia Consalvo and Susanna Paasonen. Oxford: Peter Lang Publishing, 2002, 275–91.

———. "Teknologinen nationalismi." In *Suomineitonen hei! Kansallisuuden sukupuoli*, edited by Tuula Gordon, Katri Komulainen, and Kirsti Lempiäinen, 211–29. Tampere: Vastapaino, 2002.

Woodhead, Linda. "The Turn to Life in Contemporary Religion and Spirituality." In *Spirituality and Society in the New Millennium*, edited by Ursula King and Tina Beattie, 110–23. Portland: Sussex Academic Press, 2001.

7

Authenticity Matters: Reflections on Lutheran and Muslim Perspectives of Individual Religiosity in Post-Secularity

Anne Birgitta Pessi and Nadia Jeldtoft

Introduction

Large-scale explanations of what is often termed the secular, secularism, or the post-secular are often focused on grand narratives such as the decline of religion in the public sphere, the privatization of religion, increased individualism, and the decline of religious authority. Such narratives are often accessed through the use of large quantitative studies and they focus on the macrolevels of society. With an empirical basis in two different cases, we will in this chapter present a qualitatively based analysis of the post-secular. Our analysis will illustrate microlevel workings of the macrolevel explanations offered in theories of the post-secular. In other words, we will investigate what role religion plays in the daily lives of individuals who are not active in churches, mosques, or other formalized, religious institutions. What kinds of views, expectations, and experiences do individuals who are passive in the institutional, public, religious domain have concerning their personal religiosity and religious institutions?

Both of our empirical cases are framed within the theories of the religion of everyday life, but they have different empirical points of departure and stem from two different research projects: case A is a study of the Finnish members of the majority Lutheran church, who have individualized and passive (in relation to institutions) religiosities. Case B is a study of the religious identities and practices of Muslim minorities in Denmark and Germany, who are not active in Muslim/Islamic organizations. Thus, both cases consist of individuals who have a weak or no attachment to religious institutions; their religiosity is individualized and in some cases privatized in relation to a public, institutionalized religion, and thus both cases are deeply fascinating in relation to post-secularity. It is extremely relevant to look at the differences and similarities of the two cases as members of majority churches and Muslim minorities are rarely explored in the same study. Furthermore, as the effects and structures of the post-secular are often studied in surveys, it is valuable to investigate the concrete workings of the post-secular in a qualitative study. We apply the framework of lived religion to our cases in order to be able to investigate the conditions of the post-secular on a microlevel: *we scrutinise the meanings of a religious community, particularly truth, values, and religious experience[1] with individuals who primarily live out their religiosities outside religious institutions.* In doing this we argue, with the illustrations of our original findings, that authenticity, authority, and a sense of belonging to a moral community are still relevant aspects of individuals' religious self-understandings in what has been termed post-secularity. We thus offer an empirically based critique of some of the tenets of the theories of the post-secular which do not take into account that individuals' religious lives are not as individualistic as is often assumed. Authenticity matters: religious experience, community, values, and truth are all valid and important aspects of how people make sense of their religious lives in a post-secular age.

The Post-Secular and Everyday, Lived Religion

A prerequisite for investigating post-secularity is that we view the world as influenced and structured by late modernity. One way of conceptualizing modernity is to focus on processes of differentiation: societal domains, including religion, are conceptually and functionally produced from other domains.[2] Scholarly debates have previously focused on how religion has lost its significance in this process; religion has become individualized, and many argue, privatized.[3] The more recent tendency in research is to investigate how religion and religious institutions play significant roles in people's lives and/or in public spheres by studying various forms of what has been termed "the revitalisation of religion" (i.e., the post-secular).

So what are the tenets of the post-secular? "A post-secular society" has been defined as one with a renewed interest in spiritual life, but which also combines a number of signs indicating both the continuing process of secularization and increasing illustrations of religious revitalization.[4] "Post-secularity" combines research into the increasing number of signs indicating the continuing process of secularization with research illustrating an increase in religious revitalization. It indeed overcomes the antagonism of secular and religious concerns and assumes their compatibility: the concept of post-secularity recognizes the limitations of a secularized society and gives way to religion as a social source/force without denying the potential of secularism and autonomous rationality.[5] Jürgen Habermas[6] has attributed post-secularity to three phenomena: (1) global conflicts changing public consciousness, (2) religion gaining influence as it forms communities of interpretation in the public arena, and (3) immigration. Many recent empirical studies indeed point in similar directions, particularly concerning Habermas's second notion; for instance, the unexpected prominence of the European churches in public debate and welfare action over the last two decades—and individuals' respect and trust in this—has been studied widely.[7] Still, and as noted by Habermas, the controversial term "post-secular society" can only be applied to the affluent societies of Europe, or countries such as Canada, Australia, and New Zealand, where people's religious ties have steadily, or rather, quite dramatically, lapsed in the post-World War II period.[8] One particular definition (and one of the pioneering ones) of post-secularity has been put forward by the Centre for Postsecular Studies at London Metropolitan University,[9] here the term "postsecular" means:

- a renewed interest in the spiritual life
- a relaxation of the secular suspicion toward spiritual questions
- a recognition that secular rights and freedoms of expression are a prerequisite to the renewal of spiritual enquiry
- a spiritual and intellectual pluralism
- a cherishing of the best in all spiritual traditions, East and West, while recognizing the repression sometimes inflicted on individuals or societies in the name of 'religion.'"

This definition, however, has been criticized for its usage of the category of society (not distinguishing between state and society); for not defining the term "spiritual," and for assuming a Western perspective toward spirituality which moves from the presecular through the secular to the post-secular (the emphasis being too much, according to Dalferth, on "hope for religion" and on too simplistic a historical view). Dalferth has criticized other scholars too[10] for giving normative accounts—for wanting to bring a particular religion or practice of spirituality (private and/or public) back into the center of social concern.[11]

Our critique—or wariness, prudence—in relation to the post-secular-discussion is, however, different. First of all, theories of the post-secular are orientated toward the religiosities of the national majorities and do not take into consideration the ways in which the large, or smaller, immigrant groups with other religious backgrounds are producing and reproducing the conditions of the post-secular. This, however, should be one focus in the post-secular discussion, looking (to say the least) at the third notion by Habermas, above. Second—and this relates to both minorities and majorities—most theorizing, as well as empirical studies, concern the public role of religion, such as the public roles of majority churches or global conflicts rooted in religious traditions. Individual (or lay) experiences and meanings, and their expressions in an everyday, lived context, are explored much less often in the post-secular framework. As noted by Riis and Woodhead, scholars of religion have been far more interested in religions with texts, doctrines, beliefs, and much less in forms of religion that have more to do with supporting the everyday lives of ordinary people.[12] The same is the case with the post-secular debate, in most cases it is used in association with claims or notions—deepening the view that religion is "returning" to the public sphere. We aim to contribute by filling these two particular gaps in the research: minority versus majority, as well as individuals and their everyday experience. The multifaceted, grass-roots level, individual experience of post-secularity is thus our focus and core contribution.

With our analysis and original findings we will, in our discussion, ponder and evaluate the usefulness of the post-secularity perspective for a study of individual experiences. Indeed, extensive surveys and quantitatively based research projects have scrutinized the meanings and effects of the post-secular by investigating the significance of, for instance, spirituality,[13] belonging versus believing,[14] and the public roles of religious institutions.[15] Theories of the post-secular offer macrolevel explanations of and perspectives on religion and society. As noted above, in this study we approach the issue of post-secularity from a different angle: the analytical framework of everyday, lived religion.

Such a perspective allows an exploration of the microlevels at which people actually make sense of their religious lives in post-secularity. Everyday, lived religion is the basis of a general analytical, empirical approach to studying expressions of religion and forms of religiosity which are not dependant on institutionalized structures or settings.[16] Everyday, lived religion can also take place in institutions and more formal contexts,[17] but the analytical framework always focuses on the how, when, and why people make sense of their religion in their day-to-day lives. This is often conducted by focusing on the religiosity of individuals, as opposed to more established traditions[18] and thus exploring how religious traditions, or the larger frameworks of religion, are adapted and informed in "the tactics of everyday life."[19] The focus is then on religion as it is practised: the everyday thinking and doing of individuals.[20] Our approach to religion in everyday life is not about highlighting individuality,[21] but investigating how individuals as social agents navigate through larger societal structures.[22]

Everyday, lived religion does not necessarily imply that religion is "private" or "privatized." In this chapter we understand privatization as being strongly connected to the processes of individualization, but not as an intrinsic part of the European, post-secular religious landscape. That religion is individualized does not make it private—it can be shared, explored, performed in networks and communities of various sorts which do not confine themselves to the theoretical distinction between public and private religion. We consider such multilocality of religions, indeed, to be an integral part of (what may be called) the post-secularity of religion. As noted by Woodhead,[23] the old paradigm in the sociological study of religion focused on public and privatized religion, while the more recent paradigm focused on private religiosity; the emerging paradigm sees religion as multilocated.[24]

Religion in late modernity has increasingly become an arena of individual choice.[25] This subjective turn in religiosity implies that sources of truth are subjective and that individuals wish to combine symbols, meanings, and traditions from various sources. Personal spiritual experience and personal truth is emphasized, even in institutional forms of religion.[26] This naturally underscores the multilocality of religiosity too.

In the next section we will describe how we have analytically worked with the investigation of the post-secular and its relation to the microlevels of everyday life. While acknowledging that privatization is one modality of religious expression in the post-secular, we offer an empirically based critique of some of the tenets of the theories of the post-secular which do not take into account that people's religious lives are not as individualistic and locally, spatially restricted as one might assume at first glance. Authenticity matters: religious experience, community, values and truth are all important aspects of how people make sense of their religious lives in a post-secular age.

Authenticity as Community, Religious Experience, Values, and Truth

To investigate the microlevel workings of everyday, lived religion and the larger societal structures of the post-secular, we have selected certain concepts which aid us in exploring what people perceive as authentic and legitimate in relation to the larger frameworks of their religion on a day-to-day basis. We have chosen these very concepts based on a recent, data-determined study of interview material[27] focusing on the meaning of a religious institution to religiously passive individuals; the study concludes with the authenticity model of the individual church relations.[28] The data-determined model indicates the central nature of *values* (both expectations of the church and personal values in relation to the church), *religious experiences* (rites, traditions, and emotions), and *truth* (frameworks for reflection, supply of religious activities, clear standpoints, and space for individuality)—as well as *authenticity* as the common denominator of these three—in religiously privatized individuals' relations to a religious *community*. The authenticity model illustrated, for instance, that religious communities are expected to have a clear ethical stance and ideas of the truth, and that such value standpoints are expected to be consistent and explicated in concrete actions of (particularly) love and care. Such demands exist in a dual process of authenticity: on the one hand, the churches are expected to offer the individual clarity, and on the other, to give plenty of space for individual reflection and viewpoints.[29] Similar illustrations of authenticity are evident throughout our cases, as illustrated below.

All in all, these five concepts (as illustrated above in italics) have been the conceptual tools in our analysis. Notwithstanding the strong emphasis on the grassroots, everyday experiences captured by qualitative data, our analysis was driven also by theoretical concepts. Our analysis is thus both data and theory driven; data and theory in strong dialogue.

In our analysis we are interested particularly in the concept of *authenticity*; both our cases indicate that the individualistic approaches to religious tradition and authority are tied up with larger frameworks of meaning which are important aspects of understanding how people make sense of their religion in their daily lives. Authenticity is about knowing what one is and (then) being it, or about one intuitively/automatically being what one is. Authenticity thus carries with it the notions of consistency and coherence—both consistency over time and in different situations and different contexts.[30] Starr, after conducting a concept analysis of various fields, defines authenticity as "realising personal potential and acting on that potential."[31] Along similar lines, Corey notes three elements of authentic existence: being aware of the present moment, choosing how to live one's life in the present, and taking responsibility for that choice.[32] All in all, two overall cores of authenticity can be detected in these notions: awareness/self-discovery and consistency.[33]

Indeed, all three elements of Pessi's authenticity model of individual church relations resonate deeply with both of these aspects of authenticity, as will be illustrated also in our findings below. They (the experiences, values, and truth) also all resonate with our overall notion of *religious community*; our analysis is fundamentally about the individual meanings, experiences of religious community (or of a distance from it) of our (public, institutional) religiously passive interviewees. Religious community, similarly to authenticity, is thus a red thread running through our analysis. For instance, what is the role of a religious community in individual religious experiences?

Sociologists have by and large ceded the study of *religious experiences* to other disciplines—partly due to the emphasis on individual and noncognitive aspects.[34] A classic definition by William James of religious experience is "feelings, acts, and experiences of individual men in their solitude, so far as they apprehend themselves to stand in relation to whatever they may consider the divine."[35] Our analysis includes various colorful elements related to religious communities' rites and traditions, as well as emotions they (not only they, but particularly they) evoke. Moreover, the interviewees in most cases described these elements particularly as religious experiences.

In the social sciences, *values* are often referred to by cognate terms (such as needs or desires). On the basis of a literature review, van Deth and Scarborough conclude that values can be seen as "conceptions of the desirable which are not directly observable, but are evident in moral discourse and relevant to the formulation of attitudes."[36] Our analysis will show various value elements, such as expectations, views, and experiences concerning the religious community's values as well as the interviewees' own values. Our findings will furthermore indicate that our interviewees have such broad conceptualizations of what religion is that, it is often impossible to distinguish religious and nonreligious values.

Truth has six classical usages: fidelity, constancy; the state of being the case; the body of real things, events; a transcendent fundamental or spiritual reality (a judgment, proposition, or idea that is true or accepted as true); the property (as of a statement) of being in accord with fact, fidelity to an original or to a standard (true); and God. Religious institutions have traditionally been contexts of the last-mentioned, as well as places that offer views and words of truth, particularly in this "transcendent fundamental or spiritual reality" sense. In our cases, as in Pessi's,[37] however, various other themes also arose that can usefully be gathered under the main category of truth: frameworks for pondering and discussion, the supply of religious activities, clear ethical standpoints, and space and flexibility.

With this analytical strategy we will now investigate, through our empirical cases, what it may mean to be religious in post-secular Europe today for those who are not active in religious institutions.

Case Studies of Individualized Religiosity: Muslim Minorities and Majority Church Members

As noted above, we analyze two empirical cases: the first (case A) concerns passive (in relation to public religiosity) members of the majority church of the Lutheran Church of Finland. The second (case B) concerns Muslim minorities living in Denmark and Germany, who are not members of religious organizations or institutions. Our cases are both Northern European, yet intriguingly different. Our aim is not to offer a comparative analysis, but an empirical analysis of two divergent Northern European cases of lived religion in what is seen as a post-secular situation. Our cases are complementary and together provide an interesting constellation of everyday, lived religion. The majority churches are textbook examples of passive religiosity with high levels of membership. The everyday, lived religious experience of Muslim minorities in Europe is underexposed in the research on Muslims: we do not know much about the forms of Islam that exist outside the religious organizations. In combination, these two cases provide crucial information on the meaning and depth of everyday, lived religious experience in the post-secular conditions. In spite of the similarities in terms of attachment to institutions, even if passive, and the shared geographical setting of the Northern Europe, we are analyzing two very different cases in terms of social status: a majority and a minority group. Muslims are now the second largest religious group in Western Europe but it is not this numerical attribution which makes it relevant to study them as a minority.[38] Minorities can be defined on the basis of the asymmetrical power relationship that they are involved in through a relation to a majority.[39] In relation to the two groups that we are dealing with in this study, the different offset in terms of power relationships is affecting how they can each meaningfully navigate and make sense of their religion.[40]

Our majority case, from Finland, is constituted by members of the national majority church, the Lutheran Protestant church (as in other Nordic countries). National identity and religious identity are still symbolically related to each other in the Nordic countries, even if this connection is becoming looser. There are also legal connections between the majority churches and the Nordic states. Although there is freedom of religion, it is up to the state to decide which groups and communities are acknowledged as "a religion." The power to structure and decide what religion is thus rests upon the majority via the state and may be easily (even if not correctly) associated with the church. Members of the Finnish national church (slightly over 80 percent of Finns) are mostly also national citizens with a Finnish background. Nationality, ethnicity, and religion are intertwined on a symbolic level which makes it possible to speak of the Finnish members of the national church as representatives of the majority. They can also be rendered as members of the majority because they enjoy religious rights and hegemony that new, smaller religious communities must apply for. These circumstances effect how it is possible to live out one's religion, and we will ponder this in the discussion.

Case A: Passive members of the Finnish majority church. In her study of the meaning of a religious community to individuals with privatized religiosity, Anne Birgitta Pessi interviewed seventeen Finns. Finland represents a particularly interesting Western European case for a study of late modern privatized religiosity; in comparison to the rest of Europe, Finland is a very strong example of active private religiosity (e.g., prayer) and of the most passive religious participation (e.g., going to church). Still, two out of three Finns consider themselves religious whether or not they go to church, and a majority thinks that "there is a personal God." In addition, two-thirds (63 percent) trust in the church.[41]

The original data first included twenty-five in-depth interviews,[42] but two categories; interviewees not belonging to a religious community and religiously very active individuals, were both omitted. The final data then consists of ten women and seven men, fifteen are members of the Evangelical Lutheran church, and two of the Pentecostal church. Their ages range from nineteen to seventy-eight, the majority being nineteen to forty years of age. Grounded theory methodology, developed by Glaser and Strauss,[43] was utilized in the analysis.[44]

Case B: Muslim minorities in Denmark and Germany. In her study of everyday, lived Islam within Muslim minorities, Nadia Jeldtoft carried out thirty-five qualitative life story interviews with Muslim minorities in Denmark and Germany from November 2008 through October 2010.[45] She also conducted participant observation with selected interviewees. All the interviewees were selected by means of two main criteria: (1) they could not be active in Muslim organizations and institutions and (2) they must self-identify as Muslims. All the interviewees have immigrant backgrounds and they were aged between nineteen and sixty-seven, the mean age being thirty-four. Jeldtoft interviewed slightly more women than men (57 percent). Fourteen interviews were carried out in Germany (Hamburg) and twenty-one interviews in the two Danish cities of Copenhagen and Aarhus. The vast majority of the interviewees were born and raised in Denmark or Germany, or had arrived in early childhood; the rest were refugees. The interviewees' countries of origin are Lebanon, Palestine, Turkey, Syria, Iran, Afghanistan, and Morocco. For the recruitment of potential interviewees, Jeldtoft adapted a variation of what is usually termed as "the snowballing method."[46] To avoid the obvious biases that this method carries in relation to the representativeness of age, occupation, sex, etc., Jeldtoft made sure to spread her contacts across a wide variety of networks. Jeldtoft made a particular effort to recruit interviewees who would expand the range of the sample in terms of ethnic background and socioeconomic status. This recruitment method was a useful way of getting in contact with people whose type of religiosity is not easily accessible, because it is not expressed in formalized contexts such as mosques and other religious institutions and organizations. The main method was the life story interview, a variation of the semistructured interview. The interviews were centered on the interviewees' own formulations of their lives, past and present, and Jeldtoft asked probing questions on the significance of religion at different stages of the interviewees' lives. The life story interview renders the narrative structure of the interview as a central part of the interview. Although interviews as the main method will, of course, primarily capture such expressions of religion as can be verbalized and reflected upon, the narrative structure was a useful strategy to gain information on types of religiosity which are not normally accessible to the eye of the observer, for example, privatized forms of religiosity. In the secondary method, the participant observation with interviewees selected, for example, during the month of Ramadan has given a valuable window onto the practical day-to-day life and the strategies which are embedded in the everyday life.

Findings: Authenticity Indeed Matters

Findings from Case A: On Experience

Experiences were chosen as one of the main categories in the analysis as it covers several primary elements of the everyday, lived meaning of a religious community in the data: rites, traditions, and emotions.[47] All the interviewees found religious traditions—particularly the annual celebrations, the feasts which form part of the liturgical year—meaningful and emotional. As experiences, they are considered to be "kind of tranquilising" (M 32 Lut) and they awaken various emotions, often strong ones: "I think Easter time in the church is wonderful; there is, for example, Good Friday, when the feeling is very gloomy and grim and that I find so great!" (F 23 Lut).

However, seasonal celebrations and traditions—and particularly their connections to religiosity and the church—also evoked mixed emotions. On the one hand, they are seen as a holiday time in which religiosity is not apparent. For instance, "You don't really think (of Christmas) as a Christian thing, so to speak. Maybe one thinks of it more as a vacation" (M 24 Lut). On the other hand, many interviewees criticize the commerciality of Christmas and are vexed about the way Christianity is "not sufficiently visible" (F 54 Lut) in the celebrations of their own family.

Furthermore, not only the church's seasonal traditions, but likewise the church's rites and traditions related to the course of life are appreciated and regarded with enthusiasm. Interviewees speak of their own, often very emotional experiences, which are positive, without exception.

Overall, it is not always even significant which religious community provides the spiritual emotion-provoking experiences of the sacred. "Experiences are good—say a concert" (M 32 Pent) notes a member of the Pentecostal church when asked if he wants anything from the majority Lutheran church. It is, however, considered significant that the feelings and experiences be genuine and authentic, both in the way they are experienced by the individual and offered by the religious communities.

All in all, traditions and rites—and particularly the strong emotions they may evoke—are indeed personal experiences in relation to religious communities. Such experiences maintain the relationship to a religious community, even if only in the mere sense of not resigning church membership: "Well, I don't really fancy paying (church) taxes and all, but then I think that when it comes to it, I want to be blessed for burial in that church" (F 78 Lut). Most of the elements related to experiences are often beyond words: "Q: Why do you think you are a Lutheran? A: Well, it's hard to say anything other than it just feels right." (M 65 Lut).

On Values

Expectations of the church: acts of assistance and words of justice. In their everyday experiences of the meaning of a religious community, interviewees strongly underscored their appreciation of acts of assistance, especially by the Evangelical Lutheran church. A central message arising from the data is that the church's relief activities are expected to be strong, visible and unprompted; there are, all in all, very high expectations of the church. The interviewees also felt strongly that the church should inform people better and more often about the various forms its social work takes. Relief activities are sometimes even seen as the primary function of the church: "In my opinion the purpose of the congregation is philanthropy" (F 59 Lut).

However, even though a clear majority of interviewees have high expectations and appreciation of support from religious communities, this does not apply to all. There were a couple of interviewees in the data who saw such support as the responsibility of other actors, especially the public sector. They thought the church should help people only via discussion, chatting, and offering somebody to talk to. For instance, for the elderly "the church should not take care of practical matters but, for example, arrange home communions" (M 35 Lut). In these cases, the meaning and the expectation concerning the church is primarily spiritual.

Still, even among these interviewees the appreciation of support is particularly apparent in their expectation that the church will *talk* about aid and justice. Indeed, all the interviewees greatly appreciate actions by religious communities, particularly the majority church, as a voice for justice and altruistic values, for instance, an active discussion of justice, as well as the values of corporate life. There is also hope that this will be a rising trend in religious communities. Such vanguard battles for justice are seen as urgent during the current "time and values of selfishness" (F 27 Lut). Religious communities, and specifically the church, are also expected to set an example here: "Maybe the congregation could like really speak out more.—The church could speak out for that . . . for caring. The church could act as a voice, a mouthpiece for caring so that people would wake up themselves—Surely they could be more visible out there" (F 53 Lut). For many, this—like the acts of giving relief—is a central reason for paying the church tax, and thus maintaining a continuous bond with the church community.

Church values versus personal values. The interviewees sometimes also reflected on church values in relation to their personal ones. As the focus of this study is the meaning of a community in religiosity, these elements are indeed of great interest. However, for the same reason, the analysis does not include interviewees pondering on their personal values per se. Discussion of the church values versus personal values most often concerned the themes, explored above, of aid and justice. Many of the interviewees emphasized the fact that values—particularly of altruism—are built into all church activities. In their view, this separates the church from all other actors, such as the municipalities, making the church a unique institution. One interviewee commented that: "they (in the church) have this written background ideology and the Bible on which they can build all that aid work. Well, of course, the public helpers have some laws, but that's a little different, so, in that respect they differ. So in principle the message of the Bible is there in the background" (M 24 Lut). Moreover, as already noted, religious communities are seen to specifically represent the value of love for one's neighbor, helping and caring:

> [i]n my opinion the church promotes, although it's a massive institution and that's why you cannot really feel it's really your own, the church promotes, the values it promotes are in my opinion really good.—it promotes such nice values like caring for your neighbour in a not-so-caring society.—Without it society would probably be a somewhat colder place. (M 24 Lut)

The interviewee here contrasts the values of the church with his experience of being distanced from it: the values of the church are

169

appreciated and considered necessary even if "you cannot really feel that (the church is) really your own."

At an even deeper level than appreciation, some of the interviewees indicate that they have been able to build their personal values from what the church offers. For them, the church values are "the basic life philosophy" (M 32 Lut). Thus, it is not only that people appreciate church values, but that they are experienced as personally meaningful. Thus, like-minded people may also be found in religious communities:

> Q: So, since the feeling of community is a relatively important value to you, do you feel a sense of community with your own parish?
>
> A: Well, maybe not my parish. However in a certain way surely with the people who are in the church, or I'd hope that—there would perhaps be like-minded people there, like with respect to values. That they also care about other people. (F 27 Lut)

This positive statement comes from a young lady who does not have any particular connection with her parish; she is speaking hypothetically. But this quotation illustrates her image of the church and her expectations of it.

On Truth

The youngest and the oldest interviewees in particular said they like to discuss religious matters and spiritual issues in everyday life with their immediate relatives and friends. They see religious communities as being like mirrors—a framework, although a fairly remote one, for their own reflections and pondering about such questions as truth, values, and spirituality. That is, religious communities are needed to offer frameworks for discussion and the pondering of facts, actuality, and fidelity—to use the dictionary terms. Some of the interviewees underscored their conviction that the church would offer them dialogue and a discussion partner, *if* they ever needed to or wished to reflect upon these matters with someone: "If I wanted to discuss something, like, thoroughly (in the church) then that's going to be ok and here it is, kinda like—and there are pastors who are, like, ready to discuss and (who understand) pretty sort of broadly about many things" (F 40 Lut). Thus, notwithstanding the privatized religiosity, the church still seems to be the institution that is used—if any is to be used—as a framework for one's ruminations on spiritual issues. Most interviewees are by no means looking for religious or spiritual alternatives. The data also shows examples of how the feeling of community in relation to a religious community and hope for both discussion and support might be available at a time of crisis.

Furthermore, all the interviewees, with their privatized religiosity, still emphasize the fact that religious activities must be arranged; a supply of these needs to be provided. This experience is linked with the idea above that *if* needed, there should be someone to talk to in the church, a community to belong to, activities in which to participate: "At the moment there is probably hardly anywhere, nowhere (in which I feel a sense of community). But I do think it's good to have like a spiritual home, where . . . Or a kind of religious group. In the background. I know I have experienced that. But maybe not just at this very moment, I have no such place. But it is necessary for it to be there" (F 24 Pent).

Deeply essential, and also closely connected to this "if I needed it" feeling, is the fact that religious communities offer space for individualistic, privatized religiosity. This may be apparent, for instance, in open discussions on truth(s) and on ethics: people want to have flexibility from the church to form their own views. One interviewee noted: "I'm more of a private person in this respect (religiosity). In the Lutheran church that is possible" (M 65 Lut). Indeed, religious communities are seen as *supporting* one's religiosity by providing space for it.

All in all, the picture is two-sided: at the same time as individuals want to have space, they also long for clear mirrors and reflection points for their own pondering. Most interviewees urge the church to have clear standpoints on various issues, particularly ethical ones. In their view religious communities should have unambiguous stances, a coherent doctrine. They note that the church's theological debates (related to, for instance, women priests and homosexuals) distance them from the church. There is thus a clear overall expectation of coherence, a common policy. Consistency is crucial; the church should stand in unison. Theological disagreements erode respect for and trust in the church, and the interviewees even see them as tragicomic. "Well, I think that when it comes to these female pastors—like when some people don't want to work with them, that's ridiculous—isn't it the same whoever preaches the word of God, whether it's a man or a woman, if they stand behind their words?—So maybe this is a little distracting, disruptive (to the church), these grumpy old men." (N 59 Lut).

Interestingly, interviewees noted that clear ethical and theological standpoints would be respected by them in the everyday, even if they might not always agree on them personally. They just seem to wish to know that the community does have a clear stance on fundamental matters, one that they can *relate* to—agree or disagree with—in their own view.

Findings from Case B: Muslim Minorities in Everyday Life

To illustrate the interviewees' attitudes and narratives on authenticity, we will start out by describing three different identity types that we have identified in the data, which gives the necessary overall picture of how the interviewees live out their Islamic faith. Before moving on to this description it is important to stress that we view religiosity and religious identity as relational and situational concepts. What constitutes the content of an identity is defined in social processes, which always involve power struggles.[48] As such, the religious identity is informed by other relevant identity positions. This means that we view the religious identity as a Muslim (or as a Christian) as something which makes sense in some situations and relationships, and not in others.[49] The following demarcation of the interviewees' religious identities, is thus to be understood as analytical archetypes, which describe some of the characteristic ways in which these Muslim minorities make sense of Islam in their daily lives.

Nonpractice, Reconfigured Practice, and Orto-praxy

The three identity types all relate to the issue of practice. At the same time, these three identity types tell us something relevant about the relationship between authenticity and individualism—also in its privatized forms. The first one, "nonpractice" describes the discourse and lack of practice which is characterized: (1) by the individual's self-definition as a Muslim and belonging to a community that is taken to be Muslim in one way or another; (2) a minimum, or no, performance of religious practices, combined with a relatively strong awareness and notion that "real" Islam is about practising. Often the interviewees with this identity type have a rather critical and individualistic approach to religious authority figures, and to the Islamic tradition. These interviewees say that they are aware that Islam is about practice, but that they choose not to do so. They emphasize that Islam is about your personal intention and not about what you do.

The second identity type is termed "reconfigured religious practices." This describes how Muslims reshape and reformulate religious practices in highly individualistic, inclusive, and pragmatic ways. They cut a heel and a toe in order to make Islamic rituals make sense for them on a personal level. Examples that can be used to illustrate this identity are interviewees who choose to fast on random days throughout the year instead of fasting during Ramadan. Another example is choosing to meditate instead of praying, as prescribed by the Islamic tradition, or to pray inside oneself. Reasons given for transforming religious practice are both pragmatic and spiritual: it is not possible to fast or pray five times a day because of work, family life, etc. Meditation and praying inside oneself is explained as giving a peaceful feeling of contemplation. These reconfigured ritual practices often have a privatized quality: when you pray inside yourself, the prayer is internalized and thus not visible to others. When not fasting during Ramadan but on other days, this practice also becomes invisible.

The third identity type is called "orto-praxy" and it covers Muslims who practise more or less as prescribed by the Islamic tradition. They do not necessarily seek out information on Islam on their own, and they see Islam as part and parcel of their ethnic identity.

These three identity types can be seen as a backdrop which illustrates the interviewees' experiences of being Muslims in their everyday life. In the following section, we will analyze more closely the meaning of authenticity.

Doing Islam and Knowing Islam

Two potent narratives characterize the material and cut cross the identity types: doing Islam and knowing Islam. The nexus between these concepts touches upon the meaning of authenticity: what the interviewees render as true and legitimate within Islam as a religion. These notions of authenticity are further connected to powerful notions of community and values. Doing Islam describes how the interviewees articulate and perceive Islam as an entity which is separated from other arenas in life. As such, living as a Muslim in daily life becomes a question of picking and choosing parts of Islam as a religion. The choices are based on the concrete circumstances in one's life. In this way it becomes a task. One female Danish interviewee with a Pakistani background, Aisha (27),[50] expresses it like this:

> It [Islam] is a bit like, say, if you had grown up with football, then it's a part of your life . . . well, if you have done more than just watching it on TV, right? And if you as an adult say "Ok, cool: I'll join a football club," then it becomes a project. In the way that you need to work, you need to work deliberately on getting better at it. Of course if

> it becomes a part of your life and you keep on doing it, then [it is different] than if you just do it a couple of times a week, or when you have five minutes to play with the ball, or something like that, right? (March 26, 2009)

In this version of doing Islam, Aisha describes Islam as something you can jump in and out of: "a project." Meanwhile, this strongly individualistic interpretation also contains an understanding that Islam is about a certain, demarcated community: it is a "club," defined by a group of people who are all Muslims, and as such the individualism is tied to larger, as above noted, "communities of interpretation" which both serve as a mirror, and vouch for the authenticity of, individualistic interpretations.[51]

"Doing" Islam can also be described as an experience; as something fun and festive—or even spiritual, as with the practice of meditation. The interviewees explain that the month of Ramadan, is fun, even if they do not observe the fast: it is a fun time where you get to eat special foods, and spend time with your family and friends. A Danish interviewee, Yunus (thirty-three), who was born and raised in Denmark by Afghani parents, is married to a non-Muslim. When they got married they had the official ceremony at the city hall, and then in addition to this, the couple decided to have an Islamic ceremony. Yunus explains why:

> . . . we already had the marriage certificate, so we really didn't need it [the Islamic wedding ceremony]. It was more out of a concern to make it more official . . . For me it [the decision to have an Islamic wedding ceremony] had something to do with having been to a lot of weddings, seen that it was fun; of course I also wanted to experience that . . . And I also wanted to give my wife that experience: it was a really good day, a fun day, where people were happy. (February 25, 2009)

The experience aspect is emphasized by Yunus, but it is equally important for him that the wedding somehow becomes part of what he sees as a real, authentic marriage by inscribing him and his wife into the Islamic tradition by virtue of the authenticity of the wedding ceremony. In order for his marriage to be rendered as "official" for himself, his wife and for his "Muslim Others," he needs the Islamic ceremony and the community which contributes to the making of its authenticity.

The narratives of "knowing" Islam, the other strand of the nexus, underlines the relationship between authenticity and community further, while showing the importance of the generational aspects, which Aisha talked about in the above quote: Islam is something that you must be initiated into as a child, otherwise it becomes a project in your adult life. Almost all the interviewees talk about how it is important that you "know Islam," i.e., knowing how to pray, knowing the Qur'an and the Islamic tradition. For most this initiation into knowing Islam takes places in Qur'an school when they are children, or as they are taught by family members. But later in life this "knowing Islam" stops for most of the interviewees, and this is described as problematic: not knowing Islam makes you vulnerable in the public debates that link Islam with, for example, terrorism and the suppression of women. Jamileh (twenty-seven), a German-born woman with an Iranian background, explains that she did not go to Qur'an classes as a child, but she did learn how to pray at home as her mother encouraged her to read bits from the Qur'an. She explains that although her family in Iran is "religious" and her mother prays, she did not grow up with a strong sense of what Islam actually was, and this led her to study Islam at the university:

> Because I am from Iran and the family of my father is religious and he is from a religious family, I wanted to see and know more about it than just what others tell me. So I started to study Islam in university. (February 27, 2009)

The individualistic approaches to living Islam are thus adopted possibly by virtue of its connection to both social, ethnic, and cultural communities, and to a notion that Islam as a authentic framework is "out there." For living as a Muslim it is important to at least have a minimum of knowledge about the authentic framework, so you are able to base your individualistic practices and interpretations within it.

In the narratives of knowing Islam, values and morality play a crucial role, and here Islam is often defined very broadly, or very minimally depending on how you look at it, with an emphasis on its universality. Roya (fifty-three) restates what many other interviewees also define as Islam:

> Islam for me is a feeling that I am Muslim. It is about values . . . you can't be mean, and you can't make others sad. You can't do anything illegal. It's about values when I think about it . . . (February 25, 2009)

Others emphasize that Islam and what it says in the Qur'an is almost the same as Christianity or Judaism. Islam is thus interpreted as being primarily about morals and values: it is your intention and your moral behavior which is important. Many interviewees explain how they use ideas "from Islam" when they ponder on concrete moral issues in their life. Islam is thus seen as a framework of interpretation upon which the individual can rest his or her own life.

This analysis has showed that the notion and experience of community is relevant for even the most individualized types of religiosity and religious practice. Community, truth, religious experiences and values are all part and parcel of how the interviewees live as Muslims in their daily lives. Religiosity in the post-secular situation is often connected to liberal notions of free choice.[52] When we are investigating the experience of lived religion for a minority group, it is important to keep in mind that choices are always made within given norms: the question of how, when, and why minority religiosities are shaped in the way they are is always influenced by the asymmetrical power relation to a majority which holds the power to define what religion is and is not. As such, eclectic ritual behavior—for example—which results in privatized forms of religion, or a focus on Islam as primarily about morals and values can also be seen as an expression of a minority strategy that serves the purpose of making the minority less visible and abnormal in relation to the majorities' religion.

Discussion

Applying the frameworks of authenticity and of lived religion to our cases has enabled an investigation of the meanings and depths of the post-secular at a microlevel. We have scrutinized the meanings of a religious community—particularly truth, values, and religious experience—with individuals who primarily live their religiosities outside religious institutions. Our two divergent cases reflect the multiplicity of European modernity—seeing Europe "as a story of continual constitution and reconstitution of a multiplicity of cultural programmes."[53] The idea of authenticity is a thread running through all of our three dimensions of everyday religiosity: truth, values, and experiences. Elements of individualism and collectivism are inextricably interlaced in our findings; authenticity epitomizes this interrelatedness.

Our cases have provided intriguing windows onto post-secularity. In this respect, one element in our authenticity-centered findings seems particularly crucial, Habermas's notion of "communities of interpretation": religion gaining influence as the basis of interpretative communities in the public arena.[54] Religion is thus understood as something abstract, as something which is "out there," available for specific, individual interpretation. Our overall findings indicate that religious communities, understood as Habermasian communities of interpretation, offer the opportunity for groups to be vocal and consistent, yet to leave room for individual pondering and reflection, both in our Christian and Muslim cases. Although the notion that religion must be authentic is prevalent for all our interviewees, it is important to note the differences in points of reference when it comes to the articulation of what is experienced as authentic. The majority church members with passive religiosity hold the church as an institutional entity, responsible for upholding a certain moral standard. The Muslim minorities articulate their notions of authenticity up against social communities of other Muslims, as there is no one unified and institutionalized religious community which sanctions what Islam is and is not. This difference points to the fact that Muslim minorities and national majority church members face different religious realities which affect how they can meaningfully navigate and make sense of their religiosities. Muslim minorities in Northern Europe are constantly faced with different and competing interpretations of what "real" Islam is, and this creates a certain openness to individualized interpretation.[55] Authenticity for the national majority of this study is much more tied to the views and understandings offered by the church; they are expected to be unified and authentic, even if individuals might not always agree with them. The church is still, at the same time, expected to offer room for various personal (personally authentic) viewpoints of individuals. One outcome of the asymmetrical power relationship between the majority and the minority is thus different possibilities for establishing frameworks of interpretation.

According to Habermas,[56] religious organizations can exert influence on public opinion by making contributions on key issues, irrespective of whether their arguments are convincing or objectionable: "Our pluralist societies constitute a responsive sounding board for such interventions because they are increasingly split on value conflicts requiring political regulation. Be it the dispute over the legalization of abortion, or voluntary euthanasia, on the bioethical issues of reproductive medicine, questions of animal protection or climate change—on these and similar questions the divisive premises are so opaque that it is by no means settled from the outset which party can draw on the more convincing moral intuitions." Both cases indicate that such "interventions" by religious communities are expected to be particularly prolove, procaring: about having good morals and values which affect how you treat other human beings.

Habermas, as do most other scholars, focuses on the role of institutions and institutional religion in the post-secular society. Our focus, the depth of individual understanding, has illustrated vivid, multifaceted elements of religiosity. Such elements are easily missed in survey research—and such, and similar, elements were surely missed by previous research carried out with the expectation of secularization in mind. Discussion of the post-secular must in the future be particularly sensitive to the colorful range and complexity of individual religious expressions and searching. Indeed, as van Peursen has noted on such searches: "signs of a 'post-secular' era are becoming visible, but we might ask: to whom are the signs visible?"[57] Might the focus of the secularisation thesis miss some of the manifold and diverse expressions of religion by asserting that religion and the secular are two separate things? Rather than ultimate relativism and scepticism, there is a growing effort to discover the horizons beyond human manipulation, technological power and the naturalistic and supernaturalistic fallacies." Similarly Reemtsma has underscored the age of post-secularity as an age (resembling Habermas's communities of interpretation) in which there is a need for a truth beyond that offered by conventional science.[58] Actually the entire post-secularity discussion encapsulates a paradox. As noted by Eder, "in secular societies like those in Europe, we have a growing religious discourse: On one hand, we speak of secular society, but, on the other hand, more and more people discuss religious matters."[59]

Our study has contributed to the post-secular debate a case focusing on both minority and majority perspectives, and particularly from the perspective of individuals. Casanova has noted in an intriguing manner: "[b]ecoming post-secular does not mean necessarily becoming religious again, but questioning our stadial consciousness, de-stabilising if not our secular immanent frame, at least the possibilities of transcendence within the immanent frame, and being open, receptive, at least curious to all the manifold forms of being religiously human."[60] In a similar tone, Charles Taylor concludes in his book *A Secular Age:* "We are just at the beginning of a new age of religious searching, whose outcome no one can foresee."[61] Looking at surveys, it is premature to speak of a post-secular age in today's Europe—however, looking behind the statistics, looking at individuals' experiences, as we have done in this study, reveals also a different story; not a contradictory but a complete one. Our findings from the everyday, lived experiences of individuals seem rather to be posing researchers the question as to whether people were ever really as secular as researchers thought them to be? Are our interviewees rather, not post-secular, but "still" religious, in their own authenticity emphasizing ways?

So, what then actually is the usability, usefulness of the post-secular perspective for a study of individual experiences, according to our study? Our findings reflect elements of post-secularity both at the level of individuals and of societies: individuals' religious activities in daily life seem complex, multilocal, and various, and the social roles of churches are not only rather active, but particularly highly respected by individuals. Furthermore, our findings have illustrated that even surprisingly traditional elements—such as community and truth—may play a surprisingly central role in individualistic, often passive and subtle, religiosity. Post-secularity does indeed seem to be a valid concept for analysis in the sociology of religion—but scholars need to acknowledge that religion is not necessarily experienced as something separate or sui generis by people adhering to religion in one way or another. Nor might people consider themselves as either "religious" or "nonreligious," at all times and in all situations. Religion should not be viewed as an either/or category (for example, inside versus outside religion/the religious community). Religion is not something totally individualistic and private, or totally communal; our findings have revealed fascinating mixtures of these. Future studies of various contexts would be greatly beneficial in the future.

One particularly valuable point in the thesis of post-secularity is that religion is fluctuating and not easily defineable. This point carries important methodological questions, ones underscored by our findings too: how are we to study religion that is not necessarily experienced as "religion" by the people who constitute our objects of study? One way of doing this is to look at agency: how people actually explain and make sense of their religious worlds, instead of asserting that they are religious by some previously given standard. By asking questions as to how people appropriate religion on larger and smaller scales, we are able to move beyond the assumptions of the post-secular, and show how the macrolevel explanations of post-secularity can be applied as analytical tools to understand ways and forms of being religious on a microlevel. Post-secularity at its best, as an analytical tool, encourages us to be alert also in relation to subtle expressions of religiosity.

Notes

1. In our section on methodology, entitled "Authenticity as Community, Religious Experience, Values, and Truth," we will explain the background of these exact concepts.

2. See Talal Asad, *Formations of the Secular: Christianity, Islam, Modernity* (Stanford, CA: Stanford University Press, 2003); José Casanova, *Public Religions in the Modern World* (Chicago, IL: University of Chicago Press, 1994).

3. See, e.g., Thomas Luckmann, *The Invisible Religion* (New York: Macmillan, 1967).

4. Ingolf U. Dalferth, "Post-Secular Society: Christianity and the Dialectics of the Secular," *Journal of the American Academy of Religion* 78, no. 2 (2010): 317–45; Hans-Georg Ziebertz and Ulrich Riegel, "Europe: A Post-Secular Society? International Report," *International Journal of Public Theology* 13, no. 2 (2009): 293–308.

5. Hans-Georg Ziebertz and Ulrich Riegel, "Europe: A Post-Secular Society? International Report," *International Journal of Public Theology* 13, no. 2 (2009): 294, 299–301, 305–7; see also Hans-Georg Ziebertz and Ulrich Riegel, "Post-secular Europe – a Concept Questioned – Europe: Secular or Post-Secular?" *International Practical Theology* 9 (2008): 9–42; Stefanie Knauss and Alexander D. Ornella, eds., *Reconfigurations. Interdisciplinary Perspectives on Religion in a Post-Secular Society* (Berlin: LIT, 2007), 43–58.

6. Jürgen Habermas, "Notes on a Post-Secular Society," *Signandsight.com* (2008), http://www.signandsight.com/features/1714.html (accessed April 19, 2010).

7. E.g., Anders Bäckström and Grace Davie, eds., *Welfare and Religion in 21st Century Europe Volume 1: Configuring the Connections* (Aldershot: Ashgate, 2010); Martha Middlemiss Le Món, "The In-between Church: A Study of the Church of England's Role in Society through the Prism of Welfare" (PhD diss., Uppsala University, 2009); Anne Birgitta Pessi, "Religion and Social Problems: Individual and Institutional Responses," in *The Oxford Handbook of the Sociology of Religion*, ed. Peter B. Clarke (Oxford: Oxford University Press, 2008), 942–61.

8. E.g., Jürgen Habermas and others, "Secularism's Crisis of Faith," *New Perspectives Quarterly* 25, no. 4 (2008): 17.

9. "Defining Post-secular" (Centre for Postsecular Studies, London Metropolitan University), http://www.jnani.org/postsecular/definitions.htm (accessed October 2, 2010).

10. J. S. Diamond, "The Post-Secular. A Jewish Perspective," *Cross Currents* 53, no. 4 (2004): 1–17; Frank Morales, "The Post Secular Age," *Dharma Bhasha* (2007): 1–6.

11. He has proposed a view of post-secularity society which does not focus on those in which everyone is free to inquire into, or refrain from, religious questions, or those in which religion plays an important role in the public sphere (for this is also characteristic of presecular societies), but rather on those which define themselves no longer, even implicitly, by any reference to questions of religion or spirituality. That is, a society is post-secular if reference to religion or spirituality is no longer of basic, principal, or of

any importance for its self-understanding. Truly post-secular societies thus are neither religious nor secular, neither for nor against private or public religion (Dalferth 2010, 320–24). For concrete examples of post-secularity, see Abeysekara (2008).

12. Ole Riis and Linda Woodhead, *A Sociology of Religious Emotion* (Oxford: Oxford University Press, 2010), 4.

13. Paul Heelas and Linda Woodhead, *The Spiritual Revolution: Why Religion is Giving Way to Spirituality* (Malden: Blackwell, 2005).

14. Grace Davie, *Religion in Britain since 1945: Believing without Belonging* (Oxford: Blackwell, 1994).

15. Casanova, *Public Religions in the Modern World.*

16. Meredith McGuire, *Lived Religion. Faith and Practice in Everyday Life* (Oxford: Oxford University Press, 2008); Nancy Ammerman, *Everyday Religion. Observing Modern Religious Lives* (Oxford: Oxford University Press, 2007); "Golden Rule Christianity: Lived Religion in the American Mainstream," in *Lived Religion in America: Toward a History of Practice*, ed. David D. Hall (New York: Princeton University Press, 1997), 196–216.

17. Lena Löwendahl, *Religion utan Organisation: Om Religiös Rörlighed blandt Privatreligiöse* [Religion without Organization] (Stockholm: Stockholm Symposium, 2005).

18. McGuire, *Lived Religion*, 11.

19. Michel de Certeau, *The Practice of Everyday Life* (Berkeley: California University Press, 1984), xix.

20. David D. Hall, "Introduction," in *Lived Religion in America*, vii.

21. de Certeau, *Practice of Everyday Life*, xi.

22. Ben Highmore, *The Everyday Life Reader* (London: Routledge, 2002).

23. Linda Woodhead, "Old, New, and Emerging Paradigms in the Sociological Study of Religion," *Nordic Journal of Religion and Society* 22, no. 2 (2009): 103–21.

24. See also Anne Birgitta Pessi, "Public and Private Religion," in *Encyclopedia of Global Religions*, ed. W. C. Roof and M. Juergensmeyer (New York: Sage, forthcoming).

25. Karen Dobbelaere, *Secularization: An Analysis at Three Levels* (Bruxelles: Peter Lang, 2002), 173.

26. Heelas and Woodhead, *Spiritual Revolution*; Wade Clark Roof, *A Generation of Seekers: The Spiritual Journey of the Baby Boom Generation* (New York: Harper Collins, 1993).

27. Anne Birgitta Pessi, "Privatized Religiosity Revisited: Building an Authenticity Model of the Individual-Church Relations," *Social Compass* (forthcoming).

28. This chapter utilizes the same data in its case A. The analysis of our case A builds on the earlier analysis (Pessi 2011), and the analysis of our case B, as noted here, uses the core findings (the above noted concepts) of Pessi (2011) as its starting point, yet taking them further into the Muslim case. Also this conceptual section of ours builds on Pessi's earlier text.

29. Pessi, "Privatized Religiosity Revisited," forthcoming.

30. Similarly, according to the Merriam Webster Dictionary, authenticity means, among other things, "not false or imitation" as well as "true to one's own personality, spirit, or character"; the Oxford English Dictionary then

defines authenticity, among other things, as "being genuine" and "being real, actual."

31. Sharon S. Starr, "Authenticity: A Concept Analysis," *Nursing Forum* 43, no. 2 (2008): 55.

32. Gerald Corey, *Theory and Practice of Counseling and Psychotherapy* (Monterey: Brooks/Cole, 1982) on counseling.

33. Pessi, "Privatized Religiosity Revisited."

34. Courtney J. Bender, "Touching the Transcendent: Rethinking Religious Experience in the Sociological Study of Religion," in *Everyday Religion: Observing Modern Religious Lives*, ed. Nancy T. Ammerman (New York: Oxford University Press, 2007), 204–5.

35. William James, *The Varieties of Religious Experience* (New York: Penguin, 1903; repr., 1982), 31.

36. Jan W. van Deth and Elinor Scarbrough, *The Impact of Values* (Oxford: Oxford University Press, 1995), 46.

37. Pessi, "Privatized Religiosity Revisited."

38. Jørgen S. Nielsen and others, *Yearbook of Muslims in Europe, Vol.1* (Leiden: Brill, 2009).

39. Henri Tajfel, *The Social Psychology of Minorities* (London: Minority Rights Group, 1978), 38; Helen Krag, *Mangfoldighed, Magt og Minoriteter. Introduktion til Minoritetsforskningens Teorier* [Plurality, Power and Minorities. Introduction to Theories of Minority Studies] (Frederiksberg: Forlaget Samfundslitteratur, 2007).

40. See Johansen and Possing (2011) for a critical discussion of the minority concept in relation to Muslim minorities in the West.

41. Kimmo Kääriäinen and others, *Facing Diversity: The Evangelical Lutheran Church of Finland from 2004 to 2007* (Tampere: The Church Research Institute, 2008).

42. The interviewees were recruited via a survey that included 1,051 respondents (representative of Finns; response rate 30.03 percent) and focused on altruism, religiosity, and happiness. All quotations from this case include information concerning the gender of the interviewees (F for women, M for men), their age, and the religious community they belong to (Lut for the Evangelical Lutheran majority church, Pent for the Pentecostal church).

43. By Barney G. Glaser and Anselm L. Strauss, *The Discovery of Grounded Theory: Strategies for Qualitative Research* (New York: Aldine de Gruyter, 1967).

44. In detail, see Pessi, "Privatized Religiosity Revisited."

45. Nadia Jeldtoft, "Lived Islam: Religious Identity with 'Non-Organized' Muslim Minorities," *Ethnic and Racial Studies* 34, no. 7 (2011), 1134–51

46. Bernard Russell, *Research Methods in Anthropology. Qualitative and Quantitative Approaches* (Lanham, MD: Altamira Press, 2006).

47. Pessi, "Privatized Religiosity Revisited."

48. Gerd Baumann, *The Multicultural Riddle. Rethinking National, Ethnic and Religious Identities* (London: Routledge, 1999); Richard Jenkins, "Rethinking Ethnicity: Identity, Categorization and Power," *Ethnic and Racial Studies* 17, no. 2 (1994): 197–223.

49. Nadia Jeldtoft, "Defining Muslims," in *Yearbook of Muslims in Europe: Volume 1*, ed. Jørgen S. Nielsen et al. (Leiden: Brill, 2009), 9–14.
50. All names of interviewees are not revealed for purposes of anonymity. The names used here are pseudonyms.
51. Habermas, "Notes on a Post-Secular Society."
52. Saba Mahmood, *Politics of Piety: The Islamic Revival and the Feminist Subject* (Princeton, NJ: Princeton University Press, 2005), 11–17.
53. Schmuel Eisenstadt, "Multiple Modernities," *Daedalus* 129, no. 1 (2002): 1–29.
54. Habermas, "Notes on a Post-Secular Society."
55. Frank Peter, "Individualization and Religious Authority in Western European Islam," *Islam and Christian-Muslim Relations* 17 (2006): 105–18.
56. Habermas, "Notes on a Post-Secular Society."
57. Cees A. van Peursen, "Towards a Post-Secular Era. A First-World Contribution," *The Ecumenical Review* 41, no. 1 (1989): 38.
58. Jan P. Reemtsma, "Must We Respect Religiosity? On Questions of Faith and the Pride of the Secular Society," *Eurozine*, December 2, 2005, http://www.eurozine.com/articles/2005-12-02-reemtsma-en.html (accessed September 15, 2010).
59. See Giancarlo Bosetti and Klaus Eder, "Post-Secularism: A Return to the Public Sphere," *Eurozine*, August 17, 2006. http://www.eurozine.com/articles/2006-08-17-eder-en.html (accessed September 15, 2010).
60. José Casanova, *"Are We Still Secular? Exploring the Post-Secular: Three Meanings of "the Secular" and their Possible Transcendence,"* presentation at a workshop with Jürgen Habermas at the Institute for Public Knowledge, New York University, October 22–24, 2009.
61. Charles Taylor, *A Secular Age* (Cambridge, MA: Harvard University Press, 2007), 535.

Bibliography

Abeysekara, Ananda. *The Politics of Postsecular Religion: Mourning Secular Futures*. New York: Columbia University Press, 2008.

Ammerman, Nancy. *Everyday Religion. Observing Modern Religious Lives*. Oxford: Oxford University Press, 2007.

———. "Golden Rule Christianity: Lived Religion in the American Mainstream." In *Lived Religion in America: Toward a History of Practice*, edited by David D. Hall, 196–216. New York: Princeton University Press, 1997.

Asad, Talal. *Formations of the Secular: Christianity, Islam, Modernity*. Stanford, CA: Stanford University Press, 2003.

Bäckström, Anders, and Grace Davie, eds. *Welfare and Religion in 21st Century Europe Volume 1: Configuring the Connections*. Aldershot: Ashgate, 2010.

Baumann, Gerd. *The Multicultural Riddle. Rethinking National, Ethnic and Religious Identities*. London: Routledge, 1999.

Bender, Courtney J. "Touching the Transcendent: Rethinking Religious Experience in the Sociological Study of Religion." In *Everyday Religion: Observing Modern Religious Lives*, edited by Nancy T. Ammerman, 201–18. New York: Oxford University Press, 2007.

Bosetti, Giancarlo, and Klaus Eder. "Post-Secularism: A Return to the Public Sphere." *Eurozine*, August 17, 2006. http://www.eurozine.com/articles/2006-08-17-eder-en.html (accessed October 1, 2010).

Casanova, José. "Are We Still Secular? Exploring the Post-Secular: Three Meanings of "the Secular" and their Possible Transcendence." Paper presented at a workshop with Jürgen Habermas at the Institute for Public Knowledge, New York University, October 22–24, 2009.

———. *Public Religions in the Modern World*. Chicago, IL: University of Chicago Press, 1994.

Corey, Gerald. *Theory and Practice of Counseling and Psychotherapy*. Monterey: Brooks/Cole, 1982.

Dalferth, Ingolf U. "Post-Secular Society: Christianity and the Dialectics of the Secular." *Journal of the American Academy of Religion* 78, no. 2 (2010): 317–45.

Davie, Grace. *Religion in Britain since 1945: Believing without Belonging*. Oxford: Blackwell, 1994.

de Certeau, Michel. *The Practice of Everyday Life*. Berkeley: California University Press, 1984.

"Defining Post-secular." Centre for Postsecular Studies, London Metropolitan University. http://www.jnani.org/postsecular/definitions.htm (accessed October 2, 2010).

Diamond, James. "The Post-Secular. A Jewish Perspective." *Cross Currents* 53, no. 4 (2004): 1–17.

Dobbelaere, Karel. *Secularization: An Analysis at Three Levels*. Bruxelles: Peter Lang, 2002.

Eisenstadt, Schmuel. "Multiple Modernities." *Daedalus* 129, no. 1 (2002): 1–29.

Glaser, Barney G., and Anselm L. Strauss. *The Discovery of Grounded Theory: Strategies for Qualitative Research*. New York: Aldine de Gruyter, 1967.

Habermas, Jürgen. "Notes on a Post-Secular Society." *Signandsight.com*, 2008. http://www.signandsight.com/features/1714.html (accessed April 19, 2010).

Habermas, Jürgen, Tony Blair, and Régis Debray. "Secularism's Crisis of Faith." *New Perspectives Quarterly* 25, no. 4 (2008): 17–29.

Hall, David D. "Introduction." In *Lived Religion in America: Toward a History of Practice*, edited by David D. Hall, vii–xiii. New York: Princeton University Press, 1997.

Heelas, Paul, and Linda Woodhead. *The Spiritual Revolution: Why Religion is Giving Way to Spirituality*. Malden: Blackwell, 2005.

Highmore, Ben. *The Everyday Life Reader*. London: Routledge, 2002.

James, William. *The Varieties of Religious Experience*. 1903. Reprint, New York: Penguin, 1982.

Jeldtoft, Nadia. "Defining Muslims." In *Yearbook of Muslims in Europe: Volume 1*, edited by Jørgen S. Nielsen et al., 9–14. Leiden: Brill, 2009.

———. "Lived Islam: Religious Identity with 'Non-Organized' Muslim Minorities." *Ethnic and Racial Studies* 34, no. 7 (2011), 1134–51

Jenkins, Richard. "Rethinking Ethnicity: Identity, Categorization and Power." *Ethnic and Racial Studies* 17, no. 2 (1994): 197–223.

Johansen, Birgitte S., and Dorthe Høvids Possing. "Between Gaza and Here: Analytical Reflections on Modes of Identification, Minority Identity and Lived Space among Muslims in Britain and Denmark in the Course of the

Gaza Conflict 2008." In *Lived Space. Reconsidering Transnationality Among Muslim Minorities*, edited by Jakob Feldt and Kirstine Sinclair. Frankfurt am Main: Peter Lang, 29–47.

Kääriäinen, Kimmo, Kimmo Ketola, Kati Niemelä, Harri Palmu, and Hanna Salomäki. *Facing Diversity: The Evangelical Lutheran Church of Finland from 2004 to 2007*. Tampere: The Church Research Institute, 2008.

Knauss, Stefanie, and Alexander D. Ornella, eds. *Reconfigurations. Interdisciplinary Perspectives on Religion in a Post-Secular Society*. Berlin: LIT, 2007.

Krag, Helen. *Mangfoldighed, Magt og Minoriteter. Introduktion til Minoritetsforskningens Teorier* [Plurality, Power and Minorities. Introduction to the Theories in Minority Research]. Frederiksberg: Forlaget Samfundslitteratur, 2007.

Löwendahl, Lena. *Religion utan Organisation: Om Religiös Rörlighed blandt Privatreligiöse* [Religion without Organization]. Stockholm: Stockholm Symposium, 2005.

Luckmann, Thomas. *The Invisible Religion*. New York: Macmillan, 1967.

Mahmood, Saba. *Politics of Piety: The Islamic Revival and the Feminist Subject*. Princeton, NJ: Princeton University Press, 2005.

McGuire, Meredith. *Lived Religion. Faith and Practice in Everyday Life*. Oxford: Oxford University Press, 2008.

Middlemiss Le Món, Martha. "The In-Between Church: A Study of the Church of England's Role in Society through the Prism of Welfare." PhD diss., Uppsala University, 2009.

Morales, Frank. "The Post Secular Age." *Dharma Bhasha* (2007): 1–6.

Nielsen, Jørgen S., Samim Akgönül, Ahmet Alibasic, Brigitte Maréchal, and Christian Moe. *Yearbook of Muslims in Europe*. Vol. 1. Leiden: Brill, 2009.

Pessi, Anne Birgitta. "Privatized Religiosity Revisited: Building an Authenticity Model of the Individual-Church Relations." *Social Compass* (forthcoming).

———. "Public and Private Religion." In *Encyclopedia of Global Religions*, edited by W. C. Roof and M. Juergensmeyer. New York: Sage, forthcoming.

———. "Religion and Social Problems: Individual and Institutional Responses." In *The Oxford Handbook of the Sociology of Religion*, edited by Peter B. Clarke, 942–61. Oxford: Oxford University Press, 2008.

Peter, Frank. "Individualization and Religious Authority in Western European Islam." *Islam and Christian-Muslim Relations* 17 (2006): 105–18.

Reemtsma, Jan P. "Must We Respect Religiosity? On Questions of Faith and the Pride of the Secular Society." *Eurozine*, December 2, 2005. http://www.eurozine.com/articles/2005-12-02-reemtsma-en.html (accessed September 15, 2010).

Riis, Ole, and Linda Woodhead. *A Sociology of Religious Emotion*. Oxford: Oxford University Press, 2010.

Roof, Wade Clark. *A Generation of Seekers: The Spiritual Journey of the Baby Boom Generation*. New York: Harper Collins, 1993.

Russell, Bernard. *Research Methods in Anthropology. Qualitative and Quantitative Approaches*. Lanham, MD: Altamira Press, 2006.

Starr, Sharon S. "Authenticity: A Concept Analysis." *Nursing Forum* 43, no. 2 (2008): 55–62.

Tajfel, Henri. *The Social Psychology of Minorities*. London: Minority Rights Group 38, 1978.

Taylor, Charles. *A Secular Age*. Cambridge, MA: Harvard University Press, 2007.

van Deth, Jan W., and Elinor Scarbrough. *The Impact of Values*. Oxford: Oxford University Press, 1995.

van Peursen, Cees A. "Towards a Post-Secular Era. A First-World Contribution." *The Ecumenical Review* 41, no. 1 (1989): 36–40.

Woodhead, Linda. "Old, New, and Emerging Paradigms in the Sociological Study of Religion." *Nordic Journal of Religion and Society* 22, no. 2 (2009): 103–21.

Ziebertz Hans-Georg, and Ulrich Riegel. "Europe: A Post-Secular Society? International Report." *International Journal of Public Theology* 13, no. 2 (2009): 293–308.

———. "Post-secular Europe – a Concept Questioned. Europe: Secular or Post-Secular?" *International Practical Theology* 9 (2008): 9–42.

8

Combining Choice and Destiny: Identity and Agency within Post-Secular Well-being Practices

Terhi Utriainen, Tuija Hovi, and Måns Broo

Introduction

By focusing on contemporary well-being practices, this chapter proposes that the concept of destiny has its place in modern life along with individual choice. A sense of destiny can be found, for instance, in the engagements with post-secular practices where people turn toward something not quite empirical in order to gain identity and agency. We focus on contemporary religious/spiritual well-being and healing practices such as yoga, angel therapy, and faith-healing as concrete cases, examples, and figurations of the post-secular. Our examples reflect the special case of Finland in comparison to many other European societies, since Finland has long been very strongly Lutheran, something that is now slowly changing.

Religious/spiritual well-being practices often center on constructing the meaning of life upon a sense of destiny—when destiny is, in a very general manner, understood as a *sense of orientation, direction, and purpose in life*. Indeed, our working hypothesis is that active participation in the construction of destiny is one important aim of many contemporary well-being practices. We maintain, moreover, that the notion of destiny is something that connects religious/spiritual identity and agency with its structural and cultural conditions and opens it up to a future orientation.

This creates an intriguing tension in modernity, since destiny is often considered as the opposite, or antagonist, of individual freedom and choice. The question "choice or destiny?" encapsulates a real, modern dilemma. However, destiny—in the sense of meaning and direction in life—can be understood either as a predetermined course of events, or as the *unfolding of life's course through human will and action*. The latter understanding means that people often think they can, at least to a certain degree, negotiate with and construct destinies. Looking at how people use various post-secular practices in order to do this today provides, we suggest, new perspectives on modernity's possible religious and/or secular near futures. Could it be the case that people want, simultaneously, both choice and destiny? And how is this possible?

By use of the term "post-secular," we refer to the multiple ways that religion shifts from its traditional, institutional sphere and from privacy, into a more public and shared world. This also implies that the borders of previously distinct (secular versus religious) institutions may become, to some extent, blurred. Such a blurring entails a revitalization of the consciousness of religion and public attitudes toward it—both for as well as against it. The post-secular is intimately tied to the secular, whether the secular is understood as an institutional separation of religious and secular spheres of knowledge (e.g., medicine) and responsibility, as the privatization of religion, or as a lessening of tolerance toward religious presences within modern life. In the post-secular situation, all these characterizations of the relations between religious and secular are often compromised or rearticulated. Most importantly, however, the post-secular is not first and foremost a temporal indicator, but a scholarly position reminding us of the new possibilities of describing and analyzing religious worlds—including the great variety between religious and secular positions—and taking them seriously following the culmination of secularization theories and narratives and the academic culture influenced by them.

How, then, are post-secular, well-being practices—for instance, practices such as yoga, charismatic healing, and angel therapy—used as resources and what do they mean for identity formation and for agency in the post-secular situation? The complexities of identity and agency overlap and intertwine, but by identity we refer primarily to the precarious process of finding out "who I am," whereas agency is about "what I can do?" Today, both identity and agency are often seen in terms of choices to be made, but there are important conditions as well as contours around individual choice-making.

Post-Secular Practices

Aspects of contemporary religiosity have been described from various angles, for instance, as *vicarious* (letting the specialists take care of religious activities[1]), as *belonging without believing* (where some people find spiritual development and support as members of a congregation, others may use their membership as a performance of the desirable identity[2]), or believing in belonging, (finding spiritual development and support as members of a congregation[3]), as *believing without belonging*,[4] or *spiritual but not religious* (whereby people may acknowledge a spiritual aspect to their lives, in the sense of seeing meaning and social connectedness to something greater than oneself, without being tied to a certain religious tradition or deity[5]). Common to the above views is the idea that contemporary religiosity is in a process of change that emphasizes and combines such elements and processes as individualization, democratization, fluidity, hybridity, relocation, and the transgression of boundaries.

Institutions and more or less structurally fixed movements do not always provide an adequate conceptual perspective on today's post-secular practical and even pragmatic, as well as often fluid and evanescent, religiosity. This can be seen in how the study of the much debated phenomenon of New Age has moved from having first been approached as a movement, to the more recent way of seeing it, rather, as a set of disparate, but nevertheless interconnected practices that do not demand exclusive or full commitment from individuals.[6] The concrete forms that these practices take include workshops, seminars, courses, meditations, and appointed meetings. The individuals involved may be, respectively, teachers and students, providers and clients, or healers and "healees." Moreover, these more or less active roles and positions can easily be changed and/or undifferentiated within the relatively loose structures of the practices.[7]

We maintain that religiosity, seen in the post-secular way in the post-secular culture, can be fruitfully conceived of as *practices engaged in and made use of by individuals in their daily lives*. These engagements and usages can sometimes appear to be rather idiosyncratic and unstructured when compared to earlier times and situations. *Lived religion*, i.e., religion as a part of people's everyday lives, endeavors, and passions, is structured more as (often flexible and even compromised) embodied and material religious practices than as a prescribed set of (sacred) religious ideas or beliefs.[8] This implies that religion is not necessarily logically coherent, but rather requires *practical coherence*—it needs to make sense in one's everyday life, and it needs to be effective in the sense of accomplishing some desired end, such as, for instance, healing.[9] A familiar tradition, or parts of it, may be used to shape and interpret an individual experience, but this connection is not necessary. Many individuals rather believe in and do practices selected from multiple religious or cultural resources. As Meredith McGuire reminds us, "humans are creative agents, not merely over-socialised automatons."[10] It is these creative agents in the post-secular landscape and its practices that we want to learn to know better. In order to achieve this, we first need to think about *practices* in general and in particular in the post-secular situation. After that we will more precisely define what we mean by identity and agency with regard to these practices.

Practices are in some ways regular or structured, often strategic actions, wherein such things as meanings, emotions, and positions are recognized, pursued, created, negotiated, manipulated and, sometimes, deconstructed.[11] Practice, like all "action," according to Hannah Arendt, is an intersubjective, social, and thus always potentially political phenomenon and process.[12] Practice never approaches life or the world as a completely closed and predetermined system, but always conceives of and organizes at least some place for human agency. When we examine ritual practice we see that even when rituals aim at fixing and securing seemingly eternal parameters and structures of the macro or mesocosm, they do this by means of historical and contingent human action. Some contemporary rituals, such as those studied by Åsa Trullson, whose women informants participate in femininity-focused and often healing-centered rituals around the world, provide much open space for innovation and ritual creativity.[13] Yet even they supply structure and closure.

This combination of structure and openness to change entails and implies that religious practices are always embedded in both open and subtle fields of power. Thus, they are open to inequality and oppression.[14] This applies to all kinds of ritual and other religious/spiritual practices, from imaginary and rhetoric, to spatial and physical ones. Health-related and well-being practices are no exception to this. For instance, Judith McPherson's ethnographic study of women's Reiki healing circles in Scotland shows that even those well-being practices such as Reiki, that entail self-understanding as democratic, both stem from power-structures and (re)create them.[15] Power produces difference and distinction, and thus creates social and cultural capital in a Bourdieuian sense.[16] Religious/spiritual and well-being practices are also political and ethical practices which people engage with in order to aim at some benefit or value in their lives: for better health, society, life, self, relations, and future.[17] These practices are thus vehicles of both conscious and unconscious desires, linked to such fundamental structures and relations of human life as gender, sexuality, embodiment, and emotion.

Furthermore, as Ole Riis and Linda Woodhead write: "[o]ur emotional life is shaped by encounters not only with living beings, but with dead ones, imagined ones, transcendent ones, and inanimate ones. [. . .] Religious emotion has to do not only with social relations in the narrow 'human' sense, but with 'super-social' relations—such as those we may have with sacred sites, landscapes, artifacts, and beings."[18] Also, as Rosi Braidotti writes, the post-secular turn demands that we pay closer attention to other than human actors and aspects in order to understand agency in its full range, variety, and implications.[19]

Relocations of Healing and Other Well-being Practices

What has been said above concerning religious practices applies also very much to the flourishing field of (more or less alternative) "spiritual" practices, as well as practices within the less explicitly religious, well-being culture of today. Both spiritual and well-being practices also often occur in the form of courses, workshops, seminars, and the like. Moreover, religion/spirituality and well-being intersect and overlap both in traditional, modern, and contemporary cultures. Our task is to explore in what, potentially specific, ways they relate and intersect in the post-secular situation in different contexts. With this aim in mind, we should not separate religion and spiritual as analytical concepts—at least at the present stage of our project. Instead, their separations, as they occur in the field studied (that of health and well-being practices) are of utmost importance and interest to us. Therefore, in order to retain both their connection as well as their potential separation, we write them as linked together with a slash (religious/spiritual).

With regard to the holistic well-being culture of today, we can take the definition used in the *Handbook of Religion and Health* as a heuristic starting point. Synonyms for well-being include happiness, joy, satisfaction, enjoyment, fulfillment, pleasure, contentment, and other indications of a life that is full and complete. Nonreligious predictors of well-being have been mapped in several well-designed surveys, revealing that there is no single variant that explains well-being. Rather, it is determined by a large number of different factors, including biological forces, developmental influences, positive and negative life events, as well as current situational factors. Contrary to most expectations, economic wealth or age do not function as self-evident predictors of happiness.[20]

In numerous studies, the most obvious predictors of well-being have rather been defined as including education, income, and occupational status, as well as marital satisfaction and family, certain active involvements, certain social contacts and such psychological factors as optimism, sense of purpose in life, high self-esteem, extroversion, personal control over one's life: in short, a sense of self-efficacy.[21] However, health seems to be the strongest predictor of well-being irrespective of gender or age. Well-being has been more strongly related to measures of subjective health (personal experience) than to objective measures (disease checklist or physician ratings).[22]

Psychologists of religion since William James have studied how religion contributes to or distracts from well-being. We do not believe that religious involvement as such is automatically advantageous for well-being. There is, of course, much evidence to prove quite the opposite effect. However, it has also been demonstrated that religious (or spiritual) involvement may promote certain behaviors or attitudes which increase happiness, satisfaction, and general well-being. Persons with high religious involvement are, for example, less likely to misuse alcohol or drugs, something that has direct beneficial effects on health.[23] Thus, even though the connections between well-being and religion are not straightforward, they are intriguing. In what ways might religion figure as an aspect in contemporary well-being practices with different kinds and degrees of religious/spiritual self-understanding?

Since post-secularity in one sense means a situation where religion has moved out of its institutional sphere and out of privacy into the more public and shared world, post-secular well-being practices would take place in multiple places and settings—both concrete and rhetorical (as well as in the virtual world of the Internet). This also implies that the borders of previously distinct (secular and religious) institutions may become, to some extent, blurred.[24] And, even though blurring boundaries (for instance, in the name of "holism" within some alternative therapies) may be aimed at by some social actors, for others such vagueness may cause anxiety and provoke reactions of altogether different kinds. The post-secular situation is thus far from monolithic but, rather, full of potential tensions and shifting positions. Healing is a good example of this.

Healing has been exercised within practically all religious traditions, particularly in the context of popular and lived religion.[25] Healing practices touch upon and deal with the precarious questions of life such as death and frailty, as well as the continuity and coherence of individuals and society in the quotidian sphere. Moreover, caring and healing have been practised within both medical and religious institutions throughout modernity. Some individuals may, in order to alleviate their often complex sufferings, turn both to medical doctors and religious healers as, for instance, McGuire's classic study of the 1980s North American urban healing scene shows. However, there has been a rather clear boundary between these two authorities, epistemologies and practices. With the relative exception of pastoral counseling provided by Christian churches in the Western medical institutions, the organizational, spatial, professional, and legal demarcation lines between medicine and religion have been quite clear in Finland for a long time. What we witness now may be an upsurge and creation of some new *in-between spaces* for healing practices.

In-between spaces are created within, as well as between, the two conceptual and institutional territories, known as the secular and the religious, which used to be relatively separate in modern societies. In the typically modern north-European nation-state of Finland there have been hitherto officially secular spaces, such as hospitals which now include "pockets" where religious language (but in a changed form, as we will soon see) or other practices are increasingly found. Health care is a good example of a context of secular modern technical specialization and expertise. However, individuals sometimes have the sense of becoming merely the objects of many distinct medical disciplines. Thus, for some people secular biomedicine is not enough; they would also like to see the secular medical institution hosting spiritual practices.

This trend is particularly clear within palliative care (care for the dying). It has been the sector in the modern health care system which has led the way in including "holistic" and "spiritual" care in their service provision for some decades now, a trend which has spread almost all over the world. However, the issue and interest of spiritual, holistic, and alternative care is not restricted to palliative care, but reaches out much more widely within the modern health care system. In Finland, it has been observed that within the complementary education of nurses there is a growing willingness among the predominantly female students to take responsibility also for spiritual care—even though nurses do not receive religious/spiritual training. Along with Christian pastoral care and a more general, even generalized and often very positively viewed spiritual care, alternative therapies are also welcomed.[26]

The attitudes of Finns toward alternative medicine and healing have become more positive in recent decades.[27] Holistic healing, or energy healing, can be roughly divided into three categories: psychic healing, spiritual healing, and faith healing. In psychic healing, the energies are supposed to be found in the subject himself. It is an attempt to enhance the body's own healing activity. A spiritual healer (such as an angel therapist) rather attempts to channel the supernatural or universal healing powers or life force. Correspondingly, faith healing is an elementary aspect of especially charismatic Christianity, where the power of the Holy Spirit is claimed to cause miraculous healing effects, channeled through the charismata of believers. The methods used in energy healing typically involve contact (touching), prayer, or distant healing. Among the latest (imported) alternative healing methods in Finland are ayurvedic medicine and chakra healing.

This new situation and an increased supply of alternative healing methods have provoked anxiety within the official medical and health care sector in Finland. Several medical doctors have voiced their concerns about the growing impact of alternative therapies. One recent indication of this concern is the investigation ordered by the Ministry of Health and the subsequent law, proposed in 2008, to restrict alternative and belief-based medicine practices in Finland. The most important aim here was said to be to protect vulnerable individuals such as children, pregnant mothers, and the mentally ill. It is also possible to see this concern as anxiety over the boundaries of "pure" secular medical treatment vis-à-vis religiously contaminated "humbug." While this specific law proposal was eventually dropped, plans still remain for legally restricting alternative medicine in other ways.

Not only institutions of health care, but also other formerly secular institutions may become places for religious/spiritual practices. This is, as of now, not as visible in Finland as in some other Western countries, and thus it provides us with a very intriguing case for comparison. Anne-Christine Hornborg offers an analysis of some of the various ways in which the Swedish public sector today engages with alternative spirituality. For instance, explicitly spiritual workshops are offered in the supplementary education of teachers, for unemployed people, or in helping young children with their psycho-social problems. This often happens under the umbrella of such words as "therapy" and "life-coaching," or sometimes "spirituality." In some of the cases given by Hornborg, the participants were ritually led to meet their spirit guides—something that provoked strongly ambivalent and even negative responses among some observers.[28] Social work university lecturer Beth R. Crisp's book, *Spirituality and Social Work*, provides a description of the ways in which spirituality is and, according to the writer, should be, making its way into the world of social work and academic education of social workers, so that they may more "holistically" orientate themselves in the lives of their clients.[29]

We maintain, very much on the lines of Hornborg, that "therapy," "holism," and "spirituality" may be some of the key labels by the use of which religious practices and beliefs enter many public and formerly secular institutions and places. These labels can in themselves sometimes be regarded as using a double language: they reveal the simultaneous absence and presence of religion—and the sensibility and tolerance toward religion—in contemporary culture. Religion may be absent as "religion" but present as "spirituality." Sometimes the separation between religion and spirituality is a strongly evaluated one, and spirituality is quite often seen as something more universal and more deeply existential, or "human," than religion. "Spirituality" can often be regarded as more beneficial or liberal than "religion." According to Steven Sutcliffe, "spirituality" can be chosen instead of "religion" also because it allows more fluidity and positive ambiguity: "[s]pirituality, understood as an expressive and holistic mode of personal behaviour encouraging strategic interaction on the part of the practitioner between natural and supernatural realms, is an attractive proposition for modern individualists, since its fuzzy boundaries and malleable praxis is to occupy ambiguous, multivalent ground between realms elsewhere more categorisable (and hence potentially open to stigma) as 'religious' and 'secular.'"[30] These kinds of evaluations have even at times entered scholarly studies.[31]

The Spread of "Spirituality" in Western Societies

Spirituality can be seen to be spreading even more widely in civil society. Even in Finland (though it lags behind such European countries as Sweden and Britain) it is no longer necessary to go to special organized fairs in order to access alternative spirituality and therapies. Instead, some of these are provided in community-run adult education centers. In 2010, such centers in the Helsinki and Vantaa (capital area) provided under the category "speciality" (cf. in England "personal skills" Bowman 1998, 185.) courses in, for instance, Reiki and astrology. Under the category "physical exercise" one would find, for example, yoga, Chi Kung, and Shakti-stretching. We find religion/spirituality today also in contemporary art museums. The Helsinki contemporary art museum Kiasma hosted two large exhibitions successively on religion in spring 2009.[32] Moreover, both exhibitions depicted religion/spirituality as a very positive existential phenomenon which people are much in need of today. In an interview with one of the present writers, the museum curator said that she would like to see contemporary art museums in the future being deployed as sacred places where urban people could come to meditate and relax in the midst of their daily lives. This positive evaluation of religion (as spirituality) would not have been as open in the relatively secular Finnish art world at the end of the 1900s, when interest was more focused on gender and sexual politics.

Dick Houtman and Stef Aupers argue that research has not, so far, paid enough attention to the subtle ways in which new spiritualities become socialized today.[33] We maintain that all the above-mentioned practices in various in-between spaces, such as spiritual care, alternative therapies, Eastern physical exercise lessons and religion in the frame of contemporary art may prove to be vehicles for the socialization of religion/spirituality in post-secular culture. Moreover, we find several beauty salons and spas offering, along with conventional beauty and well-being treatments, courses, and workshops on astrology and chakras; energy healing is also available. It is noteworthy that these nonconventional treatments are offered by independent entrepreneurs. This tells us how many well-being practices are organized in the neoliberal society as small enterprises, often run by middle-aged women.[34]

This also implies that one of today's trends is to borrow Bowman's and Sutcliffe's words: "towards formalizing and marketing traditions that were previously informally or privately transmitted and practised, or pursued in quite different cultural contexts."[35] These contexts include books and other publications, TV series, the Internet and, also, sometimes, the discipline of religious studies, as Kelly Besecke reminds us.[36] In Finland, the small publishing house *Basam Books* has been a big player in the field of publishing widely on diverse religions, spirituality, and well-being, especially during the 2000s. However, today the large commercial publishing houses also invest more in spirituality, mind-body, and well-being titles than before. The academic publishers *Gaudeamus* recently published a Finnish translation of a classic yoga text, geared not only toward academics, but also toward yoga practitioners, a move that apparently had not been possible even a few years ago.

One important venue for familiarizing the predominantly female audience and clientele with these practices are women's magazines.[37] This often happens by means of providing long articles recounting the life, moments of crisis, and choices made by individuals who have shifted from more ordinary professions to become providers of alternative well-being practices, or who have made major improvements in their personal lives through the use of such practices. Besides being descriptions of religion-related well-being practices, these kinds of accounts are, in themselves, rhetorical practices within the same field. Thus, there seems to be rhetorical space for religion, and even for the promotion of it, not only in the alternative but also in the mainstream media.[38]

Thus, on one hand there would seem to be more space than some time ago for what Robert Orsi calls "religious presence," not only in people's private lives, but also in the ways in which they express and present themselves in more public settings. By religious presence, Orsi refers to nonempirical others (forces or entities) that people include in their lives and communicate with—quite in line with Riis' and Woodhead's thinking, cited earlier.[39] Abby Day's study in which she interviewed over 200 people in Britain likewise shows that regardless of how people identify themselves in regard to religion, they have experiences of meeting spirits (such as their deceased relatives) and engage in practices to communicate with them—even including self-professed atheists.[40] Sometimes these presences remain a private truth, but increasingly the same issues become shared topics in popular culture and language. Hence, what Kelly Besecke calls "the cultural possibilities of transcendent meaning in highly rationalized societies" would seem to be receiving and gaining space.[41]

On the other hand, this growing visibility and tolerance of religion in the public space has also stimulated marked critical and antagonistic reactions—somewhat parallel, but varying in tone and style, to the proposed law restricting the kinds of alternative therapies mentioned above. One expression of this is the campaign of the so-called Free-thinkers in Helsinki. In 2009, they used advertisement space on public coaches to display their message "God probably doesn't exist, so stop worrying and enjoy life." In another 2010 campaign they exchanged Bibles for pornographic magazines in the city center. Religion may thus have come out of its closet (that of privatization), but so has atheism in its various guises and voices.

Thus the field, contours, and conditions of post-secular practices is under constant articulation and elaboration, but also under surveillance, governance, and (critical) interest from many sides. This indicates that the post-secular includes both religious and nonreligious (and even antireligious) revitalization. In this sense, it comes close to the diagnosis made by the coexistence theory: both religiosities and secularities can be seen to be becoming stronger in contemporary culture.[42] We give both of them in the plural in order to underline that there are not only two separate camps of religion and secularity, but a much more complex field or matrix of positions and interactions.[43] In fact, the shifting relations between the secular and religious form a dense weave in Western history and its self-understanding.[44] It seems, when looking at our case studies (praying clinics, angel therapies, and yoga practice), that many individuals move within this complex matrix and shift or adjust their identity positions and agency differently in different contexts and within different practices. How should this kind of identity and agency be understood?

Identity: Private, Social, and Religious/Spiritual

It has often been argued that both social and personal (as well as cultural and religious/spiritual) identities are becoming increasingly transitory and unstable in the present late modern society.[45] This is of course connected with the ever-increasing plethora of choices that the individual is faced with, but also with detraditionalization and secularization, and an often perceived lack of institutionalized stages of adolescence and adulthood,[46] a lack perhaps somewhat romantically or nostalgically contrasted with an opposite situation in premodern societies. Does the post-secular perspective have anything to add to the scholarly debate on identity?

Identity has been discussed in widely differing ways and from the viewpoint of several academic disciplines. In our work, following, for example, Anthony Giddens[47] and Albert Bandura,[48] we view identity as a continual process, rather than as something one attains (or fails to attain) and then tries to maintain. Because of an institutional de-structuring of habits and customs and also because of a corresponding continual institutional restructuring and differentiation, it makes sense to view identity as a reflexive and, also, contextually various, precari-ous project, engaged in for the whole of one's lifespan. As argued by Dan P. McAdams, this identity formation process creates a story, or narrative that explains or gives meaning to past actions. For an indi-vidual related to a reference group and embedded in social structure, weaving a personal narrative out of his or her life creates coherence and makes it meaningful in a certain context. This shaping of these "personal myths," as McAdams calls them, is an elementary part of identity formation, a process by which individuals negotiate with themselves who they are and what is significant in their lives.[49]

Now, how is this identity constructed and how can we analyze it within the conditions of the post-secular situation? Jürgen Habermas views identity as grounded in the relationship between individual and societal development through three analytically distinct, although empirically interacting, levels of analysis: the interactive–communi-cative level, the cognitive–affective level, and the social–structural level.[50] Specifically, identity develops through speech acts on the level of communicative action, which foster the autonomous realization of the self through dependency on interaction with others. Identity can thus be seen as embedded in social experience, symbolic com-munication, and as a reflection of institutional processes. Yet it can be potentially under the agentic control of the individual, that is, if communicative and broader social conditions allow. This correlates with Albert Bandura's, argument that, "[p]eople's success in shaping their social and economic lives lies partly in a shared sense of efficacy to bring their collective influence to bear on matters over which they can have some command."[51] The sense of collective agency can thus be seen as a guideline for social identity.

Social psychologists James E. Côté and Charles G. Levine have sug-gested the term *identity capital* to describe the resources at the indi-vidual's disposal which contribute to what they call an internal point of reference. The acquisition of this identity capital is the product of an agentic personality, and it consists of either tangible (socially visible) or intangible (socially invisible) effects, the latter including qualities such as ego strengths, an internal locus of control, self-esteem, and a sense of purpose in life.[52] Côté and Levine also point out the importance of analyzing how skilful people are in constructing and completing strategies of actions that achieve certain ends (or identities) for them, i.e., how they create their agency in different circumstances.[53] The idea of an active change or transformation is integral in defining human agency, irrespective of which aspects of it are emphasized.

Bringing all of this down to the present study again, we may ask what kind of identity capital do individuals in post-secular Finland strive for? What are the building blocks or resources that they make use of in their identity processes? And even more specifically, is there something that could be called post-secular within the well-being practices that we are studying?

Many secularization theories have been heavily tied up with the idea of a privatization of religion.[54] This privatization of religion correlates well with what could be called the privatization of identity. According to sociologists Harold J. Babbitt and Charles E. Burbach, the Twenty Statements Test (TST) developed by the sociologists of the Iowa School in the 1950s and often used in studies since then, shows that among North American college students, personal identity (defined in terms of styles of self-presentation) seems to be increasing in importance, and social identities (understood as socially recognized roles) appear to be increasingly less important. Some 80–90 percent of college students in the 1990s appear to favor personal identities compared to about 30 percent in the 1950s.[55]

However, many scholars subscribing to the notion of a post-secular society have critiqued the idea of a privatization of religion and found evidence of a contrary development. Instead of discussing the decline of religion and its loss of meaning in a society, there is a turn to the resacralization or revitalization of religion, or of reenchantment.[56] It may be that the turn from social identities to personal identities will likewise have to come under scrutiny, especially considering the blurring of the boundary between the social and the personal (or public and private) that the new media has brought with it. The same goes for the distinction between religious/spiritual and secular identities, as can be seen, for instance, in Abby Day's research, mentioned above.[57] The issue of religious/spiritual identity is very context sensitive and thus, also, in relation to research methods. It is possible to profess a religious/spiritual identity in one context and deny, or compromise it in another.

Rather than such strict categories, it may be more germane to see identity as "variable indexicality," to use Gavin Flood's apposite phrase, meaning that the content of the "I" is filled out in different ways in different contexts.[58] By this we do not intend to subscribe to what has often been called a "post-modern" understanding of identity, where there is no stable content,[59] but rather wish to emphasize a general fluidity and elasticity of identity around some internal points of reference.

Agency and Its Resources

Agency can be approached in many different, yet often interlinking ways. Agency is often seen as the altercation between structure and the individual's free choice. Exclusively choosing the first would, of course, eliminate the need for the whole notion of agency, whereas a more psychological treatment, with the focus on the self, often runs the risk of downplaying the importance of structure. Sociologists and anthropologists have also pondered upon questions such as the temporal and spatial aspects of agency, as well as various types of agency and how they are available to differently resourced people, such as sexual or religious minorities, immigrants or people with handicaps.[60]

The linguistic anthropologist Laura Ahearn provides a short, open, and practical definition of agency as "the socioculturally mediated capacity to act."[61] Thus, agency should not be considered as primarily a psychological property of the individual but, rather, as a relational field or network of action within which different individuals and groups are very unequally resourced. Thus, agency should be understood as a participatory and complex composition. This would imply that it is a matrix of often semi-invisible factors in temporal (and sometimes transient and context-bound) interplay with one another. However, Karlyn Kohrs Campbell writes that individuals (in her case, authors) are important points of articulation of agency, and thus it is justified to research agency by starting from their accounts.[62] This perspective and approach to both rhetorical and practical agency and its possibilities should take into account detailed and often subtle (life) historical, cultural, sociopolitical, and imaginary aspects—such as different kinds of "others" at work in religious worldviews and practices. Moreover, agency as well as identity should also be approached as a fragile and multifaceted potential in its various transitive moments of empowerment, but also in those of lack, suffering, and frailty.[63]

This approach would, in this way, focus on various boundaries, points of contact, and moments of transition—those between the "inner" and "outer" aspects of agency, as well as those between absence and presence, or lack and fullness of agency. Even if the accounts of our research participants were given in moments when agency is felt to be at its fullest or, at least, relatively full and strong, they often also recount moments and feelings of pain, loneliness, and suffering, i.e., a lack, or weakness of agency. It is important to detect and describe the moments and feelings of both strength and fragility in order to discern: (1) how the boundaries are crossed and, in these crossings, made visible, and (2) what kinds of actors can be seen at work at these borderlines, either as resources or as counterresources (as something that empowers or disempowers). Religion/spirituality may become, at least temporarily, one important device for transforming and enhancing agency by, for example, interweaving it with destiny, in the midst of complexities and risks of demanding and often disenchanted modern lives and choice-making.

From the starting point, that identity and the acquisition of identity capital are dependent on agentic capability and agency in general, we need to look more closely at these terms. From a social–psychological perspective, agentic capability refers directly to the individual's identity formation, and is thus applicable to our approach as it focuses on identity as a dynamic, ongoing process, rather than as a fixed state. Agency as a means for identity formation refers to a culturally specific, but inborn agentic capacity—power, intentionality, social practices, and interaction, as well as cultural schemas. Thus, agency is also connected to memories and tradition; it is interwoven in the "chain of memory"[64] and the storied life.[65] A broad discussion across sociology, social-psychology, and anthropology has produced perspectives of human agency with different aspects, with emphases applied according to each theoretical point of view. The idea of an active change—smaller or larger—is integral in defining human agency, irrespective of which aspects of it are emphasized. However, in addition to the type of agency that is aiming to change conditions in one way or another, we may see how agency is used for supporting or maintaining already existing practices which are regarded as meaningful resources. In this case, we can also talk about *habitual agency*.[66]

The classic social–psychological understanding of an agent is the idea of *instrumentality* through obedience to authority, focusing on power and control.[67] The instrumental idea of agency, as it was presented by the social psychologist Stanley Milgram, refers to a person working as a mediator for a higher authority without any control of his or her own. Thus, the classic idea of obedience to authority can also be understood in terms of a more symbolic relationship in religious everyday life—the relationship between religious believers and what they regard as an abstract "foreman" or principal, the supernatural controlling power above them. In religious life, agency in the role of an obedient mediator may also legitimize personal choices and wishes which stand out in a community of believers. It may give space and reason for activities that would not be accepted otherwise. For instance, the anthropologist Mary Keller takes instrumentality as a starting point in her analysis of Malay women's possession rituals and explains it in reference to "the power of receptivity" that makes the possessed body powerful.[68] The very same idea of instrumentality and receptivity is obvious, for instance, in Pentecostal ideas such as that of the charismata, receiving the gifts of the Holy Spirit, or praying for the sick. Thus, in certain situations, agentic receptivity legitimizes the nonobservance of conventional gender-roles.[69] Channeling, sometimes present in angel therapy, expresses the idea of receiving the divine energy.

As outlined above, representativeness, or instrumentality, actualizes in a sense the idea that agency preconceives "a foreman," be it a transcendental, God-like power, or a human authority. John Meyer and Ronald Jepperson have put the question of agency into a wider historical perspective. They indicate that the agency of individuals, organizations, and even national states has a continuing religious and post-religious evolution. According to Meyer and Jepperson, "the spiritual immanence of Western societies" may construct a modern actor as an authorized social agent for various other interests.[70] They discuss the cultural rules that constitute agentic action, and attempt to point out how they are generated by specific institutional structures within the modern Western cultural framework.

Studying the relationship of cultural structure and agency, William Sewell has defined agency as an actor's capacity to reinterpret and mobilize an array of resources in terms of cultural schemas other than those that initially constituted the array.[71] Such agency arises from the actor's knowledge of schemas, which means the ability to apply them to new contexts. Sewell's cognitive definition, which reflects the sociological practice theory of Pierre Bourdieu, refers to the attempt at making change by reinterpreting cultural structures. In such situations personal agency has also been understood as being situated in dilemmas of power and resistance within tradition.[72]

What differentiates agency from routine practices is active *intentionality*. Supporting this stance, anthropologist Sherry Ortner positions agency in a structuration process that makes and remakes cultural and social formations. Intentionality refers, in this case, to the states that are directed toward some end; agency includes all the ways in which action is cognitively and emotionally pointed toward some end.[73] However, we maintain that this end need not be specific and well defined, but might mean, for instance, opening up a locked situation, closure, exploring new possibilities, or asking new questions using such means as angel cards or horoscopes.[74]

Human agency is often analyzed as being exercised individually, as personal agency, notwithstanding its culturally specific and profoundly social nature.[75] According to the sociologists Mustafa Emirbayer and Ann Mische, agency emerges out of temporal *intersubjective* processes. It is a culturally and historically situated orientation that is based on relationality, projectivity, and interaction. Intersubjective relationality is the substratum of human agency.[76] Also, from the perspective of the personality and social structure, identity is a function of both external (social) and internal (agency) factors.[77] Intersubjectivity as a constitutive structure of human agency may expand from everyday social relations to those that take place in religious or spiritual practices (yoga teachers, angel therapists) and also to nonempirical relations which are constructed and experienced within the practices (in the forms of God, spirit guides, etc.).

Through agency a person exercises control over events and affects in his or her own life. The core aspects that Albert Bandura sees as constructing human agency are an individual's *self-efficacy*, beliefs that mean an individual's consciousness, sense and feeling of being able to control his or her own life, produce experiences and shape events. It is joined together with capacity of forethought and intentionality, orientation toward the future.[78] In his social cognitive theory, Bandura has outlined the model of an emergent interactive agent that is a result of reciprocal causation. Stretching the borders of individualism, he offers a more detailed conception of agency at different levels of social interplay. According to Bandura, social–cognitive theory distinguishes two more different modes of agency in addition to the *personal* one, namely, *proxy* and *collective* agencies.[79]

People devoted to a religious faith often appeal to a proxy agency, for instance, through prayer to a divine authority to intervene and alter an unwanted course of events. Thus, agency is used instrumentally as humble obedience, or as an appeal to a greater power.[80] Nevertheless, we may ask if reliance on a divine proxy agency enhances or detracts from a sense of personal efficacy. The question of the efficacy of prayer could be an example of this. The role, or possibilities of a proxy agency may vary dramatically depending on the religious tradition. We may compare, for instance, the very self-efficient attitude in Neocharismatic beliefs about prosperity, to the self-denying guilt in the revival of the old Pietist movement in Finland. In the first case, the idea of "God helps those who help themselves" is the typical cognitive structure for controlling one's own life, whereas in the latter, self-efficacy as such is regarded as being prideful and sinful behavior.

In both religious and nonreligious contexts, many of the outcomes people seek are achievable only through interdependent efforts, i.e., working collectively "for the cause." In spite of increased individualism in post-secular culture, the holistic practices of yoga schools or the systematically organized network of Healing Room prayer clinics are based on collective efforts. People's shared beliefs in their power to produce desired results are key ingredients of collective agency. The shared beliefs in collective efficacy influence the types of futures they seek to achieve through collective action, how well they use resources, how much they put effort into their group endeavor, etc., when collective effort fails to produce quick results or meets opposition.[81] The stronger the shared belief in collective efficacy is, the more motivated people are to keep up their efforts in spite of possible obstacles. This is a fact also in a post-secular situation. Social relationality (or intersubjectivity, interdependency etc.) is, indeed, an important aspect in theorizing human agency.[82] It is an aspect that we may use to question the dichotomy of the private and the public that has more or less been taken for granted in the study of the secular society.

Multiple Authorities and Unfolding Destinies

Sometimes contemporary (and what we here call post-secular) religious/spiritual well-being practices are regarded as providing mere resources to be used by the individual(ist) seeker and agent who is understood as the sole or main authority of her own spiritual life—or as her or his own principal in the light of the above discussion on the social–psychological construction of agency.[83] It is possible to read this argument as if the seeker had abandoned all traditional and external sources of authority. However, the picture may not be quite as simple as this. The question of authority within religious practices has changed from what it has been in traditional societies and, also, when looked at through a lens that divides religious and secular as clearly distinct categories. Yet, this change may not be just a simple relocation of authority.

Matthew Wood argues, on the basis of his ethnographic studies within various New Age settings, that instead of simply having changed from external to internal authority, individual seekers may have many authorities within their practices and lives.[84] Moreover, this plurality of authorities might in fact undermine any single and determining religious authority (or principal). Since people take part in many different kinds of religious/spiritual practices, such as reading books, consulting oracle cards, meditations, praying, various kinds of physical exercises, and healing workshops, it is less likely that the authority (guru, book, god, or inner voice) of one practice would come to govern the whole life of the individual. Thus, the contemporary field of religiosities/spiritualities and well-being practices does not necessarily imply a categorical change from external to internal authority. Rather, it indicates that *the whole question of authority becomes increasingly complex and is in flux.* Therefore, one characteristic of post-secular culture would be that this set of multiple authorities may consist of very different yet somehow interacting sources: traditionally understood religious sources as well as scientific texts and personal inner voices, etc.

This is, of course, not completely surprising. If contemporary people do not want to step outside the secular world entirely (which is what only a minority of them wants, since secularity provides many advantages and possibilities), then they try to make the best of both worlds in actively stitching these two worlds together and, while making meanings, switching from one to another. This is what has been done, for instance, by many nurses working in the modern medical hospital.[85] In order to succeed in this kind of image-processing of the two worlds together, one must be able to at least somehow recognize and identify the parameters, or schemas, of both the secular and the traditionally religious, as Besecke's reflective spirituals do.[86] With a simultaneously critical and productive practice (which seeks alternatives for the literary understandings of reality often present in science as well as in religion) they may succeed in constructing flexible and reflective identities and a sense of personal agency.

Connecting two (or more) worlds may also mean that people include some of the most valued parts of secular modernity, for instance, the air of the modern medical exactness or scientific language, in various alternative or "holistic" spaces in their reflective practices and positionings. Gordon Lynch's study on progressive spirituality shows in what ways those he calls progressives (i.e., specialists in the field of alternative religions) also engage in elaborate dialogic practices with modern science, particularly new physics.[87] We suggest that they do this at least partly in order to build positions that allow them space to move and act in culture and society, as well in this and other worlds, and a sense of identity and agency in multiple demanding contexts. This situation of multiple authorities from both the religious and, for example, scientific fields can, of course, be seen either as an advantage or a disadvantage to the individual; it provides an open field of choices, but it may also be felt to be inchoate and frustrating.

However, it is of utmost importance to remember that agency and identity are not exclusively matters of individual choice and that they are always bound to networks of power, authority, and potential manipulation, but also to structural conditions, and that the most imperative conditions today are posed by globalization and neoliberalism, with all their complexities, fragilities, and precariousness with regard to life and the future. These complexities also make it understandable that healing and well-being practices are variably and often simultaneously aimed at many levels. These levels range from that of the individual self to social relations, the future and destiny of the whole planet or universe, as well as from the psychological to the metaphysical realm. The sense that something like destiny and purpose would be unfolding in the midst of structure, authorities, and choice may be an important accomplishment gained with the help of the kinds of well-being practices that we have given glimpses of in this chapter. But what would be the place of destiny in modernity?

According to Anthony Giddens, destiny or, rather, fate, is a notion that has lost much of its hold in modernity.[88] In traditional societies, fate, in the sense of *Fortuna* as a preordained course of events, meant that in an important sense the future was not in the hands of humans but of the gods. Instead, now people want to control their futures. Post-traditional societies are increasingly characterized by a growing awareness of many kinds of risks, and, accordingly, by elaborate risk calculations and risk-management efforts at both social and individual levels. Both groups and individuals aim at what Giddens calls "colonisation of the future" by various political, scientific, and technological means; important examples of these means are economic calculation and medical technology. People today are invited to take advice and make assessments that help them rationally to navigate in a risk society and control, or at least minimize, most known risks, and thus provide themselves with futures which are as secure as possible.

However, we maintain that fate, or destiny, has not altogether departed from modernity but has its place alongside the risk-calculating ethos. It can be found, for instance, in the engagements with post-secular religious/spiritual well-being practices such as yoga, angel therapy, and faith-healing, where people open up to some instance of otherness and consult something not quite empirical. Furthermore, we would like to make a small, but important, distinction between fate and destiny. On the one hand, fate can be seen as being more connected to the nonhuman deity *Fortuna*—the Roman goddess was sometimes depicted as blind and quite merciless toward humans. On the other hand, destiny is connected to the interaction or dialogue between *Fortuna* (or providence as its more Christian version) and human action. Destiny would thus be understood as a lived and very practical sense of direction and purpose in life that unfolds partly by means of human action and agency together with something "other." This would also mean that identity and agency always become materialized in tensions between structures and freedoms.

Notes

1. Grace Davie, *Religion in Britain since 1945: Believing without Belonging* (Oxford: Blackwell, 1994).
2. Meredith McGuire, *Lived Religion. Faith and Practice in Everyday Life* (Oxford: Oxford University Press, 2008), 98; cf. Abby Day, "Propositions and Performativity: Relocating Belief to the Social," *Culture and Religion* 11 (2010): 9–30.
3. Abby Day, "Believing in Belonging: An Ethnography of Young People's Construction of Beliefs," *Culture and Religion* 10 (2009): 263–78.
4. Davie, *Religion in Britain since 1945*, 93.
5. E.g., Robert C. Fuller, *Spiritual but not Religious. Understanding Unchurched America* (Oxford: Oxford University Press, 2001), 5; Albert Bandura, "On the Psychosocial Impact and Mechanisms of Spiritual Modeling," *The International Journal for the Psychology of Religion* 13 (2003): 167–73.
6. Steven Sutcliffe and Marion Bowman, eds., *Beyond New Age. Exploring Alternative Spirituality* (Edinburgh: Edinburgh University Press, 2000), 7–8; Steven Sutcliffe, *Children of the New Age. A History of Spiritual Practices* (London: Routledge, 2003); Mathew Wood, *Possession, Power and the New Age: Ambiguities of Authority in Neoliberal Societies* (Aldershot: Ashgate, 2008), 47–50.
7. E.g., Marion Bowman, "Healing in the Spiritual Marketplace: Consumers, Courses and Credentialism," *Social Compass* 46 (1998): 181–89; Ellie Hedges and James A. Beckford, "Holism, Healing and the New Age," in *Beyond New Age. Exploring Alternative Spirituality*, ed. Steven Sutcliffe and Marion Bowman (Edinburgh: Edinburgh University Press, 2000), 169–87;

Judith McPherson, *Women and Reiki. Energetic/Holistic Healing Practice* (London: Equinox, 2008).

8. McGuire, *Lived Religion*, 12–16; see also Nancy Ammerman, "Introduction: Observing Religious Modern Lives," in *Everyday Religion. Observing Modern Religious Lives*, ed. Nancy Ammerman (Oxford: Oxford University Press, 2007), 3–18.

9. McGuire, *Lived Religion*, 15.

10. Ibid., 98.

11. Cf. Catharine Bell, *Ritual Theory, Ritual Practice* (Oxford: Oxford University Press, 1992), 69–93.

12. Hannah Arendt, *The Human Condition* (Chicago, IL: Chicago University Press, 1958).

13. Åsa Trullson, *Cultivating the Sacred. Ritual Creativity and Practice among Women in Contemporary Europe* (Lund: Lund University, Department of History and Anthropology of Religions, 2010).

14. E.g., McGuire, *Lived Religion*, 67–96.

15. McPherson, *Women and Reiki.*

16. Cf. Pierre Bourdieu, "The Forms of Capital," in *Handbook of Theory and Research for the Sociology of Education*, ed. J. G. Richardson (New York: Greenwood Press, 1986), 241–58.

17. Cf. Saba Mahmood, *Politics of Piety. The Islamic Revival and the Feminist Subject* (Princeton, NJ: Princeton University Press, 2005), 34–35; Sarah Bracke, "Conjugating the Modern/Religious, Conceptualizing Female Religious Agency. Contours of a 'Post-secular' Conjuncture," *Theory, Culture & Society* 25 (2008): 51–67.

18. Ole Riis and Linda Woodhead, *A Sociology of Religious Emotion* (Oxford: Oxford University Press, 2010), 7.

19. Rosi Braidotti, "In Spite of the Times: The Postsecular Turn in Feminism," *Theory Culture Society* 25 (2008): 1–24.

20. Harold G. Koenig and others, *Handbook of Religion and Health* (Oxford: Oxford University Press, 2001), 97–98.

21. Ibid., 98–99; cf. Albert Bandura, "Exercise of Human Agency through Collective Efficacy," *Current Directions in Psychological Science* 9 (2000): 75–78.

22. Koenig and others, *Handbook of Religion and Health*, 98.

23. Ibid., 99.

24. See, e.g., Ammerman, "Introduction," 8–9.

25. See, e.g., Bowman, "Healing in the Spiritual Marketplace", 2; McGuire, *Lived Religion*, 119–58.

26. Terhi Utriainen, "Agents of De-differentiation: Women Care-givers for the Dying in Finland," *Journal of Contemporary Religion* 25 (2010): 437–51.

27. Kimmo Ketola, *Uskonnot Suomessa. Käsikirja uskontoihin ja uskonnollistaustaisiin liikkeisiin* [Religions in Finland. A Handbook of Religions and Movements with Religious Background] (Tampere: Kirkon tutkimuskeskus, 2008), 226.

28. Anne-Christine Hornborg. "Att återförtrolla det sekulariserade samhället. Är Sverige på väg in i Vattumannens tidsålder?" *Svensk Religionshistorisk Årsskrift 2006–2007* (2008): 33–59.

29. Beth R. Crisp, *Spirituality and Social Work* (Farnham: Ashgate, 2010).

30. Steven Sutcliffe, "'Wandering Stars': Seekers and Gurus in the Modern World," in *Beyond New Age*, 17–36.

31. Liselotte Frisk, "Globalization: An Important Key Factor in Contemporary Religious Change," *Journal of Alternative Spirituality and New Age Studies (JASANAS)* (2011): http://www.asanas.org.uk (accessed December 21, 2011).

32. *Choosing my Religion* by the Finnish multimedia artist Marita Liulia and *Elixir* by the Austrian artist Pippilotta Frisk. Other contemporary Finnish art projects that have received media space are, for instance, the installation *Visitation of Mary* by Eeva-Liisa Ahtiala as well as the paintings by Kuutti Lavonen and Osmo Rauhala in the old church of Tyrvää.

33. Dick Houtman and Stef Aupers, "The Spiritual Revolution and the New Age Gender Puzzle. The Sacralization of the Self in Late Modernity (1980-2000)," in *Women and Religion in the West. Challenging Secularization*, ed. Kristin Aune, Sonya Sharma, and Giselle Vincett (Hampshire: Ashgate, 2008), 99–118.

34. Cf. Linda Woodhead and Eeva Sointu, "Spirituality, Gender, and Expressive Selfhood," *Journal for the Scientific Study of Religion* 47 (2008): 259–76.

35. Sutcliffe and Bowman, eds. *Beyond New Age*, 11.

36. Kelly Besecke, "Beyond Literalism: Reflexive Spirituality and Religious Meaning," in *Everyday Religion*, 169–86.

37. Cf. Woodhead and Sointu, "Spirituality, Gender, and Expressive Selfhood."

38. Lorraine Code, *Rhetorical Spaces. Essays on Gendered Locations* (New York: Routledge, 1995).

39. Robert Orsi, *Between Heaven and Earth. The Religious Worlds People Make and the Scholars Who Study Them* (Princeton, NJ and Oxford: Princeton University Press, 2005), 12.

40. Day, "Believing in Belonging," 263–78.

41. Besecke, "Beyond Literalism," 172.

42. Heelas and Woodhead, *Spiritual Revolution*, 77–128.

43. Cf. also Ammerman, "Introduction," 6–7.

44. See, e.g., Fenella Cannell, "The Anthropology of Secularism," *Annual Review of Anthropology* 39 (2010): 85–100.

45. E.g., Anthony Giddens, *Modernity and Self-Identity: Self and Society in the Late Modern Age* (London: Sage, 1991); James E. Côté and Charles G. Levine, *Identity Formation, Agency and Culture. A Social Psychological Synthesis* (London: Psychology Press, 2002), 6; Gary Taylor and Steve Spencer, *Social Identities: Multidisciplinary Approaches* (New York: Routledge, 2004).

46. Stephen J. Hunt, "Religion as a Factor in Life and Death through the Life-course," in *The SAGE Handbook of the Sociology of Religion*, ed. James A. Beckford and N. J. Demerath III (Los Angeles: Sage, 2007), 609–29.

47. Giddens, *Modernity and Self-Identity*; Anthony Giddens, *Beyond Left and Right: The Future of Radical Politics* (Cambridge: Polity Press, 1994).

48. Albert Bandura, "Social Cognitive Theory in Cultural Context," *Applied Psychology: An International Review* 51(2002): 269–90.

49. Dan P. McAdams, *The Stories We Live by: Personal Myths and the Making of the Self.* (New York: Guilford Publications, 1993), 5; "The Case for

Unity in the (Post)modern Self: A Modest Proposal," in *Self and Identity: Fundamental* Issues, ed. R. D. Asmore and L. Jussim (New York: Oxford University Press, 1997), 46–80.

50. According to Côté and Levine, *Identity Formation, Agency and Culture*, 49.

51. Bandura, "Exercise of Human Agency through Collective Efficacy," 75–78.

52. Côté and Levine, *Identity Formation, Agency and Culture*, 143–44.

53. Ibid., 123.

54. For the classic thesis, see Max Weber, *The Protestant Ethic and the Spirit of Capitalism* (London: Unwin Hyman, 1930).

55. Charles E. Babbitt and Harold J. Burbach, "A Comparison of Self-orientation among College Students across the 1960s, 1970s and 1980s," *Youth and Society* 21 (1990): 472–82.

56. E.g., Jürgen Habermas, "Religion in the Public Sphere," *European Journal of Philosophy* 14 (2006): 1–25; Charles Taylor, *A Secular Age* (Cambridge: The Belknap Press of Harvard University Press, 2007), 3; Christopher Partridge, *The Re-enchantment of the West: Alternative Spiritualities, Sacralization, Popular Culture and Occulture* (Dorset: T&T Clark Publishers, 2006); Besecke, "Beyond Literalism," 169–86.

57. Day, "Believing in Belonging," 263–78.

58. Gavin Flood, *The Tantric Body. The Secret Tradition of Hindu Religion* (London: I.B. Tauris, 2006), 18

59. Côté and Levine, *Identity Formation, Agency and Culture*, 40–44.

60. John W. Meyer and Ronald L. Jepperson, "The 'Actors' of Modern Society: The Cultural Construction of Social Agency," *Sociological Theory* 18 (2000): 100–20.

61. Laura Ahearn, "Language and Agency," *Annual Review of Anthropology* 30 (2001): 109–37.

62. Karlyn Kohrs Campbell, "Agency: Promiscuous and Protean," *Communication and Critical/Cultural Studies* 2 (2005): 1–19.

63. See, e.g., William E. Connolly, "Suffering, Justice and the Politics of Becoming," *Culture, Medicine and Psychiatry* 20 (1996): 251–77; Marja-Liisa Honkasalo and others, eds., *Arki satuttaa. Kärsimyksiä suomalaisessa nykypäivässä* [Sufferings in Everyday Life in Finland] (Tampere: Vastapaino, 2004).

64. Cf. Danièle Hervieu-Léger, *Religion as a Chain of Memory* (Cambridge: Polity Press, 2000), 126.

65. Cf. McAdams, *Stories We Live by*, 13.

66. Mahmood, *Politics of Piety*, 135–39.

67. Stanley Milgram, *Obedience to Authority. An Experimental View* (London: Tavistock, 1974 [1969]), 132–34; Jerry M. Burger, "Replicating Milgram. Would People Still Obey Today?" *American Psychologist* 64 (2009): 1–11.

68. Mary Keller, *The Hammer and the Flute: Women, Power, and Spirit Possession* (Baltimore, MD: Johns Hopkins University Press, 2002), 9.

69. Tuija Hovi, "Gender, Agency and Change in Neo-charismatic Christianity," *Aura. Tidskrift för akademiska studier av nyreligiositet* 2 (2010): 38–62.

70. Meyer and Jepperson, "The 'Actors' of Modern Society," 101–2.

71. William H. Sewell Jr., "A Theory of Structure: Duality, Agency, and Transformation," *American Journal of Sociology* 98 (1992): 1–29.
72. E.g., Mahmood, *Politics of Piety*, 8–10.
73. Sherry B. Ortner, *Anthropology and the Social Theory. Culture, Power, and the Acting Subject* (Durham: Duke University Press, 2006), 136; cf. Dorothy Holland and others, *Identity and Agency in Cultural Worlds* (Cambridge: Harvard University Press, 2001), 42.
74. Cf. Besecke, "Beyond Literalism," 178–80; Kristine Munk, "Det hypotetiske liv: Om brugen af astrologi i senmoderne tid." *Aura. Tidskrift för akademiska studier av nyreligiositet*, 1 (2009): 1–19.
75. Cf. Sewell Jr., "Theory of Structure," 21.
76. Mustafa Emirbayer and Ann Mische, "What Is Agency?" *The American Journal of Sociology* 103 (1998): 962–1023.
77. Côté and Levine, *Identity Formation, Agency and Culture*, 9.
78. Albert Bandura, "Human Agency in Social Cognitive Theory," *American Psychologist* 44 (1989): 1175–84.
79. Bandura, "Exercise of Human Agency through Collective Efficacy," 75–78.
80. Bandura, "On the Psychosocial Impact," *The International Journal for the Psychology of Religion* 13 (2003): 167–73.
81. Bandura, "Exercise of Human Agency through Collective Efficacy," 76.
82. E.g., Margaret R. Somers, "The Narrative Constitution of Identity: A Relational and Network Approach," *Theory and Society* 23 (1994), 605–49; Holland and others, *Identity and Agency in Cultural Worlds*, 82; Bandura, "Exercise of Human Agency through Collective Efficacy," 77
83. E.g., Heelas and Woodhead, *Spiritual Revolution*, 82–83.
84. Wood, *Possession, Power and the New Age*, 70–71.
85. Utriainen, "Agents of De-differentiation."
86. Besecke, "Beyond Literalism."
87. Lynch, *New Spirituality*, 71–72.
88. Giddens, *Modernity and Self-Identity*, 109–43.

Bibliography

Ahearn, Laura. "Language and Agency." *Annual Review of Anthropology* 30 (2001): 109–37.

Ammerman, Nancy. "Introduction: Observing Religious Modern Lives." In *Everyday Religion. Observing Modern Religious Lives*, edited by Nancy Ammerman, 3–18. Oxford: Oxford University Press, 2007.

Arendt, Hannah. *The Human Condition*. Chicago, IL: Chicago University Press, 1958.

Babbitt, Charles E., and Harold J. Burbach. "A Comparison of Self-orientation among College Students across the 1960s, 1970s and 1980s." *Youth and Society* 21(1990): 472–82.

Bandura, Albert. "Exercise of Human Agency through Collective Efficacy." *Current Directions in Psychological Science* 9 (2000): 75–78.

———. "Human Agency in Social Cognitive Theory." *American Psychologist* 44 (1989): 1175–84.

———. "On the Psychosocial Impact and Mechanisms of Spiritual Modeling." *The International Journal for the Psychology of Religion* 13 (2003): 167–73.

————. "Social Cognitive Theory: An Agentic Perspective." *Annual Review of Psychology* 52 (2001): 1–26.

————. "Social Cognitive Theory in Cultural Context." *Applied Psychology: An International Review* 51 (2002): 269–90.

Bell, Catherine. *Ritual Theory, Ritual Practice*. Oxford: Oxford University Press, 1992.

Besecke, Kelly. "Beyond Literalism: Reflexive Spirituality and Religious Meaning." In *Everyday Religion. Observing Modern Religious Lives*, edited by Nancy Ammerman, 169–86. Oxford: Oxford University Press, 2007.

Bourdieu, Pierre. "The forms of Capital." In *Handbook of Theory and Research for the Sociology of Education*, edited by J. G. Richardson, 241–58. New York: Greenwood Press, 1986.

Bowman, Marion, ed. *Healing and Religion*. Middlesex: Hisarlik Press, 2000.

————. "Healing in the Spiritual Marketplace: Consumers, Courses and Credentialism." *Social Compass* 46 (1998): 181–89.

Bracke, Sarah. "Conjugating the Modern/Religious, Conceptualizing Female Religious Agency. Contours of a 'Post-secular' Conjuncture." *Theory, Culture & Society* 25 (2008): 51–67.

Braidotti, Rosi. "In Spite of the Times: The Postsecular Turn in Feminism." *Theory Culture Society* 25 (2008): 1–24.

Burger, Jerry M. "Replicating Milgram. Would People Still Obey Today?" *American Psychologist* 64 (2009): 1–11.

Campbell, Karlyn Kohrs. "Agency: Promiscuous and Protean." *Communication and Critical/Cultural Studies* 2 (2005): 1–19.

Cannell, Fenella. "The Anthropology of Secularism." *Annual Review of Anthropology* 39 (2010): 85–100.

Code, Lorraine. *Rhetorical Spaces. Essays on Gendered Locations*. New York: Routledge, 1995.

Connolly, William E. "Suffering, Justice and the Politics of Becoming." *Culture, Medicine and Psychiatry* 20 (1996): 251–77.

Côté, James E., and Charles G. Levine. *Identity, Formation, Agency and Culture. A Social Psychological Synthesis*. London: Psychology Press, 2002.

Crisp, Beth R. *Spirituality and Social Work*. Farnham: Ashgate, 2010.

Davie, Grace. *Religion in Britain Since 1945: Believing without Belonging*. Oxford: Blackwell, 1994.

Day, Abby. "Believing in Belonging: An Ethnography of Young People's Construction of Beliefs." *Culture and Religion* 10 (2009): 263–78.

————. "Propositions and Performativity: Relocating Belief to the Social." *Culture and Religion* 11 (2010): 9–30.

Emirbayer, Mustafa, and Ann Mische. "What Is Agency?" *The American Journal of Sociology* 103 (1998): 962–1023.

Flood, Gavin. *The Tantric Body. The Secret Tradition of Hindu Religion*. London: I.B. Tauris, 2006.

Frisk, Liselotte. "Globalization: An Important Key Factor in Contemporary Religious Change." *Journal of Alternative Spirituality and New Age Studies (JASANAS)* (2011): http://www.asanas.org.uk.

Fuller, Robert C. *Spiritual but not Religious. Understanding Unchurched America*. Oxford: Oxford University Press, 2001.

Giddens, Anthony. *Beyond Left and Right: The Future of Radical Politics.* Cambridge: Polity Press, 1994.

———. *Modernity and Self-Identity: Self and Society in the Late Modern Age.* London: Sage, 1991.

Habermas, Jürgen. "Religion in the Public Sphere." *European Journal of Philosophy* 14 (2006): 1–25.

Hedges, Ellie, and James A. Beckford. "Holism, Healing and the New Age." In *Beyond New Age. Exploring Alternative Spirituality*, edited by Steven Sutcliffe and Marion Bowman, 169–87. Edinburgh: Edinburgh University Press, 2000.

Heelas, Paul. *The New Age Movement. The Celebration of the Self and the Sacralization of the Modernity.* Oxford: Blackwell, 1996.

Heelas, Paul, and Linda Woodhead. *The Spiritual Revolution. Why Religion is Giving Way to Spirituality.* Oxford: Blackwell, 2005.

Hervieu-Léger, D. *Religion as a Chain of Memory.* Cambridge: Polity Press, 2000.

Holland, Dorothy, William Lachicotte, Jr., Debra Skinner, and Carole Cain. *Identity and Agency in Cultural Worlds.* Cambridge: Harvard University Press, 2001.

Hollywood, Amy. "Gender, Agency, and Divine in Religious Historiography." *The Journal of Religion* 84 (2004): 514–28.

Honkasalo, Marja-Liisa, Terhi Utriainen, and Anna Leppo, eds. *Arki satuttaa. Kärsimyksiä suomalaisessa nykypäivässä* [Sufferings in Everyday Life in Finland]. Tampere: Vastapaino, 2004.

Hornborg, Anne-Christine. "Att återförtrolla det sekulariserade samhället. Är Sverige på väg in i Vattumannens tidsålder?" *Svensk Religionshistorisk Årsskrift* 2006–2007 (2008): 33–59.

Houtman, Dick, and Stef Aupers. "The Spiritual Revolution and the New Age Gender Puzzle. The Sacralization of the Self in Late Modernity (1980-2000)." In *Women and Religion in the West. Challenging Secularization*, edited by Kristin Aune, Sonya Sharma, and Giselle Vincett, 99–118. Hampshire: Ashgate, 2008.

Hovi, Tuija. "Gender, Agency and Change in Neo-charismatic Christianity." *Aura. Tidskrift för akademiska studier av nyreligiositet* 2 (2010): 38–62.

———. "Healing Rooms as Bodily Channeled Spirituality." CESNUR Centro Studi sulle Nuove Religioni (2010). http://www.cesnur.org/2010/to-hovi.html (accessed January 28, 2011).

Hunt, Stephen J. "Religion as a Factor in Life and Death through the Life-course." In *The SAGE Handbook of the Sociology of Religion*, edited by James A. Beckford and N. J. Demerath III, 609–29. Los Angeles, CA: Sage, 2007.

Keller, Mary. *The Hammer and the Flute: Women, Power, and Spirit Possession.* Baltimore, MD: Johns Hopkins University Press, 2002.

Ketola, Kimmo. *Uskonnot Suonessa. Käsikirja uskontoihin ja uskonnollistaustaisiin liikkeisiin* [Religions in Finland. A Handbook of Religions and Movements with Religious Background]. Tampere: Kirkon tutkimuskeskus, 2008.

———. "Uusi kansanomainen uskonnollisuus." In *Moderni kirkkokansa: suomalaisten uskonnollisuus uudella vuosituhannella* [Religion in Finland. Decline, Change and Transformation of Finnish Religiosity], edited by Kimmo Kääriäinen, Kati Niemelä, and Kimmo Ketola, 53–86. Tampere: Kirkon tutkimuskeskus, 2003.

Koenig, Harold G., Michael E. McCullough, and David B. Larson. *Handbook of Religion and Health*. Oxford: Oxford University Press, 2001.

Leming, Laura M. "Sociological Explorations: What Is Religious Agency?" *The Sociological Quarterly* 48 (2007): 73–92.

Lynch, Gordon. *The New Spirituality. An Introduction to Progressive Belief in the Twenty-first Century*. London: I.B. Tauris, 2007.

Mahmood, Saba. *Politics of Piety. The Islamic Revival and the Feminist Subject*. Princeton, NJ: Princeton University Press, 2005.

McAdams, Dan P. "The Case for Unity in the (Post)modern Self: A Modest Proposal." In *Self and Identity: Fundamental* Issues, edited by R. D. Asmore and L. Jussim, 46–80. New York: Oxford University Press, 1997.

———. *The Stories We Live by: Personal Myths and the Making of the Self*. New York: Guilford Publications, 1993.

McGuire, Meredith. *Lived Religion. Faith and Practice in Everyday Life*. Oxford: Oxford University Press, 2008.

———. *Ritual Healing in Suburban America*. New Brunswick and London: Rutgers University Press, 1988.

McPherson, Judith. *Women and Reiki. Energetic/Holistic Healing Practice*. London: Equinox, 2008.

Meyer, John W., and Ronald L. Jepperson. "The 'Actors' of Modern Society: The Cultural Construction of Social Agency." *Sociological Theory* 18 (2000): 100–20.

Milgram, Stanley. *Obedience to Authority. An Experimental View*. 1969. Reprint, London: Tavistock, 1974.

Munk, Kristine. "Det hypotetiske liv: Om brugen af astrologi i senmoderne tid." *Aura. Tidskrift för akademiska studier av nyreligiositet* 1 (2009): 1–19.

Orsi, Robert. *Between Heaven and Earth. The Religious Worlds People Make and the Scholars Who Study Them*. Princeton, NJ and Oxford: Princeton University Press, 2005.

Ortner, Sherry B. Anthropology and the Social Theory. Culture, Power, and the Acting Subject. Durham: Duke University Press, 2006.

Partridge, Christopher. *The Re-enchantment of the West: Alternative Spiritualities, Sacralization, Popular Culture and Occulture*. Dorset: T&T Clark Publishers, 2006.

Riis, Ole, and Linda Woodhead. *A Sociology of Religious Emotion*. Oxford: Oxford University Press, 2010.

Sewell Jr., William H. "A Theory of Structure: Duality, Agency, and Transformation." *American Journal of Sociology* 98 (1992): 1–29.

Somers, Margaret R. "The Narrative Constitution of Identity: A Relational and Network Approach." *Theory and Society* 23 (1994): 605–49.

Sutcliffe, Steven. *Children of the New Age. A History of Spiritual Practices*. London: Routledge, 2003.

———. "'Wandering Stars': Seekers and Gurus in the Modern World." In *Beyond New Age. Exploring Alternative Spirituality*, edited by Steven Sutcliffe and Marion Bowman, 17–36. Edinburgh: Edinburgh University Press, 2000.

Sutcliffe, Steven, and Marion Bowman, eds. *Beyond New Age. Exploring Alternative Spirituality*. Edinburgh: Edinburgh University Press, 2000.

Taylor, Charles. *A Secular Age*. Cambridge: The Belknap Press of Harvard University Press, 2007.

Taylor, Gary, and Steve Spencer. *Social Identities: Multidisciplinary Approaches.* New York: Routledge, 2004.

Trullson, Åsa. *Cultivating the Sacred. Ritual Creativity and Practice among Women in Contemporary Europe.* Lund: Lund University, Department of History and Anthropology of Religions, 2010.

Utriainen, Terhi. "Agents of De-differentiation: Women Care-givers for the Dying in Finland." *Journal of Contemporary Religion* 25 (2010): 437–51.

———. "Situated Bodies and Others Making Religion: Phenomenology of the Body and the Study of Religion." *Temenos* 35–36 (2000): 249–70.

Weber, Max. *The Protestant Ethic and the Spirit of Capitalism.* London: Unwin Hyman, 1930.

Wood, Mathew. *Possession, Power and the New Age: Ambiguities of Authority in Neoliberal Societies.* Aldershot: Ashgate, 2008.

Woodhead, Linda, and Eeva Sointu. "Spirituality, Gender, and Expressive Self-hood." *Journal for the Scientific Study of Religion* 47 (2008): 259–76.

9

Environmentalism as a Trend in Post-Secular Society

Laura Wickström and Ruth Illman

Introduction

This chapter deals with contemporary religiously inspired environmentalism, its role and relevance in the ongoing discussions concerning post-secular transformations of society, and individual religiosity. Environmentalism is an apt example of the eclectic and dynamic transformations of values and beliefs related to the post-secular. Our aim is to explore the religiously inspired environmentalism of today and to relate it to contemporary trends in the religious landscape, such as the complex processes of globalization, modernity, and post-secular value transformations. The critical dismantling of dichotomies and binary opposites is a central objective in this metamorphosis and we focus our attention on two specific strategies within the post-secular discourse that have significant bearing on the eco-debate: the blurring of the lines between secular and religious views and motives, as well as the quest for a holistic, meaningful unity between spiritual and worldly dimensions of reality, that is; between mind and body, nature and humanity.

Contemporary religiously inspired environmentalism offers an interesting context for research relating to the post-secular. The eco-movement has formed into a scene where dominant values such as economic growth, production, rationalism, and progress are criticized and where the post-secular ideals of holism and eclecticism cater for new, spiritually informed understandings of the relationship between humanity and the earth. The interest in ecological issues is indeed an urgent one: environmental threats are, together with poverty, disease, and conflict, considered as the most serious issues of our times.[1] The eco-movement provides an interesting and important case study for

217

exploring the increasing interest over recent decades in the possibility of fundamental changes in the neoliberal market system and a renewed interest in spirituality. The awareness of environmental problems has not only increased remarkably, but has also taken on a new political significance and has challenged the central values and ideologies of industrial society.[2]

Such overarching processes at the social, political, economical, and cultural levels are also altering the way religion is understood today. As mentioned above, neoliberalism as an all-encompassing ideology is currently gaining ground, celebrating the individual and her subjective right to choose her own lifestyle and worldview, and increasing the impact of consumer culture and various media landscapes. Furthermore, change is initiated by the complex trend of globalization, which involves increased mobility, migration, and urbanization.[3] This transformation is often described as a shift from secular to post-secular.

Characteristics of the Post-Secular

The religiously inspired environmentalism of today is often developed around a set of shared leitmotifs. One of the most prominent discourses is the critique of contemporary materialistic lifestyles and binary modes of thinking in modern Western societies (separating mind and body, rationality and belief, human and nature, and holy and profane). Another feature is the renewed interest and relevance attached to spirituality, embodiment, different forms of religious practice, and holistic apprehensions of reality. Many scholars have lately attached importance to the role of nature and spiritual experiences of ecological interdependence as meaning-creating elements in contemporary religiosity. Today, engaging with the environment seems to offer a profound sense of holiness and oneness to persons inside as well as outside traditional religious structures.[4]

Such trends and values lie at the heart of the post-secular discourse, which posits a critique of theoretical predictions of a slow decline or even death of religion as a consequence of increased secularization, scientific, and rational knowledge. These expectations, it is argued, have not been fulfilled. Long-established forms of religious life—for example, traditional institutions—are indeed showing a downward trend, but a vivid interest in religion thrives outside these structures in immigrant religions, charismatic movements, and health and body practices, as well as in alternative spiritualities.[5] The current era, hence, is argued to take form *after* the secular: a context in which spiritual reflections on human existence are increasingly gaining attention, but where finding truth has become secondary to finding oneself.[6]

Jürgen Habermas uses the term "post-secular" to describe societies affected by ruptures in the previously taken-for-granted patterns of secularization described above. In a post-secular society, he argues, the traditional lines between secular and religious seem to evaporate and the linear evolution of society toward a nonreligious future is questioned.[7] For Habermas, the post-secular becomes a state where secular and religious outlooks on life must coexist with mutual respect for each other. Secularization is not a simple pattern of development that affects all societies in a similar fashion, as it is always colored by historical situations and cultural patterns.[8] Hence, Habermas questions the idea that secularization is an indispensable outcome of modernity.[9] Even if secularity is replaced by post-secularity, therefore, this does not imply a return to premodern ways of thinking and acting. Quite to the contrary, it represents a truly new way of envisioning the role of religion in the societal sphere. Post-secular religiosity bears significant imprints of modernity, even if the secular values connected to this paradigm are rejected: it entails "the fluidity of religious identity, and the porosity of religious tradition."[10]

An important consequence of this debate is that the secular and the religious or spiritual are no longer fashioned as binary opposites, or as steps that follow each other successively along a human evolutionary scale. Thus, the idea of secular and religious as binary categories is muddled and confused.[11] Therefore, the pluralism of society today cannot be approached merely as a question of an increased diversity of worldviews that are either religious or secular in character. Rather, one must take into account that the elements that together form the plural situation are being continuously transformed themselves, due to their own dynamic character.[12] Worldviews are not necessarily either religious or secular; they may also combine elements of rational secularity with enchanted spirituality. This acknowledgment poses a challenge to traditional theories of secularization and differentiation, based on a perception of the secular and the religious as incommensurable perspectives on reality.

Charles Taylor's reflections on the individual as a member of the post-secular society and the traits characterizing contemporary religiosity are also relevant in this context.[13] According to Taylor, the popular notion of being "spiritual but not religious" reflects a reaction against and a disillusionment with religious authority claims: rather than following confessional leadership, contemporary individuals strive to follow their own spiritual itinerary.[14] This development amounts to a decreasing interest in institutional religions with traditional leadership, exclusive dogmatic positions and ethical rules, and an increasing interest in new forms of spirituality, emphasizing holistic experiences, inner development, and subjective choices.[15] Simultaneously, however, the increasing weight and value attached to the individual and subjective agency is paralleled by a renewed search for unity and holistic apprehensions of reality.[16]

Nevertheless, as a growing number of people prefer personally collected and constructed spiritual solutions to the ready-made packages of creed and conduct offered by traditional religious institutions, the importance of finding and justifying one's own path in the landscape of richly diversified options becomes crucial. According to Taylor, this is a world in which "the fate of belief depends much more than before on powerful intuitions of individuals, radiating out to others." Such intuitions, however, may be all but self-evident to others.[17] However, the relationship between self and community often displays rather complex characteristics and the language of individualism does not seem to exclude care and concern for community.[18] Thus, the subjective turn that is argued to have taken place is no uniform trend. Furthermore, the interest in spirituality is nurtured not only outside traditional religious institutions, but to a significant degree also within them. As Habermas notes, the trend toward individualization does not necessarily mean that religious discourses lose their influence over, or relevance in, political and cultural spheres of society.[19]

To sum up this introduction of the post-secular discourse, it rests on the observation that religious perspectives have renewed their public prominence in contemporary Western societies, but it should be understood as a critique toward overtly confident secularist theories, rather than as a plea for the return of religion to a stage which it had once abandoned.[20] Post-secular metamorphosis is no simple pattern of alteration including particular predetermined elements, values, and lines of development. Rather, it is a multifaceted process through which the concepts of modernity, secularity, and religiosity are scrutinized, deconstructed, and combined in novel, creative ways. The contemporary situation caters for the development of several different, fragmented patterns of understanding the plural situation of most societies in the world, that is, a "plurality of pluralisms."[21]

Environmentalism after the Secular

These trends are significant for the emerging field of religion, nature, and environmentalism. Today, ecological awareness has formed into a highly relevant scene of post-secular transformation, where the blurred lines between religious, spiritual, and secular are negotiated and redefined and where people search for holistic, multifaceted, and subjectively compiled outlooks on life.[22] Rosi Braidotti names several ethical concerns, related to ecology, that have grown in importance in the post-secular context: environmental holism, deep ecology, biopolitical management, and resistance toward biogenetic capitalism. Therefore, she concludes: "This eco-philosophical dimension is essential to the post-secular turn."[23]

Contemporary environmentalism thus exemplifies a context in which a critical reevaluation is taking place, questioning the sharp contrast formed between rational and spiritual, human subject and natural object.[24] However, it is necessary to emphasize the broad spectrum of those called environmentalists. This movement involves organizations and individuals acting collectively to promote environmental protection. The scope of environmentalist movements and organizations is wide, mainly because of the different types of issues they engage in and the different ways in which they mobilize around these issues, for example, in international organizations, governmental agencies, research institutions, nongovernmental organizations (NGOs), and business organizations. In the past, most of these organizations were clearly either religious or secular, but today, a growing tendency to apply spiritually saturated forms of expression and arguments can be discerned.[25]

The environmental researcher and activist Michael Moon emphasizes the confusion of ideas within the green movement and even though he sympathizes with the aspiration to clearly demarcate the various tendencies within this field, he criticizes the sharp division between ecologism and environmentalism. Whereas ecologism has the status of an ideology, environmentalism, with emphasis on the "-ism," is not viewed as an ideology of its own. Concerning the practical politics of the green movement, however, the differences between radical ecologists and environmentalists are often apprehended as marginal.[26] An interesting example of contemporary radical environmentalism is hardcore music and more specifically the "straight edge" youth movement (sXe). According to Kennet Granholm, some of the bands active in this subculture have brought renewed focus to issues of immediate political interest, such as veganism and environmentalism.[27]

The relationship between environmentalist movements and globalization is paradoxical. On the one hand, they usually oppose (economic) globalization but, on the other hand, they could not exist if it were not for the social and cultural globalization processes of which they form an important element. Not all movements are global, but they acquire global significance by working on environmental issues in short-term strategic networks, formed in order to achieve a specific result.[28] The value base for environmental work often comprises an ecological ethics founded on the respect for life in all its manifold forms. Thus, the movement is nonhierarchical and regards nature as a biotic community, which involves human action as part of the greater interdependence of the nature. Jagtenberg and McKie accentuate that space, time, and the biophysical world are all embedded aspects of the human lifeworld, and thus, ecology must be understood as a holistic perspective. Furthermore, since ecology often combines several positions, for example, eco-feminism and deep ecology, environmentalism has developed into a thoroughly pluralist movement. Shared starting points are nevertheless found in the views of environmentalism as a coherent critical voice in the global system.[29]

Environmentalists are often divided in two main groups. While some are mainly interested in preserving wildlife and the countryside, others wish to give higher priority to the protection of the environment. The latter group argues that a simple shift of priorities is not enough; if humanity is to survive, fundamental changes are needed. Many critiques stress the urgent need to reassess the reigning ideals of development and progress in society and to stop limiting the space for visionary thinking and imagination for fear of seeming too unrealistic, too radical, and too utopian.[30]

Perspectives that previously were ruled out as utopian are, nevertheless, gaining ground in contemporary environmentalist ethics. Watling, to give an example, proposes a fundamental reorientation of humanity in nature toward greater subjectivity, holism, and spirituality.[31] This vision clearly moves beyond modern, secular confines into the post-secular. On a similar note, Praful Bidwai criticizes rationality and material prosperity as the sole measures of progress and claims that truly utopian thinking today consists of believing that it is possible to go on as usual. With the financial crisis, neoliberal market fundamentalism has been shaken. A crucial question now is how far the current debate on holistic and integrated solutions to global recession, demographic pressure, and climate change can be taken.[32] A related trend is found in contemporary eco-socialism, a term used mainly by left-wing sympathizers who criticize the overemphasis on ecological questions and the underemphasis of social conditions that directly relate to the eco-crisis. By promoting the fusion of green insights into traditional socialist analysis and by combining green consciousness with radical activism (eco-fascism) and openness to eco-spirituality, the eco-socialists often clash with more conservative greens.[33]

Cotgrove and Duff also emphasize the social and class-related aspects of contemporary environmentalism. They argue that environmentalists are drawn predominantly from a specific fraction of the middle class, whose interests and values diverge from other groups in industrial societies. Environmentalism is an expression of the interests of those whose class position in the nonproductive sector is located at the periphery of the institutions and processes of industrial capitalist societies. It is a protest against alienation from the processes of decision making and the depoliticization of issues through the trespassing of policy decisions by experts. Their sense of being outsiders is reflected especially in the attitudes toward working through the existing political parties. By rejecting the belief in the efficacy of the market, risk-taking, rewards for achievements, and of the overriding goal of economic growth, the environmentalists challenge the goals and values of the dominant class. It seems that the crucial difference in values and beliefs between environmentalists and, for example, the representatives of the market sector is partly found in their relations to the core economic institutions of society.[34] Furthermore, at the individual level, Koensler and Papa argue that environmental movements are producing new ways of belonging, as participants search for new kinds of self-relating. This "new social movement" paradigm raises the issue that in contrast to the "old" movements, which mobilized primarily in order to access resources, these "new" movements are distinctive in their creation of new identities and concepts of belonging.[35]

The history and origin of the Finnish environmental movement illustrates this description rather well, even though the Finnish context appears to be relatively restrained. The modern Finnish environmental movement can be described as being formed of four waves of protest. The first wave developed as a response to the rapid industrialization and the radical political and cultural atmosphere in society during the late 1960s. The second wave took place ten years later as a protest against a social climate dominated by hard values such as industrialization, economic growth, and bureaucracy. To counter these trends, human subjectivity, local issues, and direct nonviolent activism were promoted. The third wave, inspired by international discussions of global environmental threats and sustainable development, took shape at the end of the 1980s and established the position of environmental questions in the public political debate. In the middle of the 1990s, the fourth wave introduced animal activists and sabotage. For the first time, moral arguments without scientific emphasis were introduced.[36] This development toward practical and ethical engagement illustrates the post-secular turn discussed in this chapter.

Examples of Post-Secular Environmentalism

Returning to the question of the post-secular and its relation to contemporary environmentalism, we find that the notion of post-secularity sheds light on many of the contemporary trends described above. As previously maintained, salient features of the post-secular discourse include criticism of the dichotomies of modern thinking, as well as a renewed interest in spirituality and practice. These trends will be discussed in greater detail later. Contemporary environmentalist thinking is also beginning to question the optimistic view that future generations will be better off than the current generation and that it is the obligation of the current generation to fulfill this development. Thirty years ago, this optimistic model was taken for granted. However, owing to carbon emissions, greenhouse gases, ozone depletion, and the serious threat of climate change, a more pessimistic model is rapidly gaining ground. This model anticipates that future generations will be worse off and that this cannot be avoided. Even sacrifices made now will not improve the prospects of future generations; it will only reduce the extent of a worsening situation. In the pessimistic model, the crucial question is what can and should the current generation do to impede this downward trend?[37]

To describe the green movement and its response to the changes in society described above, Michael Moon applies Thomas Kuhn's theory of anomalies and crises. In Moon's view, the environmentalist movement has now reached the point where the amount of anomalies has seriously weakened the explanatory potential of the reigning consumption-based paradigm. This has led to general disillusionment and what Kuhn would call a crisis of the entire paradigm. At this point, Moon notes, many, especially younger, practitioners are becoming outspokenly critical and start to look for alternative environmental theories.[38] These alternative theories, which are used to fill the gap left by traditional paradigms and norms, are seldom single solutions, but a mix of unspecific and diverse perspectives and claims.

A recent book, entitled "Where the soul rests" by the eco-theologian Pauliina Kainulainen, offers an example of such eclectic post-secular environmentalism.[39] Climate change, pollution, and other threats to nature and wildlife are not merely environmental challenges, she argues, they are quintessentially challenges to humanity as such: symptoms of a fundamental moral and spiritual disorder of the human body, mind, and soul. This illness is experienced as an endless yearning; an emptiness that people try to fill by consumption, Kainulainen contends. In her view, only encounters with the holy, with God, with other human beings and with nature as a sacred place in which to dwell can satisfy this spiritual hunger and create a sense of unity and meaning in our scattered lifeworlds of today.[40] By stripping nature of its sacred dimensions, modernity has turned it into a cold, lifeless, and impersonal object of exploitation and profit, claims Kainulainen. But now nature and humanity have come to the end of their wits. By rediscovering the sacredness of the environment, however, a sustainable alternative to modern consumption culture and the continuous quest for maximized profit can be reached. A profound transformation on the attitudinal level is called for, she believes: something that touches us as thinking, feeling, and embodied beings. A reenchantment of nature and human relations is also relevant for interreligious and intercultural relations. Kainulainen concludes: as all traces of the holy have been eliminated from Western thinking, it has also made it prone to conflicts, violence, and disdain toward the humanity of others.[41]

Another example from Finland is Heikki Pesonen's research on the "greening" of the Evangelical Lutheran Church of Finland, a majority church with approximately 80 percent of the Finnish population as its members.[42] As illustrated earlier, the worldwide influence of environmentalism reached Finland in the 1960s and also touched religious organizations and institutions. According to Pesonen, the environmental awakening of the Evangelical Lutheran Church of Finland took place in the early 1990s. To evaluate the environmentalism of the church, Pesonen analyzed, among other issues, how the environmental activities of the church can be viewed as strategies by which the church seeks to strengthen its importance in secular society. Environmental activities can hence be seen as a sign of the internal secularization of the church. Pesonen concludes, however, that since the 1980s the Evangelical Lutheran Church of Finland has striven to create an image of itself as both a keeper of traditions and as a modern innovator. In this process, environmental actions offer an excellent way of combining these two goals.[43]

In the United States, the image of land fostered by several groups of American Muslims can be given as yet another example of how environmentalism and spiritual practices are combined today. According to Eleanor Finnegan, farms play an important role in many Muslim communities, especially for immigrant and convert Sunni Muslims. In the textual tradition of Islam, people are allowed to use land for their own benefit as long as it does not harm others. The land is understood to be owned by God and given as a gift to God's creation. For these Muslims, Finnegan states, the apprehension of land has been influenced by experiences of farming as well as by Islamic ideas and practices. Among these groups, land has often been a scene where Muslims can embody their religious and environmental values and are free to create religious communities, institutions, and identities. It has also helped shape environmental and religious ideas and practices.[44]

In the Middle East, to give yet another example, IndyAct represents an independent environmental action. IndyAct stands for the "League of Independent Activists" and is a global league of autonomous environmental, social, and cultural activists. IndyAct started during the July 2006 war in Lebanon, when a group of activists from different countries came together to fight the worst environmental disaster in the history of the Eastern Mediterranean. During the war, more than 10,000 tons of raw oil spilled into the sea in the south of Lebanon.[45]

After the war, the group of independent activists realized that in Lebanon, and around the world, a great number of enthusiastic independent activists wished to make a difference, but were unable to join forces. Until IndyAct was created, there was no organization or structure that allowed activists to operate to their full potential. To fill this gap, IndyAct was created. One of the lodestars of IndyAct is that major changes in this world are initiated by a small number of individuals. Any organization, no matter what it does or how it is structured, is as good as the individuals running it. Therefore, the concept of "the right individual" rather than "the right organization" has more or less become a motto. IndyAct, hence, seeks to empower individuals in their respective communities, making positive and effective changes in the way of life and duty of every human being. In their view, activism is as necessary a value as any other basic human value. Activism thus becomes a core human principle. The activists of IndyAct can hence be seen as apt examples of how new, boundary-crossing forms of belonging are nurtured in contemporary environmental networks, as argued by Koensler and Papa.[46]

Abandoning the Division between Secular and Religious

In the following sections, and on the basis of the examples given above, we analyze the negotiation between, and possible merging of, religious and secular spheres, as well as the general critique of dualistic modes of thinking and the search for holistic unity and meaning within contemporary environmentalism. As shown above, contemporary environmentalism is characterized by many of the traits associated with the post-secular discourse: a critical attitude toward materialistic and neoliberal values, a holistic understanding of humanity and nature as interdependent, as well as an ethical awareness of shared responsibility toward future generations. In what follows here, the eclectic character of contemporary environmentalism is discussed further, as an example of how secular values and religious ideals that have previously been considered as incongruent are merged into novel approaches within the post-secular context.

Braidotti, whose view of ecology as an innate aspect of the post-secular was introduced above, interestingly relates her concern for the environment to concern for a vivid and valuable plurality of cultures, worldviews, and ways of living in the world. For her, natural and human diversity seem to be equally threatened by extinction.[47] This might at first glance seem contradictory, as contemporary societies appear to be more diverse than ever before. In fact, most contemporary scholars support the observation that religious pluralism is escalating today.[48] Indeed, globalization, migration, and mobility have expanded the apprehension of pluralism to include all possible religions, spiritualities, and ideologies—not just a number of variations of Christianity. This, however, has resulted in a situation where diversity may be seen as being threatened not by uniformity, but by indifference. The "taken-for-granted status" of religion, as Peter L. Berger calls it, has dramatically diminished for the individual: no matter how pious and devout you are, you can no longer disregard the striking fact that other people take other religious truths for granted.[49] Even if the new situation does not affect one's personal religious conviction, the awareness of

227

pluralism necessarily changes what it means to be religious today. To quote Charles Taylor:

> We live in a condition where we cannot help but be aware that there are a number of different construals, views which intelligent, reasonably undeluded people, of good will, can and do disagree on. We cannot help looking over our shoulder from time to time, looking sideways, living our faith also in a condition of doubt and uncertainty.[50]

Kwame Anthony Appiah contends, however, that pluralism is often employed as an ideology rather than a neutral scientific concept.[51] It is not simply about stating the fact that diversity prevails at all levels of our societies; often, discourses of pluralism are also endowed with value-based judgments of how the plural situation should be assessed and handled. Thus, even if the escalation of religious diversity can be seen as an irrevocable process of change affecting most contemporary societies, the assumptions that secularization or a certain pattern of ideological pluralism follows in its wake is debated. Modernity, it is argued, does not necessarily lead to a decline of religion.[52] Many scholars engaged in pluralism therefore argue that the core assumption of religions as unified systems with clear-cut borders—toward each other as well as toward the secular—needs to be abandoned. The search for a satisfying understanding of human and religious diversity is futile, claims Aimee Upjohn Light, as long as we "inhabit the modernist, dichotomous discourse" in which all that is known is known "binarily," as either/or.[53]

Thus, the traditional dichotomy of religious and secular is abandoned as it no longer seems to offer a strict choice of either/or in the lives of many contemporary believers who strive to formulate personally relevant worldviews.[54] Furthermore, a plurality of practices rather than beliefs seems to form the hub of this debate, thus changing the focus from a predominantly intellectual apprehension of religion toward more practical, interpersonal, and action-oriented views of religiosity.[55] The critical dismantling of dichotomies related to the modern, rational worldview is also an important impetus for contemporary environmentalism. Religions are often referred to primarily as concerned with the divine–human relationship, which aims at personal salvation. In relation to ecology, however, it is important to acknowledge that religious traditions also emphasize the importance of social and ethical relations between human beings. Thus, the interweaving of cosmological religious thought and environmental ethics offers an intriguing field of research.

The question of ecology and religion also touches upon the classical debate concerning the compatibility of science and religion, knowledge and faith. In the environmental movement, the dominant argument has been that science is constantly ready to test and reexamine hypotheses, whereas religion, on the other hand, is purely a matter of embracing a moral and spiritual code by which life is given meaning.[56] This is perhaps due to the fact that environmental movements have frequently been associated with left-wing politics, a field in which hostile attitudes toward religion are often prevalent. Today, however, there are green parties that, partly in order to distinguish themselves from other political alternatives, claim to go beyond the traditional left–right political scale and represent left-to-right. Depending on how the political terminology *left* and *right* is used, the green movement can be described as both.[57]

According to Moon, Lynn White's essay, *The Historical Roots of Our Ecological Crisis*, in which White blames Protestantism in particular for being environmentally destructive, left irreversible imprints in the history of green ideology. This controversy took the green debate beyond the conventional political discourse of right versus left.[58] Arguments claiming that one religion or the other can be deemed to be more ecologically friendly than others are today, however, dismissed as inconclusive and a deeper understanding of the interconnection between environmentalism and religion is emerging through new interdisciplinary areas of study, such as religion and nature. Within contemporary research, there tends to be an agreement that all religious traditions have both anthropocentric and ecocentric aspects.[59] Furthermore, as the discussion in this chapter demonstrates, it is becoming increasingly difficult to point to a single basis, or even a set of clear-cut ideological elements, that contemporary environmentalism is composed of. Thus, contemporary environmentalism does not seem to offer a new way of doing the old religious–secular puzzle—rather, the rules are reinvented and the pieces reshaped.

According to Moon, environmentalism is clearly a reaction against mainstream modernism. As the green movement established itself as a political force in several countries and gained parliamentary influence, however, such ideological visions were often overridden by electoral goals and realist politics.[60] In a study of environmentalism in world religions, however, Tony Watling finds that a critique of modernity is a fundamental aspect of most forms of religious environmentalism today. In these perspectives, creativity and sacredness associated with nature and humanity are regarded as alienated from this natural context, acting on the world but not within it. Thus, in all spheres of modern life, for example, education, law, mass communications, science and technology, nature is disenchanted and human powers are enchanted. Therefore, it is argued, it is urgent to deconstruct the modern worldview and instead, some kind of holistic or participating consciousness needs to be reintroduced. Contemporary environmentalism seems to offer such a turning point in the modern worldview, abandoning mechanistic ways of relating to the earth in favor of more holistic, organic approaches. According to Watling, this new paradigm could be realized economically by living renewably off nature: socially by equally and sustainably sharing its wealth, institutionally by creating cooperation instead of competition, technologically by reducing environmental impacts, morally by widening ethics to all of nature, and religiously by stressing earthkeeping as a vocation.[61] In such a vision, environmentalism clearly surpasses the modern dichotomy of religious versus secular.

Subjectively Meaningful, but Globally Interrelated

Moving from the societal to the personal level, the post-secular transformation gives rise to somewhat different questions and apprehensions—among these the second relevant feature of post-secularity, outlined above: the search for holistically meaningful approaches to existence that moves beyond the "modern" apprehension of reality in sharp dualities. Additional relevant themes that arise in this context are contemporary trends such as individualization, an increasing emphasis on personal choice and the decline in institutional influence. As argued above, the augmented status of individual agency and choice in the religious sphere are central assumptions within the post-secular perspective.[62]

Addressing the theme of subjective spirituality and meaning creation, Watling argues that the contemporary environmental crisis can be seen above all as a moral and spiritual crisis. In his view, religious environmentalism is well equipped to deal with these environmental questions, since religions entail a history of ethical and social reflections and possess moral authority. Hence, a spiritual turn could give greater consistency to contemporary environmentalism, Watling claims.[63] This holistic or eclectic spirit influences not only critical apprehensions of

230

depoliticisation

the dichotomy between religious/spiritual and secular, but also several other binary opposites that play a constitutive role in modern, rational thinking. The discussion about rationality has been prominent in several religious traditions. In the neopagan movements and in Eastern spiritualities there are long traditions of environmental engagement, but in the Judeo-Christian tradition, White's essay on Protestantism as an eco-villain became the first landmark of eco-theology. The essay gave rise to a critical discussion of the one-sided rationality and ethnocentrism included in religious traditions, but the argument also met some criticism. Gary T. Gardner, for example, targets to a controversial issue included in White's original argument, saying that it is founded merely on a few lines of scripture. A more complete reading of the Hebrew and Christian scriptures would produce a much more nuanced understanding of the environmental perspectives of these religious traditions, Gardner argues.[64]

Nevertheless, a critical conception of the Judeo-Christian worldview taught a generation of Western environmentalists to regard religion as a problem and to avoid involving religious groups in environmental work. This hostile attitude toward religion was also reflected in religious environmentalism through the dominant conception that non-Abrahamic traditions, especially Buddhism, Taoism, and Jainism, were environmentally more developed in their spiritual traditions compared to the Abrahamic faiths. Today, however, many nonreligious environmentalists are starting to reassess their attitudes toward religious movements and recognize the potential religious groups possess to spread the essential environmental message and to inspire people to manage the world in a better, more efficient way.[65] This development illustrates the general characterization of the post-secular turn presented above, claiming that the interface between religious and secular values is currently undergoing radical changes and that the strict dichotomy between the two is becoming increasingly difficult to uphold.

Contemporary environmentalism also transcends contemporary borders of locality and cultural or religious belonging. Increasing interconnectedness across the world has led to the acknowledgment of global identities and, consequently, many environmentalists today identify themselves as global citizens. There is a potentially universal appeal in the environmentalist movement and one of its most compelling arguments is the claim that the social dislocation following in the wake of environmental degradation is everybody's concern. Transnational environmental activist groups (TEAGs), such as Greenpeace, Amnesty International, and Friends of the Earth, have grown tremendously since the 1970s. TEAGs work to disseminate an ecological sensibility and they usually target international corporations rather than national governments. Because of the global character of environmentalist ethics, people around the globe can share feelings of connectedness and engagement with ecological threats all over the world.[66]

To sum up the argument on subjectivity and choice in relation to contemporary environmentalism, it is important to acknowledge the dynamics between individuality and interconnectedness which is displayed in this discussion. As noted previously in this chapter, contemporary environmentalism is increasingly becoming a component of individual quests for belonging and increased self-understanding.[67] The creative combination of secular and religious values in individual worldviews and the emphasis on subjectivity and individual agency discovered in the current analysis of contemporary environmentalism are significant to account for in connection with the discussion on post-secularity. Both trends imply a fragmentation of worldviews in pluralistic societies, but this does not mean, however, that all societies and all individuals today have separate, unique, and solipsistic identities and worldviews. Even if human religiosity can no longer be defined according to neatly arranged patterns with clear-cut borders between different traditions and between the religious vis-à-vis the secular, the display of personal religious identities composed out of the bits and pieces on offer in the religious market place is not private. Equally, even if the importance and possibility of personal agency increases, identity formation is always open to and conditioned by contextual influence and public projection.[68] The spiritual influence in contemporary environmentalism supports both of these—seemingly contradictory—claims by enlarging the space for individual agency and global unity at the same time.

Conclusions

In this chapter, we have discussed the wide-ranging issue of contemporary post-secular value transformation and its relationship to contemporary religious environmentalism. In this discussion, special attention was given to two post-secular strategies that proved significant for the context of environmentalism: the blurring of the previously rigid lines between secular and religious views and motives, as well as the quest for a holistic, meaningful unity between spiritual and worldly dimensions of reality, between mind and body, nature and humanity.

The analysis has shown that contemporary, religiously inspired and spiritually informed environmentalism offers a relevant platform for research on post-secular practices and value transformations. Even though the green movement, according to Moon, has been criticized for being overemotional and unable or unwilling to think through its positions and proposals, contemporary environmentalism provides an intriguing example of the trends connected to a post-secular understanding of society and personal religiosity. The eco-movement has formed into a scene where dominant values such as economic growth, production, rationalism, and progress are criticized and where the post-secular ideals of holism and eclecticism cater for new, spiritually informed understandings of the relationship between humanity and the earth.[69] Scholars such as Kainulainen and Watling, discussed at length in this chapter, are good examples of this trend in contemporary research in spiritual environmentalism, strongly advocating a rediscovering of the sacredness in the environment and the reenchantment of nature.

Combining elements of secular and religious values in a personal outlook on life may seem incoherent on a theoretical level. Nevertheless, it may prove meaningful and fruitful in practice for persons who live their lives according to such complex standards. As Appiah notes, a person's life can be psychologically integrated by existential narratives and practices without being logically integrated into a single traditional narrative, either of a secular or religious character.[70] For many contemporary individuals, the ecological movement seems to offer such a holistic, creative, and intrinsically plural scene.

Notes

1. Jonathan Benthall, *Returning to Religion. Why a Secular Age is Haunted by Faith* (London: I.B. Tauris, 2008), 138.
2. Stephen Cotgrove and Andrew Duff, "Middle-Class Radicalism and Environmentalism," in *The Social Movements Reader. Cases and Concepts*, ed. Jeff Goodwin and James M. Jasper (Oxford: Blackwell, 2002), 72.
3. Michael S. Hogue, "After the Secular. Toward a Pragmatic Public Theology," *Journal of the American Academy of Religion* 78, no. 2 (2010): 356.
4. Whitney A. Bauman and others, "Introduction," in *Grounding Religion. A Field Guide to the Study of Religion and Ecology*, ed. Whitney A. Bauman, Richard R. Bohannon, and Kevin J. O'Brien (Oxford: Oxford University Press, 2011), 2.

5. Miroslav Volf, "A Voice of One's Own: Public Faith in a Pluralistic World," in *Democracy and the New Religious Pluralism*, ed. Thomas Banchoff (Oxford: Oxford University Press, 2007), 271.

6. Inger Furseth, *From Quest for Truth to Being Oneself. Religious Change in Life Stories* (Frankfurt am Main: Peter Lang, 2006), 296.

7. Jürgen Habermas, "Notes on Post-Secular Society," *New Perspectives Quarterly* 25, no. 4 (2008): 17–18.

8. Austin Harrington, "Habermas and the 'Post-Secular Society,'" *European Journal of Social Theory* 10, no. 4 (2007): 545.

9. Habermas, "Notes on Post-Secular Society," 19.

10. Hogue, "After the Secular," 357.

11. José Casanova, "Rethinking Secularization. A Global Comparative Perspective," in *Religion, Globalization and Culture*, ed. Peter Beyer and Lori Beaman (Leiden: Brill, 2007), 108.

12. Volf, "Voice of One's Own," 276; Nancy Ammerman, "The Challenges of Pluralism: Locating Religion in a World of Diversity," *Social Compass* 57, no. 2 (2010): 155.

13. Charles Taylor, *A Secular Age* (Cambridge: The Belknap Press of Harvard University Press, 2007), 534.

14. Ibid., 535.

15. Reinhold Bernhardt and Perry Schmidt-Leukel, "Zur Einführung," in *Multiple religiöse Identität. Aus verschiedenen religiösen Traditionen schöpfen* [Multiple Religious Identities. Drawing from Different Religious Traditions], ed. Reinhold Bernhardt and Perry Schmidt-Leukel (Zürich: Teologischer Verlag Zürich, 2008), 8.

16. Hogue, "After the Secular," 358.

17. Taylor, *Secular Age*, 531.

18. Furseth, *Quest for Truth*, 311.

19. Habermas, "Notes on Post-Secular Society," 19.

20. Harrington, "Habermas," 547.

21. Ole Riis, "Modes of Religious Pluralism under the Conditions of Globalization," in *Democracy and Human Rights in Multicultural Societies*, ed. Matthias Koenig and Paul de Guchteneire (Aldershot: Ashgate, 2007), 251.

22. Tony Watling, *Ecological Imaginations in the World Religions. An Ethnographic Analysis* (London: Continuum, 2009), 3.

23. Rosi Braidotti, "In Spite of the Times: The Postsecular Turn in Feminism," *Theory, Culture, Society* 25, no. 1 (2008): 16.

24. Watling, *Ecological Imaginations*, 8.

25. David L. Downie and others, *Climate Change. A Reference Handbook* (Santa Barbara, CA: ABC-CLIO, 2009), 237.

26. Michael Moon, "Green Ideology and its Relation to Modernity. Including a Case Study of the Green Party of Sweden," (PhD diss., Lund University, 2008), 12–13, 20–21.

27. Kennet Granholm, "Metal, the End of the World, and Radical Environmentalism: Ecological Apocalypse in the Lyrics of *Earth Crisis*," in *Anthems of Apocalypse: Popular Music and Apocalyptic Thought*, ed. Christopher Partridge (Sheffield: Sheffield Phoenix Press, forthcoming).

28. Kathryn Hochstetler, "Environmental Movements," in the *Encyclopedia of Globalization*, ed. Roland Robertson and Jan Aart Scholte (New York: Routledge, 2007), 392–93.

29. Tom Jagtenberg and David McKie, *Eco-Impacts and the Greening of Post-modernity. New Maps for Communication Studies, Cultural Studies, and Sociology* (London: Sage Publications, 1997), xii, 118–19.

30. Cotgrove and Duff, "Middle-Class Radicalism," 72.

31. Watling, *Ecological Imaginations*, 6.

32. Praful Bidwai, "The Convergence of Fundamentalisms and new Political Closures – What Next in the Struggle for Pluralism?" in *What Next Volume II. Case for Pluralism*, ed. Niclas Hällström and Henning Melber (Uppsala: Dag Hammarskjöld Foundation, 2009), 41.

33. Moon, "Green Ideology," 41–42, 249.

34. Cotgrove and Duff, "Middle-Class Radicalism," 76–77.

35. Alexandra Koensler and Christina Papa, "Political Tourism in the Israeli-Palestinian Space," *Anthropology Today* 27, no. 2 (2011): 13

36. Yvonne Terlinden, "Människa – moral – miljö. En undersökning av livsåskådningar i finländskt miljötänkande" (PhD diss., Åbo Akademi, 2007), 24–26.

37. Tim Mulgan, *Future Generations. A Moderate Consequentialist Account of our Obligations to Future Generations* (Oxford: Clarendon Press, 2006), 215–16.

38. Moon, "Green Ideology," 186–87.

39. Pauliina Kainulainen, *Missä sielu lepää* [Where the Soul Rests] (Helsinki: Kirjapaja, 2010).

40. Ibid., 7–8.

41. Ibid., 15–16.

42. Heikki Pesonen, *Vihertyvä kirkko. Suomen evankelisluterilainen kirkko ympäristötoimijana* [A Greening Church. The Evangelical Lutheran Church of Finland as an Environmental Actor] (Helsinki: Suomen Tiedeseura, 2004).

43. Ibid, 40, 51–55, 102–09, 113.

44. Eleanor Finnegan, "Case Study. Images of 'Land' among Muslim Farmers in the US," in *Grounding Religion. A Field Guide to the Study of Religion and Ecology*, ed. Whitney A. Bauman, Richard R. Bohannon II, and Kevin J. O'Brien (London: Routledge, 2011), 73.

45. Official webpage of IndyAct: http://www.indyact.org/ (accessed June 29, 2011).

46. Koensler and Papa, "Political Tourism," 13, 15.

47. Braidotti, "In Spite of the Times," 19.

48. Riis, "Modes of Religious Pluralism," 251; Ammerman, "The Challenges of Pluralism," 156.

49. Peter L. Berger, "Pluralism, Protestantization, and the Voluntary Principle," in *Democracy and the New Religious Pluralism*, ed. Thomas Banchoff (Oxford: Oxford University Press, 2007), 23.

50. Taylor, *Secular Age*, 11.

51. Kwame Anthony Appiah, "Causes of Quarrel: What's Special about Religious Disputes?" in *Religious Pluralism, Globalization, and World Politics*, ed. Thomas Banchoff (Oxford: Oxford University Press, 2008), 44–45.

_. Berger, "Pluralism," 21.
53. Aimee Upjohn Light, "Post-Pluralism Through the Lens of Post-Modernity," *Journal of Inter-Religious Dialogue* 1 (2009): 72.
54. Casanova, "Rethinking Secularization," 104.
55. Hogue, "After the Secular," 364.
56. Benthall, *Returning to Religion*, 124.
57. Andrew Dobson, *Green Political Thought* (London: Routledge, 2007), 19.
58. Moon, "Green Ideology," 48.
59. Benthall, *Returning to Religion*, 128.
60. Moon, "Green Ideology," 281–82, 312.
61. Watling, *Ecological Imaginations*, 16–19, 23–24.
62. Habermas, "Notes on Post-Secular Society," 17–18.
63. Watling, *Ecological Imaginations*, 38, 59.
64. Gary T. Gardner, *Inspiring Progress. Religions' Contributions to Sustainable Development* (New York: W. W. Norton, 2006), 15.
65. Benthall, *Returning to Religion*, 128, 139.
66. Paul Wapner, "Transnational Environmental Activism," in *The Social Movements Reader. Cases and Concepts*, ed. Jeff Goodwin and James M. Jasper (Oxford: Blackwell, 2003), 203–4, 207; Hochstetler, "Environmental Movements," 395; Dobson, *Green Political Thought*, 17.
67. Koensler and Papa, "Political Tourism," 13, 15.
68. Furseth, *Quest for Truth*, 296, 302.
69. Moon, "Green Ideology," 52–53.
70. Appiah, "Causes of Quarrel," 58.

Bibliography

Ammerman, Nancy. "The Challenges of Pluralism: Locating Religion in a World of Diversity." *Social Compass* 57, no. 2 (2010): 154–67.

Appiah, Kwame Anthony. "Causes of Quarrel: What's Special about Religious Disputes?" In *Religious Pluralism, Globalization, and World Politics*, edited by Thomas Banchoff, 41–64. Oxford: Oxford University Press, 2008.

 Bauman, Whitney A., Richard R. Bohannon II, and Kevin J. O'Brien. "Introduction." In *Grounding Religion. A Field Guide to the Study of Religion and Ecology*, edited by Whitney A. Bauman, Richard R. Bohannon II, and Kevin J. O'Brien, 1–9. London: Routledge, 2011.

Benthall, Jonathan. *Returning to Religion. Why a Secular Age is Haunted by Faith.* London: I.B. Tauris, 2008.

Berger, Peter L. "Pluralism, Protestantization, and the Voluntary Principle." In *Democracy and the New Religious Pluralism*, edited by Thomas Banchoff, 19–30. Oxford: Oxford University Press, 2007.

Bernhardt, Reinhold, and Perry Schmidt-Leukel. "Zur Einführung." In *Multiple religiöse Identität. Aus verschiedenen religiösen Traditionen schöpfen* ["Introduction." In Multiple Religious Identities. Drawing from Different Religious Traditions], edited by Reinhold Bernhardt and Perry Schmidt-Leukel, 7–13. Zürich: Teologischer Verlag Zürich, 2008.

Bidwai, Praful. "The Convergence of Fundamentalisms and New Political Closures – What Next in the Struggle for Pluralism?" In *What Next Volume II. Case for Pluralism*, edited by Niclas Hällstöm and Henning Melber, 23–41. Uppsala: Dag Hammarskjöld Foundation, 2009.

Braidotti, Rosi. "In Spite of the Times: The Postsecular Turn in Feminism." *Theory, Culture, Society* 25, no. 1 (2008): 1–24.

Casanova, José. "Rethinking Secularization. A Global Comparative Perspective." In *Religion, Globalization and Culture*, edited by Peter Beyer and Lori Beaman, 101–20. Leiden: Brill, 2007.

Cotgrove, Stephen, and Andrew Duff. "Middle-Class Radicalism and Environmentalism." In *The Social Movements Reader. Cases and Concepts*, edited by Jeff Goodwin and James M. Jasper, 72–80. Oxford: Blackwell, 2003.

Dobson, Andrew. *Green Political Thought*. London: Routledge, 2007.

Downie, David L., Kate Brash, and Catherine Vaughan. *Climate Change. A Reference Handbook*. Santa Barbara: ABC-CLIO, 2009.

Finnegan, Eleanor. "Case Study. Images of "Land" among Muslim Farmers in the US." In *Grounding Religion. A Field Guide to the Study of Religion and Ecology*, edited by Whitney A. Bauman, Richard R. Bohannon II, and Kevin J. O'Brien, 73–77. London: Routledge, 2011.

Furseth, Inger. *From Quest for Truth to Being Oneself. Religious Change in Life Stories*. Frankfurt am Main: Peter Lang, 2006.

Gardner, Gary T. *Inspiring Progress. Religions' Contributions to Sustainable Development*. New York: W. W. Norton, 2006.

Granholm, Kennet. "Metal, the End of the World, and Radical Environmentalism: Ecological Apocalypse in the Lyrics of *Earth Crisis*." In *Anthems of Apocalypse: Popular Music and Apocalyptic Thought*, edited by Christopher Partridge. Sheffield: Sheffield Phoenix Press, forthcoming.

Habermas, Jürgen. "Notes on Post-Secular Society." *New Perspectives Quarterly* 25, no. 4 (2008): 17–29.

Harrington, Austin. "Habermas and the 'Post-Secular Society.'" *European Journal of Social Theory* 10, no. 4 (2007): 543–60.

Hochstetler, Kathryn. "Environmental Movements." In *Encyclopedia of Globalization*, edited by Roland Robertson and Jan Aart Scholte, 392–97. New York: Routledge, 2007.

Hogue, Michael S. "After the Secular. Toward a Pragmatic Public Theology." *Journal of the American Academy of Religion* 78, no. 2 (2010): 346–74.

Jagtenberg, Tom, and David McKie. *Eco-Impacts and the Greening of Postmodernity. New Maps for Communication Studies, Cultural Studies, and Sociology*. London: Sage Publications, 1997.

Kainulainen, Pauliina. *Missä sielu lepää* [Where the Soul Rests]. Helsinki: Kirjapaja, 2010.

Koensler, Alexander, and Cristina Papa. "Political Tourism in the Israeli-Palestinian Space." *Anthropology Today* 27, no. 2 (2011): 13–17.

Light, Aimee Upjohn. "Post-Pluralism Through the Lens of Post-Modernity." *Journal of Inter-Religious Dialogue* 1 (2009): 71–74.

Moon, Michael. *Green Ideology and its Relation to Modernity. Including a Case Study of the Green Party of Sweden*. PhD diss., Lund University, 2008.

Mulgan, Tim. *Future Generations. A Moderate Consequentialist Account of our Obligations to Future Generations*. Oxford: Clarendon Press, 2006.

Pesonen, Heikki. *Vihertyvä kirkko. Suomen evankelisluterilainen kirkko ympäristötoimijana* [A Greening Church. The Evangelical Lutheran Church of Finland as an Environmental Actor]. Helsinki: Tiedeseura, 2004.

Riis, Ole. "Modes of Religious Pluralism under the Conditions of Globalization." In *Democracy and Human Rights in Multicultural Societies,* edited by Matthias Koenig and Paul de Guchteneire, 251–66. Aldershot: Ashgate, 2007.

Taylor, Charles. *A Secular Age.* Cambridge: The Belknap Press of Harvard University Press, 2007.

Terlinden, Yvonne. "Människa – moral – miljö. En undersökning av livsåskådningar i finländskt miljötänkande." PhD diss., Åbo Akademi, 2007.

Volf, Miroslav. "A Voice of One's Own: Public Faith in a Pluralistic World." In *Democracy and the New Religious Pluralism,* edited by Thomas Banchoff, 271–82. Oxford: Oxford University Press, 2007.

Wapner, Paul. "Transnational Environmental Activism." In *The Social Movements Reader. Cases and Concepts,* edited by Jeff Goodwin and James M. Jasper, 202–9. Oxford: Blackwell, 2003.

Watling, Tony. *Ecological Imaginations in the World Religions. An Ethnographic Analysis.* London: Continuum, 2009.

Internet

IndyAct: http://www.indyact.org/ (accessed June 29, 2011).

10

Grappling with Liquid Modernity: Investigating Post-Secular Religion

Mika Lassander

Introduction

In this chapter I will set out the ideas and concepts upon which I base my view that actor-network theory (ANT)[1] can be a fruitful approach for studying beliefs and worldviews in those Western societies which are experiencing relatively rapid changes in their religious landscapes. In the backdrop of these changes are wide-ranging transformations in people's priorities—such as an increasing openness to change and a loosening of traditional norms of conformity—but also more particular signs of the long-term processes whereby the ideal of individual freedom has started to outweigh the sense of collective duty. Eventually, these processes have led to a situation where individualization is the expected norm and the ties between colleagues and peers outweigh the binding ties that have held traditional collectives together.[2]

Liquid modernity is a term Zygmunt Bauman uses to describe the state of the contemporary world.[3] He contrasts liquid modernity with the kind of modernity—or the idea of modernity—where institutions and social forms and structures have had time to take on solid and relatively predictable forms in people's minds, serving as frames of reference for their actions and for the lives they envision. Through processes of globalization and technological and social developments, individuals' life settings have become increasingly complex and varied, tasking people to find ways to navigate this complexity by themselves, to adapt to continuously changing opportunities, limitations, and social contexts, and often to plan their lives in episodes rather than as a foreseeable and progressive sequence. The institutions have become fluid, porous structures, and people's lives more complex. Utriainen, Hovi, and Broo discuss this kind of endemic uncertainty as a motive for individuals to look for advice in their life navigation. A feeling of destiny—understood as a practical sense of direction and purpose in life—is an essential ingredient of subjective well-being and, as their case studies exemplify, there is a range of alternative strategies for realizing that destiny.

A consequence of the lack of solid, nonporous containers is that things which are not solid by nature do not stay in regimented forms, and this appears to be the case with religion. As Teemu Taira observes, in liquid modernity religion itself has become fluid, but at the same time more visible.[4] By emerging from its former containers into places where we are not used to seeing it, and by blending with other liquid things, religion has become noteworthy. This fluidity and blending has caused problems for the study of religions. In our field of study, the range of alternative routes in the pursuit of purpose and destiny has resulted in much conceptual confusion. The scope of the category of religion has become broader, as Moberg and Granholm observed in Chapter 5, resulting in a perceived increase of phenomena classified under "religion" or related categories, such as "spirituality." On the other hand, some instances that we, the scholars, observe as being religions are not necessarily seen as such by the people involved in them themselves. In this volume Valaskivi explores this kind of research strategy.

In religious studies, the focus of research has contracted from descriptions of the World Religions, to studying religious movements and, finally, as in Pessi and Jeldtoft's work, to studying subjective experiences and meaning making. The blending of things formerly seen as religious and those seen as secular challenges and blurs the boundary circumscribing the category "religious," as is shown by the Illman and Wickström's study. Further, the religious institutions also react and adapt their strategies, creating a need to rethink, for example, the locus of religious authority and the role of media, as discussed by Martikainen and Moberg and Granholm.

So, the boundaries and the contents of the category "religion" are being stretched, reformulated, and questioned. The alternative meaning-making strategies are not simply inducted from new religious movements, nor are they, for that matter, necessarily religious in any earlier sense of the word. With these challenges in mind, I submit this chapter as a contribution to the methodological reflections many scholars claim we need today, and particularly as an example of what it could mean to account for "religion" in liquid modernity. In my view, ANT is an exploratory methodological perspective for empirical investigations at a time when the concepts and categories that have been used previously in religious studies—including the concept of religion—have been challenged.

Background

Marion Bowman highlights the role of methodology borrowed from folklore in the study of religion, and contrasts the study of religions as entities with the study of religion as it is lived.[5] Building on Leonard Primiano's theory of vernacular religion, she sees religious belief as a process involving complex linkages of acquisition and the formation of beliefs through conscious and unconscious negotiations of and between believers. Because of these negotiations and bidirectional acquisitions, religious belief is always vernacular—in other words, domestic and functional—rather than being a grand, institutional design. What Primiano says about folklorists studying religion applies to religious studies in general: there is a tendency to generalize and leave out much personal creativity. In order to capture this individual creativity, focus should be placed on the actual contents of people's beliefs—and the motivations underlying these beliefs—rather than on observations of how and what people express religiously.[6] Further, rather than focusing solely on the individual, one should pay attention to what factors influence and interact with the creative individual and how these factors and interactions appear in the verbal, behavioral, and material expressions of the religious beliefs of the individual.[7]

In the late 1980s, an approach similar in aim to Primiano's was developed in science and technology studies by Bruno Latour, John Law, Michel Callon, and others.[8] The purpose of this was to facilitate the study of large and complex sociotechnical systems. In what came to be known as ANT, these systems are seen as negotiated orders where social, political, and cultural values affect scientific research and technological innovation, and these in turn affect society, politics, and culture. As a departure from the structuralist approaches, ANT discards the idea that predefined structural forces determine and de-limit individuals' abilities to act. A major contribution of ANT to social research lies in paying attention to the active role nonhumans play; how things—such as the geography of Glastonbury, the hot springs of

Bath, a ring of standing stones, or a doorbell—make people do things. An actor-network is, therefore, any collection of human and nonhuman things that participate in some specific and identifiable activity in some fashion for some period of time, ultimately taking part in the shaping of negotiated orders.[9] Recently, ANT has found broader application in social and cultural studies because it offers conceptual tools and a methodology for describing and exploring complex social processes.[10] Thus, in this chapter I use Bruno Latour's concept of the *quasi-object* to describe vernacular religion as a negotiated system that does not necessarily have any predefined identifying properties, or a structure that determines it.[11] I see religion as a complex assemblage of various human and nonhuman actants, only some of which we are used to regarding as having something to do with religion or spirituality.

From this perspective, religion is a nonentity: it is not an object or a structure independent from an individual and yet it is not entirely endogenous. Consequently, I see religious change as an ongoing, creative process, where new assemblages of actants emerge. Apparent secularization of individuals' worldviews can be seen as an effect of the process where more and more of these actants are things that we are not used to seeing as pertaining to religion or spirituality.[12] Conversely, some actants which are normally seen as being religious or spiritual—even those that are believed to be integral to a particular religion—cease to be relevant, or active, in these assemblages; for example, the crucifix for those Christians who see Jesus primarily as a teacher—or a guru-like character—rather than a figure whose narrative emphasizes sin and salvation.[13]

I have postulated that one aspect of religious change is that in these new assemblages, the actants are held together by different types of connections than they were before and that this change is motivated by a general change in individuals' priorities.[14] I describe this change as a move from a quasi-object religion that is oriented toward security, conformity, and tradition, to one that is oriented toward self-expression and individuality. The first type provides security by giving a familiar form and clear, prescribed norms, acting as a template for behavior and belief. The second type offers tools for individuals, enables them to use these in ways that suit different needs and purposes, and it also legitimizes the resulting multitude of ways to co-opt religious and other phenomena in the process. The change is, therefore, a move from providing the boundaries of survival and security to providing resources for identity and self-expression, and the difference between the types of connection is the difference between prescribed normative communities versus elective conditions of association. To quote Kevin Hetherington, the new type of legitimating framework is "a form of sociation that reflects the topological complexity of identity politics rather than one that smoothens things out."[15]

This change is most notable in new religious movements, but it is likely also to happen under the label of more traditional religions observable in, for example, the popularity of new forms of community and practice. I shall discuss the methodological implications of the approach I am outlining in more detail below. Finally, I shall give an example of the potential complexity of networks by describing a specific site where various kinds of actants gather. This example aims to illustrate the kinds of actants and interactions that are involved in the networks and the places where these meet and take effect. It is not meant to be an exhaustive or definitive account of the movement. Rather, it is meant as one view of the potential of applying ANT in the study of religions.

Vernacular Religion as a Departure from the World Religions Paradigm

Religious studies scholars have been exercised about the meaning and use of the term "religion" in the same way that anthropologists worry about the meaning of "culture."[16] In *The Meaning and End of Religion*, Wilfred Cantwell Smith argues that the concept "religion" in the West has evolved through a long-range reification process, whereby religion has become "a thing" in people's minds. Religion has gradually become conceived of as "an objective systematic entity." Further, integral in this development is "the rise into Western consciousness in relatively recent times of several so conceived entities, constituting a series: the religions of the world."[17] This inherited "world religions" approach has led scholars to view religions as objects with certain essential qualities and boundaries, and upon which different external and internal forces then impose influence.

While the entity model of religion may have deeper roots than Smith appreciates, changes in the religious landscape of Western societies have called for its dismantling.[18] Meredith McGuire points the finger at sociologists who have "for too long, assumed that religion is an object with enduring characteristics and is as such factually given rather than being a product of historical, social and cultural discourses and processes."[19] According to McGuire, lived religion is messy, multifaceted, and diverse, and therefore she calls for an ethnographic and "bottom-up" approach in the study of religion.[20] Departing from the world religions paradigm, the lived religion approach explores how people assemble combinations from a range of religious repertoires. According to McGuire, the focus in the study of religion should be on how ordinary people practice, experience, and express spirituality in their everyday lives, and how they inject spiritual meanings into mundane things and spaces.[21] Only by studying the individual religious expressions, it is possible to get a glimpse at an authentic religion; only such an approach can reveal the fundamental hybridity of contemporary religious identities and account for individual agency in the formation of these hybrids.[22]

Along the same lines as McGuire, Primiano argues that the process of reification has led both believers and scholars to regard religious institutions as representing the "valid" and the "official" religion. Rather than viewing it as an ideal type, this institutional religion has been mistaken for the religious reality itself. However, Primiano continues, not even the members of such institutions—or religious elites—live an "officially" religious life. Even while representing the most normative aspects of their religious tradition, some element of accommodation or reflection on lived experience influences how these individuals direct their religious lives: they—along with other believers—practice what Primiano calls vernacular religion. In order to acknowledge this, Primiano, Bowman, and McGuire, among others, advocate a research strategy that steps away from the world religions paradigm and focuses instead on the lived realities and vernacular practice of religion.

Nevertheless, and in a departure from McGuire's more person-centric view, vernacular religion theory is not suggesting that the individual is an entirely free agent. The approach sees religion as a process and, rather than emphasizing individual agency, it points to local influences that are an integral part of the process—in a similar manner as regional dialect influences the formation of one's mother tongue. The individual is entwined in various internal and external relations. Factors such as physical and psychological predispositions, the natural environment, family, community affiliations, religious institutions, the socialization processes, tradition, education and literacy, communication media, as well as political and economic conditions, influence the individual believer, interacting with the individual mind. Furthermore, individuals' religious expression and disposition radiate and influence the surrounding environment. Seeing religion as a process acknowledges the presence of these bidirectional influences of environments upon individuals and of individuals upon environments.[23]

Primiano maintains that even though the category of official, or institutional, as opposed to private religion is a customary classification in the study of religions, in practice there is no such thing as an official or institutional religion. Religious beliefs are always vernacular, including the interpretation and performance of elements of institutional religions, such as oral and written statements, rituals, sacraments, and observances.[24] As a concept used by religious believers themselves, "official" or "institutional religion" can refer to, for example, authenticity, authority, and hierarchy, or it can be used as a method of classification differentiating between oneself and people of other religions. In sum, vernacular religion theory points out that ultimately religion is a product of the personal creativity taking place in the contexts of individuals' daily lives and, consequently, the concept of world religions as a category of definable entities becomes meaningless.

The Actor-network Model as a Departure from the Durkheimian Concept of Religion

Network theories that can be seen as predecessors of, or parallel to, ANT started to emerge in the latter half of the twentieth century. These were motivated by the growing realization that "society"—which was seen as a logical, modern-day follow-up to community—does not describe, or no longer describes the actual mode of belonging together. People are not tied to others in the same ways as they used to be; the collectives that have been seen as constant and immutable have been called into question and what "we" means is becoming less and less obvious.[25] Focus started to shift toward chains or networks of individuals and the methods of connections applied to these. Anatol Rapoport and Mark Granovetter explore the flow of information through chains of connections of varying intensity and via individuals with varying numbers of connections.[26] Harrison White explores how social networks are resources for identity and, at the same time, bundles of normative ties.[27] On a more general level, these models aim to describe better the nature of social interaction. Nevertheless, interactions were still seen as being immersed in an abstract and taken for granted social context. By exploring what the social is actually made of, and how it is constructed, ANT takes the examination a step further.[28]

Bruno Latour and other proponents of ANT criticize the kind of sociological approach that postulates "the social" as a specific kind of thing or domain, separate from other domains such as psychology, economics, biology, and politics. In this kind of approach—which Latour calls a sociology of the social—"the social" is used to illuminate that which cannot be understood, interpreted, explained, or accounted for by the other domains.[29] In this way, in the study of religions, "religion" is seen as an entity that can be approached from all these distinguishable angles—focusing on its various aspects—but that is also immersed in a "social context," bound by "social limitations," influenced by "social factors," or possessing "a social dimension" that accounts for some residual phenomena. A sociology of the social can provide a useful shorthand to designate the things that have already been established as ingredients of the collective realm—such as, culture, social capital, socialization, and peer pressure—but it cannot provide explanations or accurate descriptions.[30] In other words, the ANT approach disagrees with the idea that "the social" is a Durkheimian sui generis force, the study of which can expose, for example, the structures or powers that operate backstage.[31]

As an alternative, Latour suggests studying the social as a principle of connections between varying assortments of human and nonhuman things, all of which aim to make these connections durable.[32] Latour calls this approach a sociology of associations. Accordingly, the social is not a context at all, rather, it is an interacting collection of stabilized bundles that are made of interconnected things. The things are not put into a social frame, or seen as subject to social forces: there is nothing behind or above the bundles. The social, therefore, is a product of the constituent things enmeshed in the bundle and the means by which they are connected. In other words, the "social" is not an explanation, rather, it is the thing that needs to be explained.[33] Furthermore, the "actor" in an actor-network is not seen as the source of action. Rather, it is a feature which is "made to act" by many others; a heterogeneous array of things connected to it and engaging it in some way. The "actor" therefore is a relational effect of these connected things.[34] Nor is subjectivity an inherent trait of humans. The world is not made of passive object entities, perceived by subjective observers that are separate from the entities. Sidestepping the subject–object distinction, ANT sees subjectivity as a property of the gathering of things, and it grants objects the potential of being active agents by affecting and stabilizing interactions in these gatherings.[35]

Therefore, according to ANT, causing things to happen does not require intentionality, consciousness, or motive. Qualities such as intention, reflexiveness, and morality emerge from the network re-lationships, not from actors themselves.[36] Insofar as anything makes an individual act in some way rather than another—such as a low doorway to a shrine that makes people stoop, or sheep cohabiting an outdoor ceremonial site, making people focus some of their attention on where they step—it must be included in the array of actants that potentially affect the negotiation of associations.[37] Like vernacular religion theory, ANT does not see the actor as a free agent, or as a singular point which is at the mercy of numberless influences from numberless things. Instead, the actor is construed as a star-shaped whole—an actor-network—that is entwined with other actor-net-works. Nevertheless, the complexity of this entwining can be such that sufficient different influences converge, and ultimately put the actor in a position to choose.[38] The complexity also makes it difficult to trace back to any sort of singular reason why the actor does anything.

To summarize, the "network" in the actor-network is not a stand-in for the sociological concept of structure. It is not an abstract entity, or existing on a different level, as in macro versus micro. It is the explora-tion of a thing and its relationships rather than an explanation of or for the thing. The term "network" refers to something very concrete and very local: namely, the various constituent people and objects, the connections between them, and the locations where choices and calculations are being made.

ANT as an Open-ended Methodology for the Study of Religion

As a methodological framework for exploring the changing religious landscapes in Finland and elsewhere, I suggest rethinking or reassem-bling the notion of "religion" as a creative, individual process that is affected by and affects various factors. I see ANT as an open-ended methodology that offers simply a minimal toolkit of concepts and is not particular about the methods used. The ANT approach does not aim to explain or define religion, but instead it works toward tracing the network of objects that play an active role in the process of the creation of vernacular religion.

The conventional categories employed in the study of religions—such as the divisions between religion and spirituality, extrinsic, intrin-sic, and quest types of religiosity, or the church, sect, denomination, and cult typologies—come with assumptions about the location of similarities and differences between the things they are used to de-scribe and divide, or the nature of the thing referred to. The purpose of ANT is to avoid these predefined methods of classification. An ANT approach to religion sees "religion" and all its characteristics as outcomes of varied processes of translation—or mediation—through which different "bits and pieces" of the sociomaterial world are brought into association with one another, thereby "forming relationally configured networks of people and things that are stable enough to produce such effects as 'religion.'"[39] A consequence of this approach is that the boundaries of the object of study are fuzzy and its topography is not defined. They must also remain so; the field should be entered without an a priori decision about what is the nature, shape, and extent of an interaction or of some social aggregate: in ANT studies, the focus of any investigation is on why, how, and with whom the connections are made.[40]

Apart from the basic building blocks, namely, the "actant" and the "actor-network," ANT introduces a few other concepts that are useful tools in rethinking religion as an interactive process. An "immutable mobile" is a thing that represents an actant that is not actually present in the actor-network, enabling it to act from a distance.[41] This avoids using loaded concepts, such as idol, symbol, and altar, and prefabricated distinctions, such as a separation between sacred texts and other texts. An immutable mobile is a concrete thing—a book, an illustration, a statue, an artifact, or a report from an archeological dig—that is fixed in time (i.e., is immutable) and takes the form of a transportable (i.e., mobile) object. It does not easily deform or degrade and it can travel across long distances of geographic, cultural, and political spaces to regulate activity.[42] This concrete thing is recognized as being immutable and mobile only insofar as it affects the mobility or stability, or the combinability of the elements in an actor-network, for example, by dictating terms for assemblages of actants, providing means to connect with other actor-networks, or enabling the inclusion of actants into the actor-network.[43]

Another concept, "a center of calculations," avoids giving special status to some places—a shrine, for example—and thereby seeing the action that takes place in these as more important than action taking place somewhere else. Centers of calculations are any concrete sites where "calculations"—such as decisions for action, value judgments, and interpretations—are made over issues presently at hand. It is necessary to point out here that even though "calculation" draws an image of a purely cognitive process, this is not the case. Emotions play an important role in the calculations, as does rhetoric and other means of influencing the emotions. A center of calculation can be situated on board the bus a group of people regularly take to the Sunday Service, a café people meet at Santiago de Compostela after completing the pilgrimage, or the occult section of a bookshop. Individuals make the calculations in these centers, based on the information that is gathered there. The information is brought in and translated—given meaning and purpose—there and then by the actants physically present and by the immutable mobiles that shape or delineate the actualities and limits of knowledge and action taking place at the particular locale.[44]

The Religious is not a Special Kind of Stuff

What I have outlined so far entails: (1) avoiding prejudice by prior commitment to social theories, particular structure, content or extent of the aggregate, layered explanations—such as micro and macro—or preset coordinates for study—such as power and hierarchy; (2) grounding the object of study in concrete locations of calculation and in specific situations related to what the individual construes as religious (or any other related emic classification); (3) including as active members in a network both human and nonhuman actants; and (4) tracing the connections between these in order to find the centers of calculation, to identify the disparate actants and immutable mobiles that are active in these, and to learn what is their role in the network.

ANT extends vernacular religion theory by insisting that things we are used to seeing as religiously meaningful, such as icons, altars, or hymnals, should not be primarily seen as representations of something, or classified according to an overtly religious function. Instead, these and mundane objects present and active in the actor-network are all given equal status as initiators and modifiers in the process of vernacular religion. Similarly, religious rituals and other acts and locations are not defined by their overt religious purpose, or described in religious terms, such as invocation, sacrifice, blessing, or sacred. Instead, these are described according to what actants are brought together and what takes place in these that creates and maintains connections between the various human and nonhuman actants.

To put this in other words, religion, like society, is not a specific kind of stuff—distinguishable from other stuff. Instead, religion is a principle of connection within a heterogeneous assemblage of actants. Furthermore, religious codings are not innate, static, or necessarily coherent. Networks of actants produce them and they vary from individual to individual and from one localized instance to another,

249

through a process of differential negotiation and renegotiation of the connections between the actants.[45]

A consequence of this idea of distributed agency is that the individuals are not seen as completely unfettered agents but rather—as Primiano expressed—they are involved in processes of bidirectional influences of environments upon individuals and of individuals upon environments. In these processes the individual is neither independent, nor at the mercy of some abstract social forces.[46] The interdependent processes of innovation and negotiation are aiming for the construction of a stable and self-sustaining actor-network, a quasi-object. The "mechanics" that are used to effect closure, or, how boundaries are created and how stability and order of the actor-network are effected, is a central point of interest in ANT research.[47]

A phrase frequently used in ANT is "following the actors"—trying to keep pace with the innovations actors have established in order to make everything fit together. The "making everything fit" part is important. Individuals are faced with actants that compel them to act in ways that are not necessarily congruent with each other. To make these fit together requires creativity on the part of the individual; the creativity refers to the way people relate to complexity and conflicts that occur due to the instability in the various related networks. Further, because "the social," "culture," "tradition," or "socialization" are also seen as products of other actor-networks, they cannot be employed as aids to explain, describe, or understand religion. Instead, the researcher has to put effort into finding the best account that describes the associations that have been established.[48] In this manner, Latour points out, religion needs not to be accounted for by some kind of force external or internal to the individual because it is a peculiar kind of linking together of various things that are not themselves inherently parts of some kind of social or religious order. Social forces, cognitive aptitude, and cultural tradition can certainly play important roles in these linkages, but, in order to study religion in practice, it is necessary to explore how these linkages play the important roles they have; what things are gathered together, how they are linked, what they do, and why and to what extent these stay together.[49] The main focus, therefore, is not on the ways religions are expressed by individuals, but rather on what actants are present in the actor-network, how the actants mediate and translate knowledge to each other, and how the connections between actants are negotiated and renegotiated.

Religion as Negotiated Order—Stable but Dynamic

To recapitulate what has been said above: a question often implicitly or explicitly asked and sometimes answered in the first chapters of theses in the study of religions is: What constitutes religion, religious expression, and religious stuff? From an ANT's perspective, one cannot give a working definition of religion for the study (that would ruin the idea of ANT), nor is it important to judge a priori whether an object of study necessarily has anything to do with religion. Rather the starting point of the study can be a situation or an activity that is investigated as possibly, somehow, religious, or maybe having a role similar to religion.

When the assembled things interact, and for as long as they are successful in doing so, the actor-network becomes stable and a product of this kind of stable actor-network is an artifact, such as a religion in this case. This artifact is by nature a quasi-object, where the "quasi" indicates a lack of solidity, or essence, and the "object" indicates an object-like internal integrity: a quasi-object resists deconstruction into pristine parts.[50] The quasi-object appears to be immutable and stabilized; it has the appearance of being a self-contained and self-evident object. The messy processes of invention, negotiation, and calculation at play in its creation and continuance are rendered invisible. The important point here is that—even though it looks solid and resists dismantling—in order for the quasi-object, vernacular religion, to exist in any practical sense, the actor-network must function. If that particular constellation of actants ceases to be salient for the individual, it disassembles. Consequently, even though they appear to be stable, religions are not fixed. Their dynamic nature comes from the negotiations between actants, the dropping out of some actants, and the inclusion of new ones. Therefore, despite appearances, quasi-object religion does not have an essence that could be seen as its objective and immutable meaning, or defining feature. Instead, the meaning is generated in the negotiations between the actants; it is never fixed and it is stable only insofar as the negotiations between the actants are successful.

According to Latour, tracing the connections, actants, immutable mobiles, and centers of calculations does not mean going for a bird's-eye view of the network—seeing a lot, but little of it—but rather taking a narrow and detailed view of the specific things and connections. The desired end result of an ANT analysis is not an abstraction such as a description of a hierarchy of influences. By following the actors, the researcher tries to map the network, look into how and where definition, ordering, and maintenance is achieved in the network; what concrete things persuade, coerce, seduce, resist, and compromise with each other as they come together; and how these hinder or facilitate the processes of ordering and maintenance.[51]

Tracing the Networks of Contemporary Paganism

The term "Paganism," as it is used in contemporary Western societies as self-identification, refers to a broad and dynamic system of beliefs and practices. This system draws inspiration and imagery from pre-Christian religions (e.g., Celtic, Norse, Greek, Roman, Persian, Mesopotamian, and Egyptian), types of worldview (e.g., polytheism, animism, and pantheism), identities (e.g., shaman, wise-woman, witch, and magus), and practices (e.g., astrology, herbalism, and magic). More generally, Paganism can be described as a polytheistic nature religion that recreates old ways of relating to the Earth and all its inhabitants and does not divorce nature from the supernatural, rather seeing the sacred as entwined with the mundane.[52]

For research on Pagans, defined and demarcated special places, such as Stonehenge, are not necessarily the most fruitful places to start when looking for the centers of calculations. Certainly you can find Pagans there doing stuff, but much of the process of vernacular religion happens elsewhere. A good place to start is the local esoteric bookshop. Usually these are important centers of calculations by themselves, but by browsing their notice boards you can find adverts for regular Pagan meetings, seasonal celebrations, and other events. For example, in London and Dublin, and most likely elsewhere, there are weekly meetings of Pagans in particular pubs, where the function room is reserved for the purpose. These often begin with a short presentation on some topic, such as tarot, astrology, some important person or book, or some discovery made at an archeological dig. This presentation is followed by a break where people gravitate into cliques to discuss the topic of the day or other things. There is a Q&A after the break and some people stay for longer afterwards. If the presentation was an interesting one—or, presumably, even if it was not—the information may be shared with people who were not at the meeting, thereby processing it further, and maybe altering or adding to some of the ritual practices the individuals have or the beliefs they hold.

The nonhuman actants often play an important role in the processes of translation and accumulation. For example, when a scholar specializing in the life of Aleister Crowley—a prominent figure in late nineteenth-century esoteric circles—offers his published thesis for sale after his presentation, the book draws together a congregation of people with an interest in Western esoteric traditions. Because of the arrangement of the room these people also turn their backs on the other people in the room, creating a concrete boundary between them—the esotericists—and the others. Another example is a newspaper article that attacks Pagans in general and Druids in particular, and inspires an individual to produce slogan buttons that say "Hated by Daily Mail" and to bring them to the next Pagan meeting.

Distributed around the room these buttons bring into the process the particular journalist, the newspaper, religious freedom, and freedom of speech acts. These introduce (or emphasize) the idea of Pagans as a religious minority and thereby also the ideas that (a) Paganism is a religion and (b) there is a way of defining what Paganism is. These are not the kinds of points generally considered by the Pagans in these meetings. Whether Paganism is a religion and in some way definable are generally contestable issues among the Pagans, so the buttons started a process in the meeting that would not have started without them.

Further, the customary classifications may direct focus on objects or definable entities rather than interactions. For example, when visiting a location with special meaning for Pagans, describing it as a place of pilgrimage may be misleading. For many Pagans it looks as though stone circles are no more sacred than any other place on Earth. Rather, their importance comes from their diachronic significance as places our ancestors used for gatherings and for the conduct of important

Figure 1
A Button Distributed at a Pagan Meeting in London

functions—with various suggestions regarding the nature of these functions. ANT's view is that the nature and meaning of these sites is created for each individual through the circulation and translation of information by the various actants the individual is actively connected with.

For example, when a person with a colorful dress touches a megalith at Stonehenge with an expression of calm concentration, she may be tapping on the mystical energy of the stone, connecting with Neolithic ancestors, communing with the faery folk that come to life on the summer solstice, or just making herself stand out in the crowd.

Figure 2
Woman at Stonehenge during the 2008 Summer Solstice

But, since people do not want to disturb her she is also creating an empty space around herself, which then has to be circumnavigated more slowly because of the congestion. How does this interaction between a person and a large stone affect the way people relate to or experience Stonehenge, or recall their visit? Maybe it enhances the mystical image of the place or, indeed, imbues the stones with a sense of sacredness for the individuals. The actor in this example is not the individual or the stone, but the interaction between the two.

A Place of the Great Gathering

The neolithic complex around Avebury in northern Wiltshire is a good example of how various kinds of actants mediate information and influence each other, and how these processes take place in a number of centers of calculations. It links together an array of things, such as books, maps, standing stones, and other features that have the potential to effect change in the way individual Pagans think of Paganism or their worldview in general. The size of the area the complex covers, the variety of its features, and the ambiguity of its purpose attracts Pagans from around the world, but also archeologists, historians, authors, hikers, photographers, and others.

A vast number of studies and speculations regarding the Avebury Complex have been published, from as early as the mid-seventeenth century, and many of these will come up as immutable mobiles in one evening spent in the Red Lion, the only pub in the village.

The complex includes several interconnected sites with remains of constructions built over the span of several centuries. Most notable of these remains is a large henge and stone circle, containing the remains of two inner circles. The outer stone circle, originally made up of about 100 standing stones, is inside a 420-meter-diameter henge with an external bank and an internal ditch. Today, after over four millennia of erosion and silting, the bank is five meters high and over twenty meters wide, while the ditch is about twenty meters wide at the top and nearly four meters deep. The outer circle encloses two inner circles, originally of about thirty stones and one hundred meters in diameter. These inner circles also contain stone settings. In comparison, the outer stone circle of Stonehenge is about thirty meters in diameter. The stone circles were constructed in series of stages during the late Neolithic and early Bronze Age (c. 3000–2000 BCE). There are four entrances into the henge and the enclosing stone circle. Two of these (southern and western) connect to stone avenues of smaller stones. The southern

Figure 3a and 3b
The Great Henge in Avebury

Source: (3a) Photo by J. J. Evendon, copyright owned by The Megalithic Portal, permission to use granted by Andy Burnham on behalf of The Megalith Portal on September 20, 2011, (3b) From Google earth.

avenue, or the West Kennet Avenue, leads to a site of a stone and timber setting known as the Sanctuary. The avenue also skirts Silbury Hill, the largest man-made mound in prehistoric Europe at thirty-seven meters high, and the West Kennet Long Barrow, which is one of the longest Neolithic burial mounds in Britain at one hundred meters.[53] A third of the about one hundred stones of the outer circle, eleven stones of the internal setting of the southern inner circle, and at least nineteen stones lining the avenues appear to have been deliberately buried. The stones were buried in several episodes between the early to mid-fourteenth century and mid to late seventeenth century. The motive for this undertaking—the stones weigh on average twenty to thirty tonnes—is unclear. Some evidence points to religious motives, particularly during the Middle Ages, and some of the early accounts point to the need in the seventeenth century to free up land for culti-vation. Many other stones, including nearly all of the stones forming the inner circles and the avenues, are missing, possibly broken up for building material. Even after some of the buried stones were reerected in the early twentieth century, only thirty stones of the outer circle and only a few of the inner stones remain visible today.

The original use or uses of the complex are unknown; some researchers suggest it was used for ceremonial purposes and for demonstrating power and authority, but others argue for domestic use as a site of settlement that also included ceremonial sites and places of burial.[54] Today it serves domestic purposes as well as being

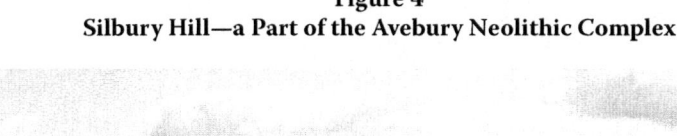

Figure 4
Silbury Hill—a Part of the Avebury Neolithic Complex

a place of gathering for people from afar: the village of Avebury is partly contained within the henge. The features of the complex have their own, sometimes contradictory, myths and narratives; some are found in books and some are told on site. Depending on the source one uses, the Avebury Complex acquires a different significance. For example, Silbury Hill can be seen as a beacon that was used to mark the beginning of major ceremonies or as the grand burial mound of King Sel, a mythical ancient ruler who is sometimes identified as King Arthur. Another popular narrative is based on the observation that the stones in the outer circle appear to have two basic shapes; they are either tall and thin, or lozenge shaped. These two shapes are believed to represent male and female, or actually to be male and female ancestors who come to life during the solstice. These and other stories like stories concerning the stone burials are numerous, and they are retold and their significance frequently reformulated in the gatherings.[55]

Figure 5
People among the Avebury Stones during the 2010 Summer Solstice

Notes: The two large stones in the middle form the southern gateway where the route via the West Kennet Avenue enters into the large stone circle. Behind and to the right of the gate are the still existing stones of the southern inner circle. The white façade of the Red Lion pub can be seen in the background to the right. The curve of the large circle continues in the left background where alternating lozenge-shaped "female" stones and straight and tall "male" stones can be seen.

For many Pagans who come to Avebury for, for example, the summer solstice, the first center of calculation they find themselves in is the Swindon coach terminal. It has a narrow concourse that collects people waiting for the same coach into a relatively small area. The coaches leave once an hour and particularly during important seasonal festivals these can be overcrowded, so people coming for the events arrive early. It is easy for individuals and groups of Pagans to spot each other here, share their plans for the event, and exchange their views, thoughts, and prior experiences of Avebury. Also, because Avebury has no designated campsite and few other options for accommodation, people frequently find unofficial places for camping. The landowners generally do not allow camping on their property, so the campsites are frequently ad hoc places in the woods around the fields, although often the regular groups use same sites. The campsites can be seen as another type of a center of calculation in the area, and, because they are often at some distance from the village, they are good examples of the ways individual actants transport and transmute information between the campsite and the various parts of the complex. On the concourse, or during the twenty-five-minute journey from Swindon, people with no plans for camping—or who are unaware of the lack of facilities—can negotiate with those who are better prepared, creating a somewhat random element in the formation of the campsites, and a potentially different set of experiences, thoughts, and assumptions regarding the solstice or Avebury in general.

In Avebury, the bus stops right next to the Red Lion pub. The pub is located at the crossroads near the center of the outer stone circle. It is where people who are coming and going between the stone circles and their campsite, those who elected to spend the night among the stones, those who visit only for the day, the police officers, and the local inhabitants meet.

There are books and magazines on the history and geography of the region, the complex, and various New Age and Pagan themes available in the pub function room and sold at the Henge Shop down the street. People also bring with them books, maps, illustrations, and their own stories on Avebury, stone circles, ley lines, and other assorted topics. In this network the various narratives and other pieces of information get translated, parceled, and moved around. There are no official or universally accepted stories telling the significance of the summer solstice at Avebury, or identifying the actual purpose and use of the complex. Instead, the significance of the event is generated

Figure 6
The Function Room of the Red Lion during a Pagan Event

there and then for the individual by the accumulation of these parcels of information.

The list of actants and immutable mobiles in the above account include, among other things, the Swindon–Avebury coach time-table, the individual Pagans, bartenders influencing the flow of the people, the town council who have not allocated campsites, the landowners pushing people out of sight into the woods, and the police officers who, mainly by walking up and down the crossroads, create an empty no man's land between the Red Lion and other areas of the complex.

Even though it can generally be said that Paganism is a polytheistic nature religion, the Gods and Nature are not necessarily the things that most influence the individual's experience of the solstice, or what they bring back from it and relate to their Pagan groups back home. When returning home, the bidirectional influences continue within the groups. These influences can potentially alter how people see themselves in relation to, for example, the Neolithic people as ancestors, the various suggested uses of the Avebury Complex, or the legends inspired by the complex, but the influences can also more fundamentally affect the ways people relate to the Gods and Nature.

Discussion

As an approach to studying what has been termed religion or spirituality, or more generally people's beliefs and worldviews, the model of vernacular religion makes explicit the view that an individual's religion is a process: but further, it insists that the process is made up of bidirectional influences. These bidirectional influences are not always clearly recognized in models that look at religion as it is lived by the individuals, emphasize the private and individualistic nature of religion, or limit the external influences to ostensibly religious bodies. ANT offers points of focus that are not tied to things that are presumed to be religious, and further allows for the mapping of highly complex networks of these bidirectional influences. The kinds of mapping of networks I have laid out in the very limited examples above are, in my view, essential for the understanding of the relatively rapid changes in people's beliefs and worldviews. This is particularly so in a situation where the increased complexity of individuals' lifeworlds has made obsolete former assumptions of similarity or continuity of beliefs under the same label—say, Christianity—or of linear unidirectional changes caused by definable factors—such as secularization or spiritual revolution.

To study religion is rather like trying to take hold of something liquid: the harder you try and the tighter you squeeze the more you lose; as when using rigid concepts to guide and direct an investigation. The categories that are believed to be immutable, or solid, are so only if they are *in reality* solid, but it is apparent that religion is not one such category. Many of the suggestions for the basic research methods laid out above are not particularly new; they are the bread and butter of folklore and anthropological studies. Participant observation and interviews stand out as the essential ingredients, but a more promiscuous approach to methodology may provide deeper and more accurate understandings of some of the associations and disassociations in the actor-networks. For example, it was necessary to use quantitative survey methods to reveal the unusual homogeneity of value priorities among contemporary Pagans. In interviews, Pagans themselves downplay any claim to shared values, emphasizing instead the heterogeneity of the movement and the importance of individual freedom from normative dogma. When participating in meetings and festivals the division of the Pagan movement into cliques and different varieties of Paganism is apparent. However, the unusual similarity of priorities among Pagans—compared to even the most religious Christians—appears to be the thing that unites Pagans regardless of the individuals' specific beliefs and worldview.[56]

At a most basic level the approach I have outlined above offers means to look at the old points of focus in the study of religions in a way that also includes otherwise unnoticed and mundane things. It also sidesteps the need for abstractions, categories, and explanatory models that appear to be defunct. A consequence of the approach is that the boundaries of the object of study are fuzzy. They have to remain so in order to avoid excluding significant actants or including those that have ceased to be process altering things. Recognizing the complexity of the networks of associations involved reveals a quasi-object religion that is not entirely socially constructed, but nevertheless is not an objective, fixed structure. Religion is neither inherently social, nor is it inherently psychological. It is a hybrid that cannot be divided or reduced into social or psychological components without acknowledging the other.

I have proposed abandoning the essentialist, or entity view of religion that underlies the world religions paradigm, where some religions are seen as textbook examples against which others are measured. Instead of defining religion as an independently real object with certain specific properties—such as origins, important people, texts, particular beliefs, or features of cosmology—one should look at what people do with religion, and how they talk about it, what actors—human and nonhuman—are involved, how they are engaged, how do they translate information, and how are the connections between actors negotiated?[57] Actor-networks that work with different prevailing strategies of interaction—the negotiation and renegotiation of connections—have different topographies. They have various constellations of actors, connected by different kinds of connectors. Therefore, a way to study this complex process is to focus attention on the differences in the strategies of interaction. This is the significant input of ANT for the study of religions.

Notes

1. Bruno Latour, *Reassembling the Social: An Introduction to Actor-Network-Theory* (New York: Oxford University Press, 2005).
2. Shalom H. Schwartz, "Beyond Individualism/Collectivism: New Cultural Dimensions of Values," in *Individualism and Collectivism: Theory, Method, and Applications, Cross-Cultural Research and Methodology,* ed. C. Kagitçibasi, Uichol Kim, Harry C. Triandis, Sang-Chin Choi, and

Gene Yoon (London: Sage, 1994), 18; Mika T. Lassander, "From Security to Self-expression: The Emergent Value Pattern and the Changing Role of Religion" (Unpublished PhD thesis, The Open University, Milton Keynes, 2010); Zygmunt Bauman, *The Individualized Society* (Cambridge: Polity Press, 2001); Ronald Inglehart and Christian Welzel, *Modernization, Cultural Change, and Democracy: The Human Development Sequence* (New York: Cambridge University Press, 2005); Mark Granovetter, "The Strength of Weak Ties: A Network Theory Revisited," *Sociological Theory* (1983): 201–34.

3. Zygmunt Bauman, *Liquid Modernity* (Malden: Blackwell Publishing, 2000), 13–15.

4. Teemu Taira, "Religion as a Discursive Technique: The Politics of Classifying Wicca," *Journal of Contemporary Religion* 25, no. 3 (2010): 379–94.

5. Marion Bowman, "Vernacular Religion and Nature: The 'Bible of the Folk' Tradition in Newfoundland," *Folklore* 114, no. 3 (2003): 285–95; Leonard Norman Primiano, "Vernacular Religion and the Search for Method in Religious Folklife," *Western Folklore* 54, no. 1 (1995): 37–56.

6. Primiano, "Vernacular Religion," 51–52.

7. Ibid., 44.

8. E.g., Bruno Latour, *Science in Action: How to Follow Scientists and Engineers Through Society* (Milton Keynes: Open University Press, 1987); John Law, *Organising Modernity* (Oxford: Blackwells, 1994); Michel Callon, "Society in the Making: The Study of Technology As a Tool for Sociological Analysis," in *The Social Construction of Technological Systems*, ed. W. E. Bijker, T. P. Hughes, and T. J. Pinch (Cambridge: MIT Press, 1987), 83–103; Michel Callon, "Four Models of the Dynamics of Science," in *Handbook of Science and Technology Studies*, ed. S. Jasanoff, G. Markle, J. Petersen, and T. Pinch (Thousand Oaks, CA: Sage Publications, 2002), 29–63.

9. Karen A. Cerulo, "Nonhumans in Social Interaction," *Annual Review of Sociology* 35, no. 1 (2009): 531–52.

10. Mark Vuuren and François Cooren, "'My Attitude Made Me Do It': Considering the Agency of Attitudes," *Human Studies* 33, no. 1 (2010): 85–101; Christopher Gad and Casper Bruun Jensen, "On the Consequences of Post-Ant," *Science, Technology & Human Values* 35, no. 1 (2010): 55–80; Karen A Cerulo, "Nonhumans in Social Interaction," *Annual Review of Sociology* 35, no. 1 (2009): 531–52.; David Lulka, "The Residual Humanism of Hybridity: Retaining a Sense of the Earth," *Transactions of the Institute of British Geographers* 34, no. 3 (2009): 378–93; Caroline Humphrey, "Reassembling Individual Subjects," *Anthropological Theory* 8, no. 4 (2008): 357–80; Paul Routledge, "Acting in the Network: ANT and the Politics of Generating Associations," *Environment & Planning D: Society & Space* 26, no. 2 (2008): 199–217; Robert Oppenheim, "Actor-Network Theory and Anthropology After Science, Technology, and Society," *Anthropological Theory* 7, no. 4 (2007): 417–93; Tony Bennett, "Making Culture, Changing Society," *Cultural Studies* 21, no. 4/5 (2007): 610–29; W. N. Kaghan and G. C. Bowker, "Out of Machine Age?: Complexity, Sociotechnical Systems and Actor Network Theory," *Journal of Engineering and Technology Management* 18, no. 3–4 (2001): 253–69.

11. Bruno Latour, *We Have Never Been Modern* (Cambridge: Harvard University Press, 1993), 51–54. Similar to what John Law describes as punctualized network patterns in John Law, "Notes on the Theory of the Actor-Network: Ordering, Strategy, and Heterogeneity," *Systemic Practice and Action Research* 5, no. 4 (1992): http://www.comp.lancs.ac.uk/sociology/papers/Law-Notes-on-ANT.pdf (accessed February 9, 2011).

12. E.g., most relevant to this chapter are: Andy Letcher, "'Gaia Told Me to Do It': Resistance and the Idea of Nature within Contemporary British Eco-Paganism," *Ecotheology: Journal of Religion, Nature & the Environment* 8, no. 1 (2003): 61–84; Douglas E. Cowan, *Cyberhenge: Modern Pagans on the Internet* (New York: Routledge, 2005), 3–6.

13. E.g., Robin R. Meyers, *Saving Jesus From the Church: How to Stop Worshiping Christ and Start Following Jesus* (New York: HarperCollins Publishers, 2010), 13–15.

14. Lassander, "From Security to Self-Expression," 203–08.

15. Kevin Hetherington, *Expressions of Identity: Space, Performance, Politics, Theory, Culture & Society* (London: Sage, 1998), 53.

16. Most relevant for this chapter is: Bennett, "Making Culture, Changing Society."

17. Wilfred Cantwell Smith, *The Meaning and End of Religion* (Minneapolis, MN: Fortress Press, 1991), 51–79.

18. Victoria S. Harrison, "The Pragmatics of Defining Religion in a Multi-Cultural World," *International Journal for Philosophy of Religion* 59, no. 3 (2006): doi:10.1007/s11153-006-6961-z.

19. Meredith B. McGuire, *Lived Religion: Faith and Practice in Everyday Life* (New York: Oxford University Press, 2008), 43.

20. Ibid., 3.

21. Ibid., 12.

22. Ibid., 185–214.

23. Ibid., 44.

24. Primiano, "Vernacular Religion," 41–46.

25. Latour, *Reassembling the Social*, 5–8.

26. E.g., Anatol Rapoport, *Mathematical Models in the Social and Behavioral Sciences* (New York: Wiley, 1983); Mark Granovetter, "The Strength of Weak Ties: A Network Theory Revisited," *Sociological Theory* 1 (1983): 201–33.

27. Harrison C. White, *Identity and Control* (Princeton, NJ: Princeton University Press, 1992), 65–71, 215–16.

28. Callon, "Society in the Making," 93; Latour, *Science in Action*, 141–44.

29. Latour, *Reassembling the Social*, 3–4.

30. Ibid., 11.

31. Bruno Latour, "On Recalling ANT," in *Actor Network Theory and After*, ed. John Law and John Hassard (Oxford: Blackwell Publishers, 1999), 17–21; Latour, *Reassembling the Social*, 8–16.

32. Ibid., 231–41.

33. Ibid., 8–9.

34. Ibid., 47–50.

35. Ibid., 217–18.

36. Daniel Breslau, "Sociology after Humanism: A Lesson from Contemporary Science Studies," *Sociological Theory* 18, no. 2 (2000): 289–307.

37. Latour, *Reassembling the Social*, 37–42.
38. Ibid., 175–83.
39. This argument is made regarding "society" in Law, *Organising Modernity*, 102–5.
40. Latour, *Reassembling the Social*, 178.
41. Latour, *Science in Action*, 89–90.
42. Bruno Latour, "Visualization and Cognition," in *Representation in Scientific Activity*, ed. Steve Woolgar and Michael Lynch (Cambridge: MIT Press, 1990), http://www.bruno.latour.fr (accessed February 9, 2011).
43. Latour, *Science in Action*, 227–28.
44. Tara J Fenwick, "(Un)Doing Standards in Education with Actor-Network Theory," *Journal of Education Policy* 25, no. 2 (2010): 117–33.
45. Oppenheim, "Actor-Network Theory," 475–76; Latour, *Reassembling the Social*, 107.
46. Vuuren and Cooren, "My Attitude Made Me Do It," 98–100.
47. Kaghan and Bowker, "Out of Machine Age?"
48. Latour, *Reassembling the Social*, 7–12.
49. Ibid., 13–14.
50. Graham Harman, *Prince of Networks: Bruno Latour and Metaphysics* (Melbourne: re.press, 2009), 63–64.
51. John Law, *After Method: Mess in Social Science Research* (New York: Routledge, 2004), 111–13; Latour, *Reassembling the Social*, 9–11; Fenwick, "(Un)Doing Standards in Education," 123–30.
52. Graham Harvey, *Listening People, Speaking Earth: Contemporary Paganism* (London: C. Hurst, 1997), 1.
53. Mark Gillings and Joshua Pollard, *Avebury, Duckworth Archaeological Histories* (London: Gerald Duckworth, 2004), 1–22.
54. Ibid., 57–76.
55. Ibid., 123–33.
56. Lassander, "From Security to Self-Expression," chap. 3 and 4.
57. Graham Harvey, "Introduction," in *Religions in Focus: New Approaches to Tradition and Contemporary Practices*, ed. Graham Harvey (Oakville: Equinox Publishing, 2010), 6–8.

Bibliography

Bauman, Zygmunt. *The Individualized Society.* Cambridge: Polity Press, 2001.

———. *Liquid Modernity.* Malden: Blackwell Publishing, 2000.

Bennett, Tony. "Making Culture, Changing Society." *Cultural Studies* 21, no. 4/5 (2007): 610–29.

Bowman, Marion. "Vernacular Religion and Nature: The "Bible of the Folk" Tradition in Newfoundland." *Folklore* 114, no. 3 (2003): 285–95.

Breslau, Daniel. "Sociology after Humanism: A Lesson from Contemporary Science Studies." *Sociological Theory* 18, no. 2 (2000): 289–307.

Callon, Michel. "Four Models of the Dynamics of Science." In *Handbook of Science and Technology Studies*, edited by S. Jasanoff, G. Markle, J. Petersen, and T. Pinch. Thousand Oaks, CA: Sage Publications, 2002, 29–63.

———. "Society in the Making: The Study of Technology as a Tool for Sociological Analysis." In *The Social Construction of Technological Systems*, edited by

W. E. Bijker, T. P. Hughes, and T. J. Pinch. Cambridge: MIT Press, 1987, 83–103.

Cerulo, Karen A. "Nonhumans in Social Interaction." *Annual Review of Sociology* 35, no. 1 (2009): 531–52.

Cowan, Douglas E. *Cyberhenge: Modern Pagans on the Internet.* New York: Routledge, 2005.

Fenwick, Tara J. "(Un)Doing Standards in Education with Actor-Network Theory." *Journal of Education Policy* 25, no. 2 (2010): 117–33.

Gad, Christopher, and Casper Bruun Jensen. "On the Consequences of Post-Ant." *Science, Technology & Human Values* 35, no. 1 (2010): 55–80.

Gillings, Mark, and Joshua Pollard. *Avebury.* Duckworth Archaeological Histories. London: Gerald Duckworth, 2004.

Granovetter, Mark. "The Strength of Weak Ties: A Network Theory Revisited." *Sociological Theory* 1 (1983): 201–33.

Harman, Graham. *Prince of Networks: Bruno Latour and Metaphysics.* Melbourne: re.press, 2009.

Harrison, Victoria S. "The Pragmatics of Defining Religion in a Multi-Cultural World." *International Journal for Philosophy of Religion* 59, no. 3 (2006): doi:10.1007/s11153-006-6961-z.

Harvey, Graham. "Introduction." In *Religions in Focus: New Approaches to Tradition and Contemporary Practices*, edited by Graham Harvey. Oakville: Equinox Publishing, 2010, 1–9.

———. *Listening People, Speaking Earth: Contemporary Paganism.* London: C. Hurst, 1997.

Hetherington, Kevin. *Expressions of Identity: Space, Performance, Politics.* Theory, Culture & Society. London: Sage, 1998.

Humphrey, Caroline. "Reassembling Individual Subjects." *Anthropological Theory* 8, no. 4 (2008): 357–80.

Inglehart, Ronald, and Christian Welzel. *Modernization, Cultural Change, and Democracy: The Human Development Sequence.* New York: Cambridge University Press, 2005.

Kaghan, W. N., and G. C. Bowker. "Out of Machine Age?: Complexity, Socio-technical Systems and Actor Network Theory." *Journal of Engineering and Technology Management* 18, no. 3–4 (2001): 253–69.

Lassander, Mika T. "From Security to Self-Expression: The Emergent Value Pattern and the Changing Role of Religion." Unpublished PhD thesis, Milton Keynes: The Open University, 2010.

Latour, Bruno. "On Recalling ANT." In *Actor Network Theory and After*, edited by John Law and John Hassard. Oxford: Blackwell Publishers, 1999, 15–25.

———. *Reassembling the Social: An Introduction to Actor-Network-Theory.* New York: Oxford University Press, 2005.

———. *Science in Action: How to Follow Scientists and Engineers Through Society.* Milton Keynes: Open University Press, 1987.

———. "Visualization and Cognition." In *Representation in Scientific Activity*, edited by Steve Woolgar and Michael Lynch. Cambridge: MIT Press, 1990. http://www.bruno.latour.fr (accessed February 9, 2011).

———. *We Have Never Been Modern.* Cambridge: Harvard University Press, 1993.

Law, John. *After Method: Mess in Social Science Research*. New York: Routledge, 2004.

———. "Notes on the Theory of the Actor-Network: Ordering, Strategy, and Heterogeneity." *Systemic Practice and Action Research* 5, no. 4 (1992): doi:10.1007/BF01059830. http://www.comp.lancs.ac.uk/sociology/papers/Law-Notes-on-ANT.pdf (accessed February 9, 2011).

———. *Organising Modernity*. Oxford: Blackwell, 1994.

Letcher, Andy. "'Gaia Told Me to Do It': Resistance and the Idea of Nature Within Contemporary British Eco-Paganism." *Ecotheology: Journal of Religion, Nature & the Environment* 8, no. 1 (2003): 61–84.

Lulka, David. "The Residual Humanism of Hybridity: Retaining a Sense of the Earth." *Transactions of the Institute of British Geographers* 34, no. 3 (2009): 378–93.

McGuire, Meredith B. *Lived Religion: Faith and Practice in Everyday Life*. New York: Oxford University Press, 2008.

Meyers, Robin R. *Saving Jesus from the Church: How to Stop Worshiping Christ and Start Following Jesus*. New York: HarperCollins Publishers, 2010.

Oppenheim, Robert. "Actor-Network Theory and Anthropology after Science, Technology, and Society." *Anthropological Theory* 7, no. 4 (2007): 417–93.

Primiano, Leonard Norman. "Vernacular Religion and the Search for Method in Religious Folklife." *Western Folklore* 54, no. 1 (1995): 37–56.

Rapoport, Anatol. *Mathematical Models in the Social and Behavioral Sciences*. New York: Wiley, 1983.

Routledge, Paul. "Acting in the Network: ANT and the Politics of Generating Associations." *Environment & Planning D: Society & Space* 26, no. 2 (2008): 199–217.

Schwartz, Shalom H. "Beyond Individualism/Collectivism: New Cultural Dimensions of Values." In *Individualism and Collectivism: Theory, Method, and Applications*. Cross-Cultural Research and Methodology, edited by C. Kagitçibasi, Uichol Kim, Harry C. Triandis, Sang-Chin Choi, and Gene Yoon. London: Sage, 1994, 85–123.

Smith, Wilfred Cantwell. *The Meaning and End of Religion*. Minneapolis, MN: Fortress Press, 1991.

Taira, Teemu. "Religion as a Discursive Technique: The Politics of Classifying Wicca." *Journal of Contemporary Religion* 25, no. 3 (2010): 379–94.

Vuuren, Mark, and François Cooren. "'My Attitude Made Me Do It': Considering the Agency of Attitudes." *Human Studies* 33, no. 1 (2010): 85–101.

White, Harrison C. *Identity and Control: A Structural Theory of Social Action*. Princeton, NJ: Princeton University Press, 1992.

List of Contributors

Måns Broo is a senior lecturer in comparative religion and a member of the project "Post-secular culture and a changing religious landscape in Finland" at the Åbo Akademi University. His research interests include yoga at the borderlines of religion and sports in contemporary Finland and ritualism in Bengali Vaishnavism, as well as aspects of urban and modern Hinduism.

José Casanova is a professor at the Department of Sociology at the Georgetown University, and heads the Berkley Center's Program on Globalization, Religion, and the Secular. His research on religion and globalization has adopted an ambitious comparative perspective that includes Catholicism, Pentecostalism, and Islam. He has published works in a broad range of subjects, including religion and globalization, migration and religious pluralism, transnational religions, and sociological theory.

Liselotte Frisk is a professor in religious studies at the Dalarna University, Sweden. She is an expert of new religiosity and new religious movements, such as ISKCON (Hare Krishna), Osho movement, Siddha Yoga, Transcendental Meditation, and Anthroposophy. In 2007, Frisk published the book entitled "De nya religiösa rörelserna – vart tog de vägen?: En studie av Scientologi-kyrkan, Guds Barn, Hare Krishna-rörelsen, Moon-rörelsen och Bhagwan-rörelsen och deras utveckling över tid" (The new religious movements – where did they go?: A study of Scientology Church, God's Children, Unification Church, and Osho movement).

Kennet Granholm is an assistant professor in history of religions at the Stockholm University, Sweden, and a docent in comparative religion at the Åbo Akademi University in Turku, Finland. His main field of research is contemporary esotericism, with a particular focus on popular culture and religious, societal, and cultural change.

Tuija Hovi is a postdoctoral researcher (Academy of Finland) and a member of the project "Post-secular culture and a changing religious landscape in Finland" at the Åbo Akademi University. Her field of interests includes the psychological and anthropological study of religion as well as narrative studies, and her current research is focused on Pentecostal-Charismatic Christianity.

Ruth Illman is a docent (adjunct professor) and senior researcher at the Donner Institute for Research in Religious and Cultural History in Turku. She received her doctoral degree in comparative religion from the Åbo Akademi University in 2004 and has since then worked as a research fellow at the Tampere Peace Research Institute and as a lecturer in comparative religion at the Åbo Akademi University. She is also the editor-in-chief of the peer-reviewed academic journal *Temenos*. Her main research interests include interreligious dialogue, peace research, philosophy of religion, and Judaism. Her book "Creative Encounters. Artists engaged in interreligious dialogue" will be published by Equinox Publications in the spring of 2012.

Nadia Jeldtoft is a Ph.D. fellow at the Centre for European Islamic Thought at the Faculty of Theology at the Copenhagen University. Her research focuses on Muslim minorities in the West, and the role of spirituality and religion for Muslims. Her research interests include Muslims and non-institutionalized forms of Islam, religious identity, and majority/minority interactions. Her latest publications include "Lived Islam: Religious identity in non-organised Muslim minorities" in *Ethnic and Racial Studies*, vol. 34:7, 2011.

Mika Lassander is a postdoctoral researcher in comparative religion at the Åbo Akademi University. His project "Viewpoints to the World" explores the worldviews and value priorities of people who are active in different social movements. His general research interest is in social–psychological study of the effects of long-term social changes on individuals' worldview. His focus is particularly on the relation of these changes to the decline of traditional religions and the emergence of new religious and spiritual movements in the latter half of the twentieth century. He also works as a consultant for the nonbelonging Christians survey in the Department of Religious Studies at the Open University, UK.

Tuomas Martikainen is a university researcher at the University of Helsinki and works in Transnational and Local: The Social Integration of Immigrant Communities project (Academy of Finland, 2010–2013).

Martikainen is also a member of the executive general management team of the "Post-secular culture and a changing religious landscape in Finland" project of the Centre of Excellence at the Åbo Akademi University, Finland. His areas of interest include religion, migration, and the consumer society. Martikainen is currently studying how recent changes in welfare state structures and policies change state–religion/minority relations.

Marcus Moberg is a postdoctoral researcher at the Department of Comparative Religion at the Åbo Akademi University in Turku, Finland. His main field of research is the contemporary intersection between religion, media, popular culture, and consumer culture and the sociology of religion.

Peter Nynäs is the head of Department of Comparative Religion at the Åbo Akademi University, Finland, and director of the Centre of Excellence in research project "Post-secular culture and a changing religious landscape in Finland." His own research is mainly in the fields of psychology of religion and intercultural encounters. He is the co-editor of *Transforming Otherness* (eds. J. Finch and P. Nynäs, Transaction, 2011) and *Bridges of Understanding: Perspectives on Intercultural Communication* (eds. Øivind Dahl, Iben Jensen, and Peter Nynäs, Oslo Academic Press, 2006).

Anne Birgitta Pessi is a docent (adjunct professor) in theology/church and social studies (University of Helsinki) and in sociology (University of Kuopio). She works as an academy research fellow and is the deputy director at the University of Helsinki, Collegium for Advanced Study. Pessi's research interests cover particularly altruism, communality, church, social work, volunteerism, and urban religion, as well as individualized religiosity. Pessi is extensively involved in various international research projects and directs currently, for instance, Finland's Academy-funded research project RiTS (Religion in Transforming Solidarity for 2008–2011) that involves seven researchers, both doctoral and postdoctoral fellows.

Terhi Utriainen is a senior lecturer in study of religions and an associate professor in both study of religions and gender studies at the University of Helsinki. She is also a member of the project "Post-secular culture and a changing religious landscape in Finland" at the Åbo Akademi University. Her research areas include women's popular religiosity, embodiment, and suffering.

Katja Valaskivi is a docent (adjunct professor) in the School of Media, Communication and Theatre at the University of Tampere. Her research interests include innovationism, the circulation of national branding, and Japanese media and popular culture. Valaskivi has previously worked as the director for the Finnish Institute in Japan, and as head of Communications and Media Relations at the Tampere University of Technology. She has also been a visiting researcher at the National Institute of Informatics, Tokyo, and at Sophia University, Tokyo.

Laura Wickström is a doctoral student at the Åbo Akademi University. She holds a master of arts degree in comparative religion and currently specializes in Islam and ecology within the Department of Comparative Religion. She also has a master's degree in public international law with specialization in human rights law.

Author Index

Subject Index

activism, environmental, 226–27, 232.
  see also environmentalism
actor-network theory (ANT)
  background of, 241–47
  Lassander on, 10
  methodology and, 261–62
  as open-ended methodology, 247–52
  paganism example and, 252–61
  religious change and, 242–43
affective resonance, 136–38
agency
  collective, 199, 204–5
  complexities of, 207
  distributed, 250
  environmentalism and, 220, 230, 232
  factors effecting, 14–15
  identity and, 188, 202
  instrumentality and, 202–3
  intentionality and, 203–4
  overview of, 201–2
  proxy, 204–5
  religious, 17
agentification, 77–78
Al-Qaida, 81
alternative healing methods, 193–96
alternative spirituality, 65n9, 112
anthropological vs. theological
  dimension, 55
atheism, 42, 198
authenticity, 162–63, 181–82n30
authorities, multiple, 205–7
Avebury Complex, 255–60
awareness/self-discovery, 163
axial age, 72

binary thinking, 217–219, 228
Birth of Biopolitics, The (Foucault), 137
Bismarckian welfare regime, 73–74

Brands of Faith (Einstein), 110
Britain/United Kingdom, 14, 33–34

case studies
  discussion of, 176–79
  experience and, 167–68
  findings of, 167–76
  methodology of, 164–67
  truth and, 170–72
  values and, 168–70
center of calculations, 248–49, 252, 259
certainty, 148–50
Chicago School of Economics, 75
China, religiosity of, 38–39, 45n13
church
  attendance statistics, 34
  definition of, 35
  state relations and, 79–80
citizens' empowerment, 77–78
collective vs. personal, 53, 62
commercialization, 15
common good, 60
communities of interpretation, 176–77
community, individuals' relations to,
  162–64
competition, 134–38, 140–41, 147
conceptual reflexivity, 63
confessionalization of states, nations,
  and peoples, 35–36
consecrating role of journalists, 144–45
conservative welfare regime, 73–74
consistency, 163, 171
constitutionalism, 78
consumer capitalism, 108–13
consumer culture, 15, 17–18, 81,
  108–13
corporatist-statist welfare regime,
  73–74